# Practical Hardware Pentesting

A guide to attacking embedded systems and protecting them against the most common hardware attacks

**Jean-Georges Valle**

BIRMINGHAM—MUMBAI

# Practical Hardware Pentesting

**Group Product Manager**: Wilson D'souza

**Publishing Product Manager**: Rahul Nair

**Senior Editor**: Arun Nadar

**Content Development Editor**: Romy Dias

**Technical Editor**: Nithik Cheruvakodan

**Copy Editor**: Safis Editing

**Project Coordinator**: Neil D'mello

**Proofreader**: Safis Editing

**Indexer**: Manju Arasan

**Production Designer**: Nilesh Mohite

First published: March 2021

Production reference: 1040321

Published by Packt Publishing Ltd.

Livery Place

35 Livery Street

Birmingham

B3 2PB, UK.

ISBN 978-1-78961-913-3

www.packt.com

*To my father. I wouldn't be who I am without you.*

# Contributors

## About the author

**Jean-Georges Valle** is a hardware penetration tester based in Belgium. His background was in software security, with hardware being a hobby, and he then started to look into the security aspects of hardware. He has spent the last decade testing various systems, from industrial logic controllers to city-scale IoT, and from media distribution to power metering. He has learned to attack embedded systems and to leverage them against cloud-scale infrastructure. He is the lead hardware technical expert in an offensive security team of a big four company.

Jean-Georges holds a master's degree in information security and focuses on security at the point of intersection with hardware and software, hardware and software interaction, exploit development in embedded systems, and open source hardware.

*I wish to thank my parents for supporting me and loving me unconditionally, Vito and Jon for giving me an opportunity when I needed it, and Ieva for accepting that this book was competing with her for my time and attention.*

# About the reviewers

**Ryan Slaugh** has been a maker and breaker of things for over 20 years. Ryan got his start in electrical systems, and augmented his learning to include the analog, digital, embedded, software, and cybersecurity fields. He continues to practice and add to his skill sets in his home lab, and this allows him to do what he loves the most: solve problems with technology. When not working with technology, Ryan enjoys traveling around the globe and exploring the less inhabited areas of the Pacific Northwest. His greatest joy is being with his family on their small hobby farm in Washington State, USA.

**Neeraj Thakur** is a manager in the risk advisory practice of Deloitte and comes with more than 9 years' experience in the area of information and cybersecurity. He holds a master's degree in cybersecurity from the Indian Institute of Information Technology, Allahabad, and has extensive experience in penetration and security testing of various embedded devices and IoT-enabled products. He is a certified ISA/IEC 62443 cybersecurity fundamentals specialist and has worked extensively in the areas of industrial automation and control system security. He has delivered multiple sessions on IoT and ICS security, as well as in the security community, including Nullcon and CySeck. Neeraj is passionate about reverse engineering and security innovations using Python.

# Table of Contents

**Preface**

# Section 1: Getting to Know the Hardware

## 1

## Setting Up Your Pentesting Lab and Ensuring Lab Safety

## 2

## Understanding Your Target

# 3

# Identifying the Components of Your Target

# 4

# Approaching and Planning the Test

# Section 2: Attacking the Hardware

## 5
## Our Main Attack Platform

## 6
## Sniffing and Attacking the Most Common Protocols

# 7

## Extracting and Manipulating Onboard Storage

# 8

## Attacking Wi-Fi, Bluetooth, and BLE

# 9

## Software-Defined Radio Attacks

# Section 3: Attacking the Software

# 10
## Accessing the Debug Interfaces

# 11
## Static Reverse Engineering and Analysis

# 12
# Dynamic Reverse Engineering

# 13
# Scoring and Reporting Your Vulnerabilities

# 14
# Wrapping It Up – Mitigations and Good Practices

# Preface

This book focuses on hardware security.

It will teach you how hardware systems are architected and how to understand the general architecture of a system. You will also learn where to find information about a system, which may exist in unexpected places.

We will examine the basic protocols that electronic devices use, look at how to attack the protocols, and learn how to leverage these attacks against the device as a whole.

You will learn how to identify the scenarios that matter for impacting the way a system works, how to test for them during a hardware assessment, and how to reach a system's 'crown jewels'.

In this book, we will teach you how to leverage attacks against hardware, with very cheap tools, to reach the software that runs on the device. You will learn how to extract and analyze this software, and how to alter the software's behavior through direct hardware/software interaction.

## Who this book is for

This book is for security professionals and researchers who want to get started with hardware security assessment but don't know where to start. Electrical engineers who want to understand how their devices can be attacked, and how to protect against these attacks, or makers and tinkerers who want to understand how they can recycle or reuse a system that seems to be locked down, will also find this book useful.

# What this book covers

*Chapter 1, Setting Up Your Pentesting Lab and Ensuring Lab Safety*, will go through what hardware to buy and when, how to arrange your lab and how to keep yourself safe.

*Chapter 2, Understanding Your Target*, explains how to understand the functionality of a system, and how to reverse engineer an embedded system.

*Chapter 3, Identifying the Components of Your Target*, will help understand how to identify chips and their relationships.

*Chapter 4, Approaching and Planning the Test*, will show how to identify the risk scenarios and threats to a target system and how to organize the test

*Chapter 5, Our Main Attack Platform*, will go over the microcontroller platform we will use to attack the target systems, and will demonstrate the usage of common hardware protocols

*Chapter 6, Sniffing and Attacking the Most Common Protocols*, covers the most common hardware protocols and how to attack them

*Chapter 7, Extracting and Manipulating Onboard Storage*, covers the different hardware formats used to store information and how to extract and manipulate them

*Chapter 8, Attacking Wi-Fi, Bluetooth, and BLE*, covers the most common forms of wireless communication and how to attack them

*Chapter 9, Software-Defined Radio Attacks*, introduces you to software-defined radio and how to intercept and attack proprietary wireless communications

*Chapter 10, Accessing the Debug Interfaces*, introduces you to hardware-specific debugging protocols and how to exploit them in order to attack embedded systems

*Chapter 11, Static Reverse Engineering and Analysis*, introduces you to binary reverse engineering tools and methodology in order to understand and attack the firmware that runs on your target system.

*Chapter 12, Dynamic Reverse Engineering*, leverages the two previous chapters to show you how to interact and attack firmware while it is running on the target system.

*Chapter 13, Scoring and Reporting Your Vulnerabilities*, teaches you how to report the problems you have found on the target system to your clients.

*Chapter 14, Wrapping It Up – Mitigations and Good Practices*, orients you towards the solutions that can be given to your clients in order to solve the problems you have found.

# To get the most out of this book

You should be familiar with Linux and be able install software on your own. All the examples and code have been developed on Debian Linux, but any distribution should work.

| Software/Hardware covered in the book | OS Requirements |
|---|---|
| Linux | Any *NIX platform |
| Bluepill board (STM32F103) | |
| Ghidra 9.2+ | |
| GCC 9+ | |
| OpenOCD 9+ | |

**While it is possible to follow all the examples on a virtual machine, you may encounter USB connectivity issues. If you experience unstable communication with your hardware tools please proceed with a real installation.**

# Download the example code files

You can download the example code files for this book from GitHub at `https://github.com/PacktPublishing/Practical-Hardware-Pentesting`. If there's an update to the code, it will be updated on the existing GitHub repository.

We also have other code bundles from our rich catalog of books and videos available at `https://github.com/PacktPublishing/`. Check them out!

# Code in Action

Code in Action videos for this book can be viewed at `http://bit.ly/3sHBxRI`.

# Download the color images

We also provide a PDF file containing color images of the screenshots/diagrams used in this book. You can download it here: `http://www.packtpub.com/sites/default/files/downloads/9781789619133_ColorImages.pdf`.

# Conventions used

A number of text conventions are used throughout this book.

`Code in text`: Indicates code words in text, database table names, folder names, filenames, file extensions, pathnames, dummy URLs, user input, and Twitter handles. Here is an example: "For example, this is adding `1` to every byte received on `ttyUSB0` and sends it to `ttyUSB1`"

A block of code is set as follows:

```
[xxx.xx] usb xxx: New USB device found, idVendor=04d8,
idProduct=fc92, bcdDevice= 1.00
[xxx.xx] usb xxx: New USB device strings: Mfr=1, Product=2,
SerialNumber=0
```

When we wish to draw your attention to a particular part of a code block, the relevant lines or items are set in bold:

```
import serial
#imports the serial module
serin = serial.Serial('/dev/ttyUSB0', 115200)
#opens serial adapter one
serout = serial.Serial('/dev/ttyUSB1', 115200)
```

Any command-line input or output is written as follows:

```
#udevadm control --reload-rules
```

**Bold**: Indicates a new term, an important word, or words that you see onscreen. For example, words in menus or dialog boxes appear in the text like this. Here is an example: "Click on the **Connect device** button and set up the analyzer"

> **Tips or important notes**
> Appear like this.

# Get in touch

Feedback from our readers is always welcome.

**General feedback**: If you have questions about any aspect of this book, mention the book title in the subject of your message and email us at `customercare@packtpub.com`.

**Errata**: Although we have taken every care to ensure the accuracy of our content, mistakes do happen. If you have found a mistake in this book, we would be grateful if you would report this to us. Please visit www.packtpub.com/support/errata, selecting your book, clicking on the Errata Submission Form link, and entering the details.

**Piracy**: If you come across any illegal copies of our works in any form on the Internet, we would be grateful if you would provide us with the location address or website name. Please contact us at copyright@packt.com with a link to the material.

**If you are interested in becoming an author**: If there is a topic that you have expertise in and you are interested in either writing or contributing to a book, please visit authors.packtpub.com.

# Reviews

Please leave a review. Once you have read and used this book, why not leave a review on the site that you purchased it from? Potential readers can then see and use your unbiased opinion to make purchase decisions, we at Packt can understand what you think about our products, and our authors can see your feedback on their book. Thank you!

For more information about Packt, please visit packt.com.

# Section 1: Getting to Know the Hardware

After reading this section, you will know how to set up an assessment lab, understand the global architecture of an embedded system, know how to identify the different components, and understand how they act together in order to make the system run. Once you are able to understand all aspects of how a system works, you will be able to follow a risk modeling methodology to plan your tests according to the threats against the target system.

This section comprises the following chapters:

- *Chapter 1, Setting Up Your Pentesting Lab and Ensuring Lab Safety*
- *Chapter 2, Understanding Your Target*
- *Chapter 3, Identifying the Components of Your Target*
- *Chapter 4, Approaching and Planning the Test*

# 1
# Setting Up Your Pentesting Lab and Ensuring Lab Safety

Embedded systems, in the broadest definition of the term, are all around us in our everyday lives (examples being our phones, our routers, our watches, our microwaves, and more). They all have a small computer inside them and take care of very critical aspects of our lives, and also collect and protect data that is very critical to us. Sadly, the embedded system industry is lagging behind the usual computing industry in terms of security. In the last 10 years, we have seen examples of how this lack of security in these kinds of systems can lead to very tangible impacts on the real world (for example, the Mirai botnet; the Stuxnet virus; a wave of attacks against routers; some countries stealing other countries' drones by spoofing the **Global Positioning System (GPS)**; and so on). This is why it is very important to train more and more people on how to find problems in these kinds of systems, not only because the problems are already here but also because there will be more and more such systems, and their ever-growing number will manage more and more crucial aspects of our lives (think about autonomous vehicles; drone delivery; robots to assist the elderly; and so on).

Helping you start with assessing the security of these kinds of systems is the first goal of this book. The second goal of this book is that you have fun while you learn because testing these kinds of systems is going to be interesting, and I take great pleasure in making the learning process enjoyable for you. You may ask yourself: *How is it going to be fun for me?* For me, it is because you are messing with the most trusted part of the system: the hardware. Not only you are messing with the most fundamental elements of the system, but you also are in direct contact with it; you will be soldering, drilling, scrapping, and touching the system to pop a shell! You will not only code to compromise your target system, but (hopefully rarely) the blood, sweat, and tears will not be figurative!

In this chapter, you will learn how to set up your lab, from a simple, low investment suitable for learning at home up to a professional testing environment. This chapter will get you up to speed on how to invest your money efficiently to achieve results and, most importantly, how not to kill yourself on the job.

The following topics will be covered in this chapter:

- The basic things you will need to get started
- The different types of (common) tools available for your labs, what to get, and at which point
- The approach to acquiring test equipment, and the difference between a company and a home lab
- Basic items you will want in a lab, what they are, what are their uses, and the approach to setting up a lab
- Examples of ramping up your lab: basic, medium, and professional labs

# Prerequisites – the basics you will need

Before going into the things you will need to buy, let's have a look at the basics you will need to go through our joint exploration of an unknown system (a Furby), and start working on your own systems.

# Languages

To be able to script activities and interact automatically with most systems, you will need to be familiar with at least one high-level programming or scripting language (I will use Python for the examples in this book, but any other scripting language such as Perl, Bash, PowerShell, and more will also work) and one low-level programming language to write your own firmware and customize the examples. I will also use C (on the attack platform) since it is the most popular programming language for embedded systems, but any language that has a compiler for your target system will work.

# Hardware-related skills

You will need to learn actual, manual skills that are not purely knowledge-based; the main obstacles people fear when starting hardware hacking are soldering and electronics. For both of these skills, you can approach them in a knowledge-based way: learn about Ohm's law; the physics of semiconductors; what is an eutectic mixture and temperature; and all of the theoretical background. To be honest, I would not recommend approaching the skills like that. Of course, you will need the knowledge down the road, but don't start with this. Solder things; make **light-emitting diodes** (**LEDs**) blink; learn how to use transistors as switches. In short: do things, accept failure, and learn from it; burning a transistor will cost you a few cents but you will not repeat your error; burning your fingers will hurt but this will heal in a few days (there are safety instructions in the book—read them very carefully). You have far more chances to disgust yourself by learning a lot of laws and formulas while never using them than by having a problem, finding the correct formula, and solving your problem with it!

# System configuration

Having a nice desktop computer will really improve your experience in the lab. Even if, in today's world, people tend to use laptops more and more, this can prove to be a challenge when you are attacking hardware. A laptop will not block you from attacking, but a desktop will definitely prove easier. A laptop's main challenge will be the very limited physical interfaces available on it (still, you can work with it).

You don't need a powerful computer to start with (I use a 7-year-old i7: nothing fancy), but really pay attention to the interfaces. It is very common for me to use 5-6 **Universal Serial Bus** (**USB**) ports when I am attacking hardware; for example, when operating on any embedded system, I typically have attached the following to my computer (not even counting my convenience peripherals such as keyboard, mouse, headset, having a dual-screen setup, and so on):

- USB:

    - A bus pirate

    - An OpenBench logic analyzer

    - One or two USB to **Universal Asynchronous Receiver/Transmitter** (**UART**) bridges

    - A **microcontroller unit** (**MCU**) board

    - A function generator

    - My programmable power supply

- Ethernet:

    - My internet connection

    - My oscilloscope

Good luck doing that with a laptop without using an external USB hub, especially when these hubs can interfere with the functionality of some peripherals (for example, the USB-UART bridges I use tend to become unstable if used over a USB hub—using a good-quality powered USB hub can help).

One of the main contention points is the operating system. I use Linux, but using a Windows-based machine (especially if you use the **Windows Subsystem for Linux** (**WSL**) for anything but access hardware peripherals) will not really limit you in the end. (I will base the examples in this book on Linux. If you don't want to install a machine with Linux, just run a **virtual machine** (**VM**) but be aware that some of the most popular and free virtualization software does not really support USB passthrough very well.)

# Setting up a general lab

The setup of the lab itself is very important and will be quite determinant in terms of your ease of use and comfort in the lab. You will spend a lot of hours thinking and hacking in there, thus the room and its furniture will be quite important to your comfort. You will need to consider the following factors:

- **Your chair**: Invest in a good wheeled desk chair with easily movable arm support and good back and lumbar support. The racecar seat-looking chairs targeted at gamers can be a good type to look into, but really pay attention to the armrests and a system that allows you to move them away and set them to the desired height easily. More often than not, they will annoy you when using your soldering iron, but you will want them to support your arms when typing, for example.

- **Your work table**: Three factors are critical—the height of the table (so you don't kill your back when operating close to a **printed circuit board** (**PCB**), for example) and its surface. For the surface, I like clear colors (to be able to easily see a component that slipped, for example) with a slightly textured surface (so the components don't skid too far too easily). Also, the larger your work surface, the better it is to spread the inevitable clutter.

- **Shelving**: You will want to have shelving on top of your work table in order to be able to have your instruments on top of your work area without them eating up the space available. I like to have the shelving approximately 50 cm higher than the surface of my work table in order to be able to easily manipulate the interface of the instruments and put back probes without having to stand up from my chair nor having to kill my neck when I look at waveforms or a specific knob or button.

- **Light**: Good and powerful lighting of your work area is crucial; not only you will be manipulating a variety of very small things (components, cables, connectors, and others), but it becomes even more important when operating under magnification (for example, for soldering).

- **Anti-static measures**: An anti-static mat is really practical to protect sensitive devices against electrostatic discharge. They come with a bracelet that ensures any electrostatic charge you may have built up is dissipated. It is also important to avoid flooring that will make you build up such charges (such as carpets).

## Safety

There are inherent risks linked with opening and interacting with live systems. Please read these carefully—safety first!

Please follow these safety tips at all times:

1.  If there is a risk of electric shock, never ever do your tests alone and be sure to brief the person who is with you on how to quickly kill the power and react. Have emergency services' number preeminently displayed; a fire extinguisher that can be used on live electricity; first aid training; and so on.

2.  Whenever your fingers or instruments go near a system, ensure it is either disconnected from the mains (that is, wall plug electricity—110/220V (where **V** stands for **volts**)) or that you are physically isolated from the mains part of the board (for example, use silicon mats to isolate the dangerous part of the power section).

3.  If a system is mains-powered, always, always use an insulation transformer.

4.  Wear adequate clothing, remove jewelry and, if you are sporting long hair, always tie this up (which will prevent it from getting in the way).

5.  If the system sports any kind of battery, insulate the battery rails appropriately (with electrically insulating sticky tape, for example). Some battery types are dangerous and can catch fire or explode if shorted. I really advise you to have a look at videos of shorted lithium-polymer batteries: you don't want this kind of catastrophic failure happening in your home, lab, or office.

6.  You will work with sharp and hot tools and objects, so having a first aid kit available is always a good idea.

7.  There is a debate about what is dangerous: voltage or current. Actually: energy kills, so both voltage and current can be dangerous. For example, you may have already survived a > 10 **kilovolt** (**kV**) electric shock from electrostatic discharge (the sparks you can feel when removing a pullover, for example), but 2,000 A at 1 V will char you to death, and people regularly get killed by mains power. The gist is, whether amps or voltage are present, treat it as dangerous.

8.  Soldering equipment is very hot and will set things on fire if you are not cautious; always have a smoke detector in your lab, along with a fire extinguisher. Use the holder your soldering iron comes with (or buy one); they are usually shrouded to avoid contact with random objects.

Safety is of the utmost importance—there is no need for all the fancy test equipment we will now go through if there is no one to operate it.

# Approach to buying test equipment

These are my personal opinions and views. Especially regarding measurement equipment and tools, you will find a lot of heated argument about the different brands, models, and tools. Engineers tend to be reasonable but they are human beings, and there will be fanboys. You will find on different forums people with their opinions and the deeply rooted belief that what is working best for them is the best for anyone. The golden rule is the following:

- Get information upfront
- Make up your mind
- Be reasonable
- Get what works best for you

## Home lab versus company lab

Some very important distinctions have to be made between your own personal laboratory equipment and what you use in a company laboratory. Not only will the money for the home lab come from your own pocket, but some options (such as renting) may not be realistic for a home lab. Additionally, a company lab is subject to the safety rules of a work environment. You should meet with your company's occupational safety manager in order to comply with the adequate regulations regarding the storage of hazardous or corrosive chemicals, ventilation/air extraction, handling of possible fire hazards, and so on (as a side note, this is a very practical and reasonable way to get out of this noisy open space).

### Hacked equipment and Chinese copies

In a home lab, one of the best reminders of why you are doing the assessment is the fact that some instrument companies are suspected by the community of actually producing hackable instruments in order to boost their sales. And their instruments get hacked. This is a reminder that there is a very real community (and not a fabled hacker hidden in their parents' cellar) that is going after electronic devices in order to get the most out of them, unlocking features that are normally paid for, and potentially costing money to the company that produces the instruments. From a hobbyist point of view, it may be not really legal, but it is a common practice for hobbyists to maximize their investment by modifying or hacking existing instruments.

Since legality and repeatability are key in a company laboratory, I would advise against hacking instruments in this context. If the current laboratory setup of your company is not enabling a test to take place, your company should have a budget to buy (or rent) the adequate instruments or be able to offset the cost to a client.

The same goes for Chinese copies of programmers and logic analyzers—you may not care about it in a private setting, but in a professional setting the lower quality can actually turn back to bite you. The gist is, as long as you are doing this as a hobby, the decision to hack your instruments is on you, but if you are doing this professionally, buy the real thing and get reimbursed, or bill your client.

# Approaching instrument selection

Measurement instruments are like cars; it's all a question of balance.... You can find the following:

- The Italian sports car type—the luxury thing that will be able to do everything (short of cooking for you), which costs an insane amount of money and actually very few people can get the most out of. It may not be worth it in an assessment context unless you have a really specific need. If it is the case, it may be smarter to just rent the instrument. Brands that I classify in this category: Teledyne-LeCroy, Rohde & Schwartz, and high-end Keysight (formerly Agilent).

- The good-quality German car that is doing everything quite well. It may be a good investment if you are actually doing this a lot and need a reliable, solid instrument that will get you far for a long time. Brands that I classify in this category: mid-range Keysight, Tektronix, Yokogawa, and very high-end Siglent or Rigol.

- Le French car type—it's going to be doing almost the same thing that the German car does, for a fraction of the price, with a lot less style, and maybe for a shorter time. Brands that I classify in this category: mid-range Siglent or Rigol.

- The no-frills, cheap Japanese car—it's going to be efficient and cheap, get you from point A to point B, but you're not going to get a lot out of it on the speedway. Brands that I classify in this category: low-range Siglent or Rigol.

- The "el cheapo" Chinese car. It is cheap; it's a box with an engine and a driving wheel, but not much more. Also, don't have a crash in it: its safety is not so well engineered. Brands that I classify in this category: OWON.

And just as with a car, you can find very interesting second-hand deals! Don't underestimate second-hand instruments—a lot of renting companies sell their used equipment second-hand, and you can score pretty sweet deals like that. (My first oscilloscope was a second-hand 100 MHz-bandwidth Phillips, which I scored on eBay and used for 3 years without a problem.)

# What to buy, what it does, and when to buy it

Here is a table of the main types of different instruments, what they are used for, and how much they are needed (0 being the highest priority):

| Instrument | Description | Priority |
|---|---|---|
| Digital multimeter (DMM) | A DMM is a fundamental tool that allows you to measure voltage, resistance, and current intensity and also to check for continuity. Advanced models allow you to measure other values such as frequency, inductance, and capacitance. | 0 |
| Soldering iron | Just as with the DMM, a soldering iron is one of the pieces of equipment you will use the most. Directly go for a temperature-controlled one. This will allow you to make your own circuits, remove and exchange components, and more. | 0 |
| Bus pirate | This is a very useful multitool to interact with in-circuit buses—more on it in the in-circuit communication chapter: *Chapter 6, Sniffing and Attacking the Most Common Protocols.* | 0 |
| Logic analyzer | A logic analyzer reads digital protocols and allows you to decode them in software later. This is extremely useful for spying on inter-chip communication, developing and debugging your custom tools, and more. | 1 |
| MCU platform | A MCU platform you will get to know well and will learn to use efficiently. This will be very useful to send fake messages on buses, impersonate a chip, and pretty much interact in a programmatic way with the target system's electric signals. We will go for a cheap and flexible one (the blue pill) later in the book. | 1 |
| JTAG adapter | JTAG (named after the Joint Test Action Group) is historically an interface to test the soldering of chips. It has been extended to offer chip-specific programming and debug interfaces and functions. | 1 |

| Instrument | Description | Priority |
|---|---|---|
| Oscilloscope | An oscilloscope allows you to measure voltage in function of time and trace the curve of this voltage. Current models can do additional measurements (frequency measurement, frequency spectrum, and more), trace voltages in function of another, decode digital protocols, and so on. | 2 |
| Hot air station | A hot air station is an advanced version of a soldering iron. It is very practical to work with surface-mounted components since it will allow you to heat all leads and underlying pads of a component at once. | 2 |
| Lab power supply | Lab power supply comes in two main flavors: variable ones (where you can set a fixed output voltage and a maximum current limit manually) and programmable ones (where you can set the voltage and current limit programmatically). The first kind is all you need to start and do most of your work. The programmable ones are more advanced and, should you need one, you'll be knowledgeable enough to know it. I personally only have a manual one and have never needed a programmable one. | 0 (var) / 3(prog) |
| FPGA platform | A **field-programmable gate array (FPGA)** is a programmable logic platform that allows you to do really fast and high throughput operations. This piece of equipment is among the more advanced that you should look into when you have become more familiar with procedural programming or if you have a specific need to do something really fast. | 4 |

## DMM

The **DMM** is your principal tool—you will be using it all the time. I really mean all... the... time....This is probably the piece of equipment you will find the most fanboy discussion around, and they can scale from a few USDs for handheld Chinese super low-end to a few thousand for a brand name, high-quality, precision-bench DMM. My first recommendation is: get two—a good workhorse from a good brand (no need to go to the super-expensive Fluke ones for your first one) for which you can make a reasonable investment, and an "expendable," low-precision one (in the 20-30 USD range). The reason behind having two DMMs is that you may have to measure voltage and current at the same time but this is not very often, so investing in two good ones isn't worth it.

## DMM basics

Your DMM will come with a manual. Read it. Even if you have used a multimeter before, you have to know the basic characteristics of the tool you will be using.

If you have never used a multimeter, it should come with at least these functions:

- **Voltage measure**: This will measure the voltage difference between the two test leads. If your DMM doesn't have an auto-range function (like most entry-level meters), you will have to set the measuring range and set it to direct or alternating voltage.

- **Current measure**: This will measure the current (the amount of electricity) passing through the leads. Again, pay attention to the range. Most of the time, you will have to change the connector one of the leads is plugged into (from V to A; sometimes there is even a mA connector for lower ranges).

- **Resistance measure**: This will measure the resistance between leads by creating a known voltage between the leads and measuring the current that the resistance lets go through. Again, pay attention to the range. The resistance is inferred by using Ohm's law:

  *Voltage* (in volts: V) = *Resistance* (in Ohms: $\Omega$) x *Current* (in amperes: A).

- **Continuity test**: When the test leads are connected with a negligible resistance, the multimeter will beep.

> **Tip**
> Never use the continuity measurement or resistance measurement modes on a live circuit—not only can the reading be false but you can also damage your DMM!

## Getting your workhorse

You will be able to find a curated list of DMMs with their characteristics and comparison on the *EEVblog* forum. (I also warmly encourage you to watch the videos from EEVblog—Dave Jones' style isn't for everybody, but I personally like it a lot and his videos are always very educative.)

The list can be found here: `https://www.eevblog.com/forum/testgear/multimeter-spreadsheet/`.

I really don't recommend going for a very cheap Chinese DMM, nor can I point you toward an exact model since it may not be valid in a few months.

The elements to pay attention to when selecting a DMM (in order of priority) are the following:

- The DMM really should be of a safety rating compatible with what you are measuring (at least CAT III, as you will be measuring main voltages at some point) and the probes should be really sharp. In a worst-case scenario, you can always buy replacement probes.

- Bandwidth, precision (the number of displayed digits), and the count numbers should be as high as your budget allows.

- The speed of the continuity test (try to find review videos)—you want it to be as fast as possible.

- The available ranges—you really want as wide a range of measurement as possible, both of **alternating current** (**AC**) and **direct current** (**DC**) (it should range from millivolts to at least 1,000 volts; from a few ohms to a few dozens of megaohms; and from a few microamps to 10 or 20 amps for current).

- The input impedance (that is, the capability of the meter to read the voltage from a circuit without disturbing the circuit)—you want at the very least 10 megaohms (the higher the better).

- A serviceable fuse that you can replace easily.

- Good back-lighting to help with screen visibility when you are working late.

## Soldering tools

Get a good temperature-controlled soldering iron with widely available replacement tips. Again, it is desirable to have a good workhorse and a lower-quality secondary iron (you will very rapidly be confronted with the necessity to rework surface mount parts; it is often tricky with a single iron and very often results in damaged PCB pads). The temperature control is very important since you will be confronted with leaded and unleaded solder, which have a different melting temperature; different-sized components with their own thermal mass (that is, how much heat does the component source from your iron before getting hot); and so on (get both irons with temperature control; the secondary doesn't need to be as precise as the main one). Some additional supplies are also extremely useful, as listed here:

- **Liquid and tacky flux**: This allows the melted solder to flow much more easily on the leads and pads. You will be constantly removing and re-soldering parts from PCBs, and flux will be helping you tremendously, especially for su**rface-mounted device** (**SMD**) parts.

- **Soldering wick**: This is an invaluable tool to remove excess solder and clean PCB pads before soldering back a part.

- **Fluxed, leaded solder**: Get two different thicknesses, one in the 0.5 mm range and the other one as thin as you can get for SMD rework. You will find leaded solder a lot easier to work with as it melts at lower temperatures, flows better, is much easier to wick out, and allows you to drown unleaded solder on multi-leaded chips to remove them. Since unleaded solder has a lower melting temperature, it is tricky to keep multiple leads in a nice melted blob of solder on all leads to remove it. Alloying the unleaded solder with additional leaded solder will help you a lot with this.

- **A third hand**: Yes—this tool's name sounds strange but it is a common tool. It is a heavy-based tool with two (or more) springy pincers that will hold components in place while you are soldering. To get how it is helpful, just imagine yourself soldering, with a soldering iron in one hand and the solder wire in the other. How would you hold parts or wires in place? These are really small, very light things that can move under the smallest shock and tend to do this at the worst moment possible.

- **Tips**: When you select your iron, try to find one for which the tips are reasonably cheap for different shapes; you will find the default conical tip that most irons come with to be actually impractical compared to a truncated cone.

- **Tweezers**: A soldering iron will get too hot for your grubby little fingers very fast. Having a nice set of cheap tweezers with different tip shapes will be very helpful to hold and manipulate small components.

- **Side cutters**: Flush side cutters are very useful to cut component leads very close to the PCB.

- **A PCB holder**: This will allow you to hold firmly a PCB (and orient it easily) while you work on it.

## Logic analyzer

Here, there are two distinct ways, either open source software-based (sigrok) or proprietary ones (there are plenty, but Saleae is well known as being easy to use). Saleae hardware is, in my opinion, a little bit expensive for the punch they pack but it is balanced by very good software. It is possible to find Chinese copies of some of their (either older or smaller) models, but I would refer to the excerpt on knock-offs at the beginning of the chapter. Sigrok is compatible with a very wide list of hardware (you can find it here: `https://sigrok.org/wiki/Supported_hardware`). I personally use both: an OpenBench Logic Sniffer (by dangerous prototypes) with sigrok at home, and Saleae at work.

Here is what to look for in a logic analyzer:

- **Sample speed**: This is the speed at which the analyzer samples the signal and determines the maximum speed of signal you can read accurately. The Nyquist criterion tells us that to read a signal accurately, you have to sample it at least at twice the speed of the signal.

- **The number of inputs**: The higher the better, but you can cover a very large percentage of buses with the basic 8-channel analyzers.

- **The input protection**: You may plug a probe on the wrong thing; you may accidentally burn a test system when fiddling with wires; your soldering iron may be badly grounded; and more.... There are a thousand things that can kill your analyzer; either have spares or good protection.

- **The input impedance**: Similar to the DMMs—at the very least, 10 megaohms.

## Bus pirate

Easy—there is only one. There is a debate about which version to use (v4 can be buggy sometimes, so go for v3). The bus pirate is a tool that will allow you to interact and play with the most common protocols used to talk with chips.

## MCU platform

The MCU platform will be the most controversial piece on the forums and on the internet in general.

I strongly recommend getting familiar with a vendor platform in the **Advanced RISC Machine** (**ARM**) family because of these factors:

1. The ARM architecture will be a very common target.

2. It is widely supported in term of compilers and debuggers with open source toolchains (GCC, OpenOCD, GDB, and so on).

3. Development boards are very cheap, plentiful, easy to find, and quite complete.

4. You can find screaming fast platforms for quite a cheap price.

5. Packages with a large number of very fast I/O are very common.

6. The necessary passive components to support the MCU can be quite low.

I am very partial to the STM32 family from STMicroelectronics. It may have its quirks, but the development boards are incredibly cheap. Some quite capable MCUs can be found mounted on cheap Chinese boards, in the 4 USD range (delivered) on popular websites (eBay, AliExpress, and so on) offering a ton of I/Os and quite decent hardware peripheral. A few bucks more will get you an official board, which includes a programmer (that can be used to program the cheap ones quite easily). This is my personal opinion and mainly comes from the fact that these cheap development boards were among the first ones I had access to and, hence, I learned to use the quirks and features of the family quite well.

Plenty of other vendors (Texas Instruments, Cypress, NXP, and so on) offer quite comparable boards in the same price range. My main advice would be: choose a vendor and a family, get well acquainted to it, and stick with it. The chances are that you'll be able to select the family member with the speed and peripheral set that will fit your needs best when you have a specific requirement set.

## JTAG adapter

JTAG, to start with, is an interface that was designed to test the soldering of integrated circuits. It was designed as a shift register that was able to activate all the leads of a CPU in order to be able to test the electrical connections. The basic design of JTAG was conceived to allow for the daisy-chaining of chips in order to have a single chain that could be leveraged to test a board. It was later enriched with CPU-specific features (that are not well standardized) in order to allow for in-circuit debugging and programming. It can be very useful for your own developments or to get access to the internal states of a chip if it is not disabled in production.

JTAG is based on a (minimum) four-wire bus (data in, data out, test, and clock). This bus is piloting a state machine in each target chip. (JTAG will be covered in more depth in *Chapter 10, Accessing the Debug Interfaces.*)

## Oscilloscope

An oscilloscope will be a very useful tool for exploring signals and probing different lines. Basically, an oscilloscope will allow you to visualize a voltage in function of time. To get a good grip on the basic operation of an oscilloscope, please refer to Tektronix's guide *XYZs of Oscilloscopes* and read your oscilloscope manual from front to back.

Selecting your oscilloscope is almost easy—the baseline is that you want to get the most bandwidth and the most memory size for your budget. The question of whether to select a two-channel or a four-channel oscilloscope is very common. As usual, it boils down to a tradeoff. If you can get a four-channel with a bandwidth of 100 MHz or more within your budget, get it. A four-channel oscilloscope is very useful if you are exploring systems where more analog electronics are used and where you want to correlate an event's occurrence relative to another event.

Before taking your decision, it is really important that you watch test videos and, if possible, teardowns to compare the usability of your different candidates and the possibilities of repairing them in the case of problems. Do not underestimate repairability, I broke the screen of a 500 USD scope and I was really happy to be able to fix it with a 30 USD Chinese screen.

## The bandwidth

The bandwidth of an oscilloscope is actually not equal to the maximal speed you will be able to measure. It is what is called a -3 **decibel (dB)** bandwidth. A -3 dB bandwidth is the frequency at which the instrument will measure a signal at half of its actual power.

This means that a 100 MHz-bandwidth oscilloscope will measure a 100 MHz, 1 V peak-to-peak p sine wave as a 0.7 V peak-to-peak signal!

To accurately read a sine wave (that is, at its actual voltage level), you will need at least three times the bandwidth of the signal.

Bandwidth is the characteristic of an oscilloscope with the most impact on the buying price. Take what the maximal and usual frequencies that you need to measure will be and make your decision accordingly.

Regarding the number of channels, it is very simple: the more channels you have, the better it is. Take into account in your decision that, most of the time, you will need one or two channels; measuring three and more signals is not something you will need every day, but you will be happy to have it when you need it.

## The probes

There are two main types of probes: active and passive. To make it simple, you can only use passive probes under 350MHz (for higher speed, you will need active probes). Passive probes are quite cheap and come with a manual switch between different "damping ratios" that can be taken into account in the oscilloscope's interface. The probes are really important, same as the DMMs; you will want very sharp probes with a wire grabber. Good-quality probes are quite common with oscilloscopes. Don't forget to compensate your probes—the procedure should be described in your scope's manual.

## Display

Most modern oscilloscopes come with additional display functions, such as **Fast Fourier Transform** (**FFT**), which allows you to see the signal in the frequency domain instead of the usual time domain); XY display (which allows you to see the signal on a channel in function of another channel); and X/Sin(X) (read Chris Rehorn's excellent paper *Sin(x)/x Interpolation: An Important Aspect of Proper Oscilloscope Measurements* and about the Nyquist-Shannon Signal sampling theorem).

## Interfaces

It is very common to find network (Ethernet) remote commands and display; **Video Graphics Array** (**VGA**) output; USB storage of measured waveforms. This can be very useful to display waveforms on your computer or extract the samples from a measurement for later processing.

## References

Just as with DMM, a list is maintained on the EEVblog forum: `https://www.eevblog.com/forum/testgear/digital-oscilloscope-comparison-chart/`.

## Hot air gun

A hot air gun shoots hot air at a controllable temperature and flow rate. This is very practical to solder or unsolder surface-mounted components. Some accessories and consumables are inseparable companions to an hot air gun: solder paste (to tin your pads, this can be deposed pad by pad with a toothpick) and Kapton tape (this is a type of heat-resistant sticky tape that can be used to protect components next to the one you are soldering or desoldering). I would recommend using leaded solder paste but this can be tricky to get in Europe or the US. The use of a hot air gun requires practice to be efficient and I would recommend watching technique videos and train on junk/broken boards before going at it on an important PCB.

Here are the things that you have to look for in pretty much all of the hot air stations you will find:

- Regulated temperature
- Regulated airflow
- Replaceable air gun head (to be able to have thin or wide flows; it can also be interesting to replace the head with a square one for bigger **quad-flat packages** (**QFPs**) or **quad-flat no-leads packages** (**QFNs**).

## FPGA platform

FPGAs are really practical for fast logic processing. Their main downside is that most of them require a proprietary programming and synthesis (the FPGA lingo for compilation). At the time of writing of this book, only the Lattice iCE40 had an open source development tool chain available (and support for the Xilinx 7 series is supposed to be coming up soon). Most of the proprietary environments are quite expensive if you want to cover most of the chips of the vendor, but some development kits come with a development environment limited to the chip that is on the board. I personally use an Artix-7 Arty board that I was trained on by Toothless Consulting's Dmitry Nedospasov, and I am very happy with it.

## Vendor

A few vendors share most of the FPGA market: Xilinx; Intel (who acquired Altera); Lattice; and Microsemi (who acquired Actel). As for MCUs, most of them are almost equivalent (short of their development environments); depending on the time you are buying, just take the best development board you can find and stick to the vendor.

## Language

A very common question is the language to develop with, being Verilog or VHDL. Verilog tends to be more common in the US, while VHDL is more common in Europe. The most important part is that both languages are equivalent; you can achieve exactly the same results and it is more a matter of taste. From my point of view, I tend to find VHDL is a bit more descriptive but as a downside, it requires more boilerplate code. I personally prefer Verilog since it is terser and easier to find examples for.

## Lab power supply

Your lab power supply will allow you to power up your circuits and your target system. Some very practical features you really want on your supply are listed here:

- **Current limitation**: This will allow you to prevent things from burning when you are messing with the circuitry. I usually measure the current consumption of the circuit in a normal context (over an hour, for example) and set the current limit 5-10% higher than the measured consumption.
- **Current measurement**: This will allow you to detect some more power-consuming behaviors in the target system, such as **radiofrequency (RF)** emission.

- **Multiple (at least two) variable outputs**: This will allow you to run some part of your target system at a voltage less than what they are intended to run at, or at a current limited to less than what they need, potentially triggering some interesting errors.

- The ability to chain outputs in case you need some higher voltage than usual.

Programmable power supplies aren't needed to start, but they can come in handy later when you need to program some behavior in function of time or other behaviors on your target system. They are usually more expensive than the simple ones but can come in handy.

## Small tools and equipment

You will need a lot of different small tools in your lab. I personally use multiple mugs and boxes to keep them ready near my work area. Some examples are listed here:

- **Tweezers**: There are different point shapes and quality. You will have a very frequent use for sharp pointy ones for very small SMD components (0201, for example) and rounded, slightly larger ones for more common packages (0805, for example). The lowest-quality ones tend to bend quite easily, and I find that investing in medium-quality tweezers can be advantageous. You can find these for quite cheap on bidding sites such as eBay.

- **Scalpels**: I tend to use n°4 medical scalpel handles with detachable blades. They replace very advantageously the usual X-ACTO knives (even if the blades are a little less sturdy) since the blades are very cheap in packs of 100 and are available in a lot of different shapes.

  I keep a stock of the following blades:

  - *n°26*: for general cutting work and scrapping traces

  - *n°23*: for cutting work that needs some force and cutting plastic

  - *n°19*: for scrapping traces

- **Screwdrivers**: You will need a set of long- and thin-precision screwdrivers with multiple heads (at least flat, pozidriv, torx, and hex) in multiple sizes. The best approach here is to buy a set of screwdrivers with multiple heads and sizes. I would also advise that, when you have to buy a set of security bits, you buy one with the following: security hex, security torx, tri-wings, tri-groove, pig noses, and clutch A and G.

Some vendor-specific and even customer-specific screw/screwdriver couples exist, but this can usually be defeated with a bi-component epoxy compound or, in extreme cases, with a bit of aluminum casting or **computer numerical control (CNC)** machining.

- **Clamps**: The type of clamps you will be most interested in are called Kelly forceps. This type is used to keep things together with a bit of force, like holding boards together while soldering or holding wires in place while glue is curing.

- **Pliers**: You will very often use cutting pliers and long-necked ones to cut leads, remove connectors, and for a variety of different tasks. Again, buying decent-quality pliers will ensure they can survive small amounts of abuse that is very common in regular usage. I would advise investing in a good-quality wire stripper plier (of the simplest, flat kind that looks like a pair of pliers with multiple teeth sizes for the different wire sizes). I find that self-stripping tools tend to rip and break the cables that usually come with embedded systems far too easily.

- **Breadboard**: A breadboard is a tool where you can plug multiple wires and through-hole components temporarily. This is very useful to make small temporary circuits to power components and to have some glue logic, level shifting, modulation, and so on. You can easily start with cheap breadboards from bidding sites but they degrade quite quickly. Better quality brands such as 3M degrade less quickly, are a bit expensive, but hold better value over time.

  Breadboarded circuits tend to be very fragile due to the way the components are mounted. Due to stray capacitance, I would not advise using breadboards with frequencies over 5 MHz. The indispensable companions to the breadboard are jumper wires (a length of wire with male or female connectors crimped at the end). Just find cheap lots of male-male, female-female, and female-male on bidding sites and buy some. I consider these consumables since I regularly cut them for ease of connection to a breadboard.

- **Perfboard/Stripboard**: These plates of PCB have either copper dots or strips you can cut and solder together in order to create circuits. They are more solid than breadboards and behave a bit better at higher frequencies.

- **Magnification**: As a first step, I recommend buying a few magnifying glasses that you can mount on your third hand (if it doesn't come with one already). At a later stage, and especially if you are working with very small components (0201 SMD or a lot of very fine-pitch MCUs, for example), a stereo microscope is very useful to see what you are actually soldering and keep a sense of depth to position your iron accurately.

## Renting versus buying

It is quite common for companies to rent their test equipment long-term. It may or may not be interesting depending on your volume of use for a certain type of equipment. For example, you may need a specialized piece of equipment (such as a high-end **software-defined radio** (**SDR**); a vector network analyzer; a very very fast oscilloscope) for a specific engagement but you will very rarely use it in your normal work; then, it may be very practical and economically right to rent the piece instead of buying it. In a professional context, my approach for it is the following:

- If it is less than 2,000€, just buy it—renting will not be worth the hassle

- If I know I will not use it again in the next 6 months or if it is over 10,000€, rent it.

- The scope in the middle is then just a matter of calculation, as follows:

  - (daily rent cost) x (number of days foreseen in the following year) < 50% price: rent it.

  - else, buy it.

Additionally, renting a piece of equipment before buying it will allow you to evaluate its interface and its performance across the spectrum of your different usages. Now that we have seen the different instruments we need to interact with components, let's have a look at those.

# The component pantry

You will need a component pantry—by that, I mean that you will need at least an assortment of common resistors, capacitors, transistors, and voltage regulators always at hand. More often than not, you will find yourself in need of a jellybean component and will actually gain a lot of time by just having it available.

## The pantry itself

Buy some of those drawer cabinets commonly sold to people that are making jewelry or doing any other hobby involving a lot of small pieces. Buy enough of them so that you can sort easily the (quite large) number of parts you will end up storing. Start by buying two to three of them; that will cover you for a few years. They are not really expensive and are really worth it.

I would advise labeling the drawers as quickly as possible and finding an organization system that suits you. For example, I have a column for through-hole resistors; another for surface mount; some drawers for capacitors; some for coils; and a column dedicated to silicon (diodes, transistors, voltage regulators, **electrically erasable programmable read-only memory** (**EEPROM**) , and others)

I also have a lot of custom shelves made out of cheap **medium-density fiberboard** (**MDF**) planks and brackets just screwed in the wall. There, I keep labeled boxes with development kits, instruments, a lot of electronic waste for cannibalization, instruments I rarely use, and others.

## The stock

To start, I would advise keeping the following in stock:

- A collection of common resistors (buy some cheap E12 resistor kit on eBay) in through-hole (THT) and surface mount (SMT— a lot in 0805 and a few in 0402).

- A (small) collection of chemical and ceramic capacitor in common values (a few in the picofarad range: 0.1μ, 10μ, 47μ mainly, and a few big ones for power decoupling). For the packages, same thing as the resistors: a mix of through-hole and surface mount.

- A few power (1N4004) and  signal (1N4118) diodes. A few Zener diodes for common voltage levels won't hurt (5, 3.3, 2.5, 1.8, 1.2). Zener diodes are designed to let current flow at a given voltage level, allowing you to protect circuitry against voltage spikes or to use them as a crude voltage conversion.

- At least a dozen fixed voltage regulators for the common voltages (5, 3.3, 2.5, 1.8, 1.2) and a few beefy adjustable ones (LM317 in a TO-220 package is very, very useful).

- Some standard transistors (both **Field Effect Transistors** (**FETs**) and **Bipolar Junction Transistors** (**BJT**), again in a mix).

- A few salvaged power supplies that can provide you with 24, 12, and 5 V (the powerful USB chargers that come with modern phones will give out a nice stable 5 V with decent amperage, are plentiful). Power supplies are very common e-waste and you can usually score a dozen for a small bill in any flea market... keeping them useful and out of the waste pile is both good for your wallet and the planet.

To keep my stock filled and enrich it, my strategy is to always order 10-15% more than I need in projects, just to cover the usage and not to have to follow individual component use (1 minute of your time is worth more money that the few fractions of cent a resistor costs).

Now, you should really play around with the components in your stock, learn about them, and make a few classical circuits to learn how they work and what they are actually doing, since keeping things you don't know how to use just for the sake of hoarding wouldn't make much sense, would it?

Now that we have looked at our instruments and components, let's have a look at a possible evolution path for your lab.

# Sample labs

In this section, we will be looking at different states of a home laboratory (from beginner to pro) that you could take inspiration from. When a piece of equipment is not described at a given level, it means that the piece is kept from the level before. Some pieces of equipment are not necessary before a given level of maturity (for example, the pro level doesn't have a new hot air station because it is kept from the amateur level).

# Beginner

At this stage, the goal is to kickstart the activity as cheaply as possible, acquire knowledge, and check that you like it without burning too much money. Have a look at the following table:

| MCU platform | A Chinese Arduino copy—start with Arduino and move later to a raw C context with avr-gcc and avrdude |
|---|---|
| Breadboard | Cheap Chinese from a bidding site |
| Oscilloscope | Any cheap secondhand 50 MHz bandwidth from a bidding site |
| Logic analyzer | A cheap bidding site Cypress FX2 repurposed board with homemade clamping diode input protection |
| Bus pirate | The one and only |
| Soldering station | Cheap bidding site temperature-controlled iron—the TS100 is very popular but you need an external supply |
| Function generator | A cheap **Direct Digital Synthesis (DDS)** device from eBay |
| Power supply | Repurposed phone chargers or **Advanced Technology eXtended (ATX)** power supply breakout (this is a small board that you can plug a computer power supply to) |
| DMM | El cheapo 10$ multimeter (do not work on mains voltage with this) |

Price: <500€.

# Amateur

At this point, you like the activity but you are starting to be limited by your equipment. You have circumvented some limitation by doing hacks, you have rolled out your own code to drive peripherals for common protocols on your current MCU and bit-banged some, but your platform is starting to become slow, your scope is not fast enough or lacking digital trigger, and more. Here are some pieces of equipment you can buy to solve these problems:

| | |
|---|---|
| MCU platform | A fast STM32F4 (such as the Discovery), in pure C with arm-gcc and stlink |
| Breadboard | A wide 3M with multiple rows |
| Oscilloscope | A low-level oscilloscope with at least 100 MHz of bandwidth, potentially a hackable one for better bandwidth or decoding of digital protocols |
| Logic analyzer | An open bench logic analyzer |
| Soldering station and hot air gun | A Chinese brand (Bekka, Yihua, OneHungLow, and so on...) combo iron and hot air gun will cover your bases for quite a long time; just pay attention to the temperature control on the iron and to the availability of replacement tips. |
| Power supply | A dual variable output with a fixed 5V power supply. It is really easy to find one on a bidding site for a quite reasonable budget. |
| DMM | A reasonably priced DMM from a reputable brand (in the 100€ range) will do the job nicely. |
| Good helping hands | The Chinese "octopus" style help hands are easy to find on bidding sites. They will allow you to hold probes easily, even if you have a four-channel oscilloscope. They have an articulation system that looks like the feet of a gorillapod. |
| JTAG programmer | Any development boards based on an FTDI FT2232H will do the job nicely (it is compatible with OpenOCD). It won't give you crazy fast speed, but this is not something you really need at this point. |

Price: <2,000€

# Pro

At this point you are doing it regularly, so you will pretty much know what you will need. Have a look at the following table:

| | |
|---|---|
| Oscilloscope | A good oscilloscope with a 350-500 MHz bandwidth from a major vendor (Rohde & Schwarz, Keysight, Tektronix, LeCroy, and so on) will be a serious investment. At this point, you will know what you need but will still need to research a lot since these instruments cost quite a bit of money. |
| Power supply | Choose a nice, programmable power supply from a mid-tier vendor with at least two variable outputs, such as the Rigol DP832. |
| Function generator | An entry-level function generator such as one from the Rigol DG900 series will cover your needs. |
| Logic analyzer | Saleae Logic Pro 16 is a very good logic analyzer with very practical software. |
| DMM | A mid-range DMM from Fluke (the DMM117, for example) will be good enough for what you will have to do. If you need something with more performance, have a look at bench multimeters. |
| JTAG programmer | A SEGGER J-Link will give you very nice speeds. |
| FPGA platform | Arty A7, S7, or Z7, depending on your needs of having an onboard ARM CPU |

Price: ~8,000€

# Summary

In this chapter, we have seen the different tools that you will use and the different elements you will need to pay attention to when creating your laboratory.

A usually underestimated aspect of the lab is comfort—you will really spend a lot of time in there, so a good chair and a lot of natural light are quite important. I hope you will find all of these tips useful in the long run and that they will avoid you having to learn the hard way (like I did...I indeed spent money stupidly and burnt myself and shocked myself and hated my chair and... well pretty much did every possible mistake I speak about in this chapter...).

In the next chapter, you will learn how to approach a target system and harvest information about it.

# Questions

1. Why would you want two DMMs?
2. What is a 3 dB bandwidth?
3. Above which frequency will a breadboard parasitic capacitance interfere with the signals?
4. Who produces the bus pirate?
5. What is an oscilloscope?
6. What is the gist of the Nyquist-Shannon signal sampling theorem?
7. What is the main difference between active and passive oscilloscope probes?

# 2
# Understanding Your Target

When we look at the current state of developments in hardware, we can see that developers rely on two assumptions:

- The hardware can be trusted.

- An attacker will not attack the hardware to threaten the software and the ecosystem.

However, if we look at the current situation, we can see that these premises are not true anymore. We own cars, phones, TVs, and other devices, and knowledge about this hardware is not reserved for a handful of electrical engineers anymore. Not only is that knowledge now widespread and accessible, thanks to the internet, but the cost of the tools necessary to mount hardware attacks has gone down drastically.

Attacking the hardware is not only interesting because the trust assumptions on which software and ecosystem security is built do not really hold anymore (and hence representing a weak link in the security chain) but because there is a direct and physical relationship with the system. Soldering, cutting, and drilling are ways to form a more direct relationship with systems than spending hours purely coding and mean we will interact at a way deeper and more intimate level of system functionality.

Now, how do these systems work? Before grabbing your trusted soldering iron, let's talk about the big blocks that compose an embedded system (or a computer in general).

Embedded systems all share common functional blocks (that is, groups of components that will achieve a function). These blocks interact with each other to provide the product's functionality.

In this chapter, we will go through functional blocks and will explain what functionality they provide. You will find that these blocks are also found in more classical (that is, non-embedded) systems. Knowing what typical blocks to expect in a system and how they interact together will help you in understanding how your target system works. Knowledge of these interactions will be important, from a pentesting point of view, to understand how they provide security properties and to help you find security issues.

The following topics will be covered in this chapter:

- The CPU block
- The storage block
- The power block
- The networking blocks
- The sensor blocks
- The actuator blocks
- The interface blocks

# The CPU block

The CPU's goal is to process information. This is the core of the system and is your ultimate target in a penetration test. In the vast majority of cases, the CPUs you will be testing will have a von Neumann architecture (that is, the bus for data and instructions is shared) and rarely a Harvard architecture (a separate bus for data and instructions). From a penetration testing point of view, Harvard architectures are less exposed to buffer overflows since these buffers typically contain data that cannot usually be executed.

## CPU roles

The CPU itself will perform the following activities:

- Executing the different arithmetic and logic instructions, such as addition, multiplication, subtraction, division, and so on
- Reading and writing memory

- Managing the different hardware peripherals that are integrated with it, such as UART, SPI, cryptographic peripherals, storage peripherals, and so on

- Reacting to interrupts from, and communicating with, the embedded hardware peripherals

In the literature, you will sometimes find references to MCUs (or µCU) and MPUs. MCU designates a microcontroller and MPU a microprocessor. The main differences between an MCU and an MPU are that MCUs have on-chip program storage while MPUs use external storage for it. Both MCUs and MPUs are forms of CPUs.

# Common embedded systems architectures

In the general computing world, the x86 (and its modern implementations found in most computers) architectures are largely dominating the market (this is the architecture found in most PCs). This architecture has its limitations, though, which make it not always suitable for embedded systems (mainly due to its power requirements and price). A processor architecture consists of the instructions and operations the CPU accepts (called an **Instruction Set Architecture** (**ISA**)) and how they are interpreted to drive the data processing. Basically, it details what to tell the processor, whether to do an addition, a subtraction, read and write to memory, and more.

The ISA is the description of the architecture:

- The list of the instructions that the CPU accepts (what they do and how)

- The description of the different registers and how they influence the behavior of the data processing

The description of an ISA and the architecture is a big corpus of data and documentation that you will study depending on your current target. It is not my goal here to describe in depth how the different architecture behaves in detail (that would fill the book, being its entire contents, and would make it quite boring).

I will go through the most common architectures found in the embedded world in order for you to be aware of their existence and their main characteristics but, if you need to dig down to the architecture level, you will need to study the details on your own.

## ARM

**Acorn RISC Machine (ARM)** is a von Neumann architecture with two execution modes with different characteristics :

- Thumb mode:

    - It is a 16-bit instruction, 32-bit data ISA (but the Thumb-2 extension added a few 32-bit instructions to provide equivalent functions to the ARM instructions).

    - Code is very compact since the instructions are 16-bit.

- ARM mode:

    - 32-bit instructions

    - Available in both 64- and 32-bit flavors (the instructions stay the same; this mainly changes the size of the operands)

This is a very popular architecture since ARM's business model makes it very easy to create CPUs with a set of companion peripherals that are targeted at a specific application (for example, for a phone, you could make a CPU tailored to your needs (for a few million dollars) with a touch display driver, inputs for a microphone, a peripheral to drive RAM, flash storage, and more, and for a much cheaper heating controller – something with just a few timers, some basic input/outputs, and that's it). ARM is actually a fabless (without fabrication) *vendor*. ARM actually designs the core of the CPU and licenses the core design to other vendors that actually put peripherals around it and make (or have them made by a third party) the final chips. This is the architecture that gives life to most of today's smartphones, TVs, and a lot of consumer electronics.

## MIPS

**Microprocessor without Interlocked Pipeline Stages (MIPS)** is an architecture that is usually present in networking equipment (routers, switches, and so on) and in some consumer products (PSP, cable routers, and so on). This von Neumann type architecture is available in 32-bit and 64-bit variants. The architecture supports co-processors natively. These co-processors are used for application-specific hardware acceleration. In late 2018, Wave Computing, the new owner of the MIPS architecture, announced the open-sourcing of the ISA for 2019 to compete with other open source architectures, such as Reduced Instruction Set Computer V, also known as RISC-V.

## Atmel AVR

The Atmel AVR architecture (present in ATtiny, ATmega, and so on) is a Harvard type, 8-bit to 16-bit RISC architecture. It is usually present in low-power Internet of Things/embedded-type consumer goods and older industrial systems. This is the architecture that powers most of the Arduino type development boards. Getting familiar with this architecture's MCUs is very practical to develop quick and cheap attack tools.

## PIC

The PIC family of micro-controllers (made by the Microchip company) is a Harvard-type architecture, available from 8-bit to 32-bit ISA implementations. The relatively low price of the PIC family ensures its pervasive presence in low-cost, low-processing power devices.

## RISC-V

The RISC-V (pronounced risk-five) silicon architecture (and its open source OpenRISC companion ISA) is entirely open source and, as of 2019, has been physically implemented by multiple companies. Due to the open source nature of the ISA, it is widely used in academic contexts (for example, I learned the fundamentals of CPU architecture at university with a lot of RISC I examples) and is believed to become a significant competitor to ARM, thanks to the royalty-free nature of the ISA. Large vendors of specialized MCUs have already announced the migration of their lines towards RISC-V (Marvell, Western Digital, and so on). It is a von Neumann architecture available in 32 and 64 bits and, in the future, also in 128-bit word length.

## Other architectures

There are a lot of other architectures on the market (HC8, Blackfin, and so on). They are less common or more targeted towards specialized markets. Testing on these infrastructures requires closer collaboration or higher research investment due to their less documented or more closed nature.

> **Information box**
>
> Check the list of CPU architectures described at `https://en.wikipedia.org/wiki/Comparison_of_instruction_set_architectures`, if you want to know more.

# The storage block

Storage blocks are components (or groups of components) used to store information. Two storage blocks are always present, the RAM (for lower-end MCUs, it is usually in the CPU chip itself and for higher-end MCUs, it is outside of the chip) and the program storage. Some optional additional long-term storage can be present (usually as flash memory on modern systems, but it can vary from spinning hard drives, EEPROMs, to diode matrix ROMs on older systems).

## RAM

RAM is very fast, tightly CPU-coupled (and usually more expensive) memory. This is where the CPU usually fetches its instructions from, stores the short-term results of its operations (they are then stored for the long term in a slower and cheaper storage medium such as flash), and so on. The main characteristics of RAM in current systems are as follows:

- Very fast compared to long-term storage (for example, EEPROM, flash, or a hard drive)

- Much more expensive compared to long-term storage (for example, EEPROM, flash, or a hard drive)

- Loses its content on power loss (this is called volatile memory)

With research advancing around a new type of non-volatile, fast memory (mainly FRAM), this paradigm could change in the next few years. From a pentesting point of view, being able to dump RAM can allow us to find pieces of data of interest such as decrypted bits of code, crypto material, and so on.

## Program storage

This is slower, non-volatile, and cheaper memory. This memory (usually flash in modern MCUs, but this is one of the roles of the hard drive on a normal computer) stores the instructions the CPU will fetch and execute after its boot sequence. Some architectures and implementations will fetch and execute data directly from it; some others will have a RAM transfer mechanism before executing the instructions. Depending on the system, this can be external to the CPU chip but it is always interesting to dump from a penetration testing point of view since the code (and sometimes other pieces of data of interest) is located here.

## Storing data

Storing data can be done in the RAM for short-term retention. The storage media can be external or internal to the CPU chip (when it's internal, it usually uses a portion of the same media that is used for the program storage). The external storage usually takes the form of a serial or I2C EEPROM on small systems. Larger systems can sport just about any kind of storage, from the smallest EEPROMs to enterprise-grade hard drives or SSDs. The largest storage forms (more than a handful of megabytes) usually embed some form of filesystem or in-house "packing" system for the firmware. This form of packing is usually used to organize the content, compressing or reducing the storage size (stripping unnecessary headers of files).

# The power block

The power block's role is to power the different parts and subsystems within the system. It is of the utmost importance that the power section is approached by taking a lot of precautions and using protection.  Some of the systems you will test *will* expose dangerous voltages or components. No test is important enough that you take the risk of maiming or killing yourself. Living to be able to do more tests and to get back to your family safe and sound is the most important part of your job as a hardware penetration tester.

## The power block from a pentesting point of view

From a pentesting point of view, studying the power block will allow you to identify the different voltage levels used within the system. Do not assume that everything happens in one physical space; in modern systems, it is very common to have power rails distribute power across the system with higher voltage, more powerful electricity sources, and local regulation that is physically near the consumer components. This allows a reduction in the risk of electrical noise disturbing components sharing the same power rail.

Some advanced attacks (for example, glitching or differential power analysis) target the power block. These kinds of attacks will not be covered in this book since they require a firm understanding of how the CPU behaves with respect to power.

---

**Information box**

If you are interested in these kinds of power attacks, look into differential power analysis and fault injection (glitching). Colin O'Flynn's website is a good start for theory, software, and hardware regarding this.

---

# The networking blocks

The networking block allows the system to communicate. This communication can be done with other systems (mesh networking), with sensors, or with the system's backend. There is a wide variety of physical transport means (wired or not) for protocols over these layers. The typical interesting scenarios on a network level all pertain to breaching the trust between the system and its communication peers.

From a system point of view, we will typically listen to the traffic as a first step to evaluate the security of the communication with its peer to verify how hard it is to impersonate a peer, for example:

- We will look into impersonating a remote sensor to fool the system into harvesting fake data or to evaluate the system's capability to handle malformed information.

- We will look into impersonating the backend to distribute malicious firmware updates to evaluate the possibility of leveraging the system for nefarious activities.

From a peer point of view, we will proceed with the same state to evaluate the possibility of impersonating the system. For example, we will look into impersonating the system to do the following:

- Evaluate the possibility of reporting erroneous data to the backend

- Harvest firmware updates for further analysis

# Common networking protocols in embedded systems

This section covers different (but far from all...) networking protocols commonly used in embedded systems.

They are further classified as follows:

- **Physical layers**: Physical layers take care of the actual signal that transports the information.

- **Transport layers**: Transport layers take care of the aspects linked with... you guessed it… transporting the information (called the payload). This model allows the encapsulation of information, allowing you to change, after the fact, what is transported or what transports what.

- **Logic layers**: Logic layers (to put it simply, check the OSI layer model if you want more details about how things are sliced) are what is finally transported and the logic attached to it.

The networking block can take different forms. Let's have a look at the most common forms of networking in embedded systems.

## Bluetooth/BLE

Bluetooth and BLE are mainly used to connect systems over short ranges (depending on the device class, from 10 cm for class 3 to 100 m for class 1). It uses a 24-channel (or 23-channel, depending on the country's regulation) system on a frequency from 2.4 to 2.48 GHz. BLE and BT2.0 are targeted at reducing power consumption. They use a frequency hopping technique to avoid interference. This frequency hopping makes the sniffing of Bluetooth a little bit less straightforward than other, simpler, radio layers. The normal Bluetooth function requires the pairing of devices (unless the device has no human interface, such as headsets and the like). This pairing (optional in BLE) allows the devices to exchange keys used to cipher communication.

## Bluetooth services

Bluetooth services are protocol submodules that provide the device consuming the Bluetooth interface with different functionalities. Let's have a look at these functionalities.

### SDP

The **Service Discovery Protocol** (**SDP**) allows you to discover services and profiles available on the device. This can reveal non-standard services that may be worth looking into.

### RFCOMM

The **RadioFrequency COMMunication** (**RFCOMM**) service acts as a communication means between a device and an endpoint or an intermediary. It allows the client to connect to the device over a serial connection. Depending on the device, it can lend you a connection to a shell on the underlying operating system, a connection expecting AT commands, or more specific interfaces.

### OBEX

The **OBject EXchange** (**OBEX**) layer allows Bluetooth devices to exchange objects over a connection-oriented protocol. Objects can be transmitted bi-directionally over different protocols on top of OBEX. Files can be transferred to the file system of the server over FTP, phone book contacts accessed over the phonebook access protocol, and more.

## Ethernet

Ethernet is the familiar network plug found at the back of almost every computer. Sniffing is easy with regular network sniffing software (Wireshark) and the availability of common attack tools will ease attacking the system. In a pentesting context, the fact that we will be providing the connectivity to the system will also ease the harvesting and attack phases.

## Wi-Fi

Wi-Fi is a popular consumer technology. Its pervasiveness also ensures that attack tools (hardware and software) are widely available. In a pentesting context, the fact that we will be providing the connectivity to the system will also ease the harvesting and attack phases. Wi-Fi provides the user with multiple (optional) ciphering modes (WPA, WPA2, and more), including an utterly broken one (WEP).

## IPv4/IPv6

Both IPv4 and IPv6 are very well known protocols that allow the transport of applicative payloads. IPv4 has a 32-bit address space and IPv6 has a 128-bit address space. Both of these protocols are widely documented and a plethora of attack tools are available.

## ISM band protocols

The **Industrial, Scientific, and Medical (ISM)** band is a set of radio frequencies that are free to use, under some conditions, without carrying a valid radio operator license. Some of these frequencies are actually reserved for some specific uses and may or may not be free to use in your own country. Please double-check with your local radio-communication authority before doing anything (the device you are testing could use frequencies that are not allowed in your own country).

## Zigbee

Zigbee is based on IEEE 802.15.4 as a physical layer. This standard can use different frequencies (based on the location):

| Frequency (MHz) | Geographical zone | Number of channels | Theoretical maximum bandwidth |
|---|---|---|---|
| 868 | Europe | 1 | 20 kbit/s |
| 915 | America and Australia | 10 | 40 kbit/s |
| 2400 | Everywhere | 16 | 250 kbit/s |

Zigbee is often used for premises automation and can be used as both star (with a central node and branches) and meshed (with a net of nodes) topologies. Zigbee's main use case is related to its very low power consumption (its cousin, Z-Wave, operates at a lower 800-900 MHz ISM band and is slower). It is a quite mature protocol, that is often used for battery-powered systems where the battery life is a crucial aspect of the product. Zigbee security mainly relies on its optional encryption settings.

## LoRa

LoRaWAN is a star topology network that uses a chirp spread spectrum technique to achieve the transportation of small data packets over long distances within a very small power budget. It has different data rates (and hence different power consumption profiles) that can be selected. It can either use a proprietary modulation scheme (that has been reversed) or **Frequency Shift Keying (FSK)** modulation for higher data rates. The security of the system relies on a 128-bit AES key for the integrity and authentication of messages. Devices and the application are identified with a 64-bit key.

LoRa uses different channels and frequencies depending on the geographical region:

| Frequency (MHZ) | Geographical zone | Number of channels |
|---|---|---|
| 433 or 868 | EU | 10 |
| 915 | US | 72 (Upload) + 8 (Download) |
| 430 | Asia | 10 |

> **Information box**
> LoRa is a stack of both physical and transport layers.

## Sigfox

Sigfox is also a star topology network. It uses both **Gaussian Frequency Shift Keying (GFSK)**, used for downlink, and **Differential Binary Phase Shift Keying (DBPSK)**, used for uplink modulation schemes to achieve the same goal as LoRaWAN (that is, the long-range, low-power transmission of short messages). It does not natively support encryption on a network level, but still, the messages are authenticated with a key of unknown nature at the time this book was written. In the Sigfox transmission model, every communication is initiated by the device, constraining the time frame for an attacker to emit a message towards the device (although the downlink message is also authenticated with a network key, which renders the device protected against simple network attacks at the time of writing).

Here are the Sigfox frequencies depending on your location:

| Frequency (MHZ) | Geographical zone |
|---|---|
| 868 | EU |
| 902 | US |

Sigfox is a stack of both physical and transport layers.

## HyperText Transport Protocol

The **HyperText Transport Protocol (HTTP)** is a clear text protocol that is very easy to deploy (using a simple web server). Its use in itself is a vulnerability since traffic is easily modifiable and readable by an attacker using commodity tools.

## HyperText Transport Protocol with Security (HTTPS)

This is an encrypted and authenticated version of HTTP. In its basic usage, the authentication part only ensures that the parties involved are indeed the ones the connection has been established with. Ensuring that the server is indeed the server it pretends to be, it requires that the certificates that are presented during the connection establishment are signed by a trusted third-party certification authority (this is called a certificate chain). Ensuring the client is indeed trusted requires some additional form of authentication. The security layer HTTPS relies upon SSL/TLS, which provides an integrated way to authenticate clients via the use of client certificates. It is not uncommon for embedded devices to validate the certificate chain incorrectly.

## Message queues

The message queue services allow the sending and receiving of messages to and from a device. Many very popular open or closed applications are used in doing so (RabbitMQ, MQTT, Apache ActiveMQ, and others). These services usually authenticate clients with a cryptographic key or username and password combinations. A very common problem is the reuse of these authentication factors across devices (the device identification being left to other means), which allows the impersonation of any device if the credentials are stolen on a single device.

## NFC

**Near Field Communication (NFC)** is a modulated magnetic field that allows communication at very close ranges (and can also power a passive device such as a card or a tag that has no local energy source). This is an interesting communication path to look into to circumvent some physical access control devices, for example.

# The sensor blocks

The sensors provide the CPU with input from the real world. Sensors are external peripherals that allow the system to sense the real world. They usually fall into two categories:

- Analog sensors
- Digital sensors

## Analog sensors

Analog sensors usually trigger a change in their electrical characteristics (through a form of voltage divider or another physical effect) relative to the physical quantity they measure and provide the CPU with a variable voltage (sometimes amplified). This voltage is read through an **Analog to Digital Converter** (**ADC**), which is a peripheral within the CPU chip itself or an external chip.

A lot of real-world physical characteristics can be read through analog sensors, as shown in the following table:

| Physical quantity measured | Example of analog sensor | How is the reading achieved? |
| --- | --- | --- |
| Temperature | Thermistor | This kind of resistance changes its value as a function of the temperature in a way that is known in advance. Using such a resistor in a voltage divider allows you to deduce the temperature from the characteristic curve of the thermistor. These are usually used in relatively low-temperature environments. |
| Temperature | Thermocouple | This interface between two metals creates a voltage difference through the Seebeck effect. This is usually amplified in order to produce a voltage level usable with modern CPUs. This type of sensor tends to be used in higher-temperature environments compared to thermistors. |
| Light | Photocell | This is light-sensitive resistance whose value changes relative to the quantity of light received. |
| pH | pH Electrodes | This measures the voltage difference between an electrode in contact with the tested solution and an electrode in contact with a reference solution. This difference is then amplified. |

| Physical quantity measured | Example of analog sensor | How is the reading achieved? |
|---|---|---|
| | Passive-resistive flex sensor | These resistances are in an arrangement engineered to change their resistance in the function of the angle they are flexed on. |
| Change in magnetic field | Coils | Coils create a current in the function of the change in the magnetic field across them. |

There is an entire field of engineering dedicated to creating analog sensors. From a pentesting point of view, it is always interesting to research how they work since it can sometimes give you creative ideas about how to circumvent or influence them in a malicious way.

## Digital sensors

Digital sensors are usually a convenient package built around an analog sensor. They free up a CPU ADC (at the expense of using a spot on a communication bus). They also free the developer from having to calibrate the analog sensor and sometimes from going through a time-consuming (hence costly) characterization phase. These kinds of sensors are as diverse as the analog sensor and they provide a digital interface too. The common peripheral interfaces they use are described in *Chapter 6, Sniffing and Attacking the Most Common Protocols.*

From a pentesting point of view, the inputs received from the digital sensor are largely considered as trusted and very well defined by developers. This tends to make the code that handles this kind of input very brittle.

# The actuator blocks

The actuators actually act on the world (these are the things that actually do things that can be perceived by humans as "the things the system does," such as triggering heating, moving, and so on). These are your servos, your motors, your power transistors, and so on.

From a penetration testing point of view, interacting with the actuators can help you with:

- Collecting data that allows you to understand how the system works. Sometimes the data itself can be interesting in a creative way to exfiltrate internal states from the system (think about the original iPod 4G firmware extraction by Nils "nilss" Schneider where he extracted the boot loader via a piezo bleeping – how cool is that?!).

- Some actuators have a feedback mechanism (for example, a linked position sensing system). These sensors' presence may not be self-evident when looking at the sensor-related chips and interfaces on the circuit board.

- Since the actuator blocks are the way the system acts in the real world, special attention should be given to them for safety-critical systems. They are a very effective way to make your client realize the potential economic and image impact that can come from their device being compromised (making a ship's autopilot change its course towards the shore or a syringe pump empty its content all at once will make the client very aware of the actual impact of a compromise).

It may seem far-fetched but there have been examples where systems were compromised through the understanding of how the system works and the abuse of the actuator. For example, the bypass of the Armatix IP1 smart gun with magnets (attack by Plore, presented at DefCON 25) where the safety of the system was completely bypassed through the external replacement of an electromagnet with a permanent magnet.

# The interface blocks

The interface block encompasses every subsystem that provides the user with feedback, being visual (screens, status LEDs, and so on) or otherwise haptic feedback. Just like the actuator block, these can be leveraged as (usually high-speed) exfiltration interfaces. Depending on how you look at it, you can classify the interfaces here that are targeted at pure point-to-point physical/bus communication (serial, USB, and so on).

# Summary

In this chapter, we went through different functional blocks in an embedded system. Not all of them are always present in a system, but having this basic understanding will allow you to classify the different components in a system. You really need to concentrate on the *Safety* section in the previous chapter, which is the most important section of the whole chapter. Don't be overconfident; be wary of electricity – nobody wins against physics.

With the knowledge of these different blocks, you will be able to better analyze and classify how a system works internally and will be able to put the different components in the block they belong to when you crack open a system.

In the next chapter, we will go through a system to learn how to map system functions and the functional blocks they belong to.

# Questions

1.  What is OBEX?
2.  What is the most prevalent CPU architecture in consumer goods?
3.  What is the ISM band? Is there a worldwide frequency band available for it?
4.  Is LoRa natively cyphered?
5.  Can the HTTP/S protocol be leveraged for client authentication?
6.  What is the main difference between Harvard and von Neumann CPU architectures?
7.  Is the RAM of an MCU usually inside or outside of the MCU chip?

# Further reading

To learn more about the topics covered in this chapter, you can refer to the following:

*   Watch conference presentations about embedded systems (any security conference – the Hackaday Supercon, or others; for example, Samy Kamkar's excellent talk at the Hackaday Supercon: `https://www.youtube.com/watch?v=tlwXmNnXeSY` or some fun x86 hardware backdoor at DEFCON: `https://www.youtube.com/watch?v=jmTwlEh8L7g`).

*   Listen to the excellent Amp Hour podcast (`https://theamphour.com/`).

# 3
# Identifying the Components of Your Target

In this chapter, you will learn, based on an easy-to-get embedded system, how to identify components, make educated guesses about which functional block they belong to, and how to set up a piece of documentation that will help us understand the relationships between the components during our test.

The following topics will be covered in this chapter:

- Harvesting information – reading the fine manual
- Harvesting information – researching on the internet
- Starting the system diagram
- Continuing system exploration – identifying and putting components in the diagram

Let's get started!

# Technical requirements

The following are the hardware requirements for this chapter:

- A test system so that you can apply the techniques and tools we will go through in this chapter. I will be using a simple children toy (a Furby, in this case; you can find one pretty easily on private sales websites or second-hand stores) as an example. You may wish to use one or more test systems (I strongly advise that you have more than a single test system available when doing hardware pentesting as it is very common to destroy components or modules during your research; a lot of things can go wrong, and having two to three test systems upfront will save you quite a bit of time) yourself if you want to follow along (some minor details could change depending on the version you get) or use another cheap kid's toy (or any other simple system for that matter) to deploy the same logic on your own.

- Some sharp tools (scalpels or hobby knives).

- Cutting pliers, wire strippers, and electrical tape.

- An entry-level multimeter will be necessary.

- Some screwdrivers may come in handy.

- A clean, white, stable working work surface, in a well-ventilated (but without an air draft) room that you can leave as-is during the course of multiple days of work (best reason ever to send the tenants of open spaces to hell...) is strongly recommended.

- If possible, try to get anti-static mats since the product you will be working with is static-sensitive (assuming that you don't know that already).

- A good quality chair, since you will spend quite a long time sitting down and working.

- Another desk with your main system set up on it and an internet connection is also a must-have.

Please read the safety tips in *Chapter 1, Setting Up Your Pentesting Lab and Ensuring Lab Safety*, again.

Install your favorite (technical) drawing program. Use one that you are familiar with, as long as it allows you to manipulate text and graphical blocks (I use LibreOffice Draw, but if you feel more at ease with any other productivity suite, Inkscape, or just paper and a pencil, that's fine by me).

# Harvesting information – reading the manual

This is a very basic and logical act, isn't it? However, you may have a different approach than the average user reading the manual. Your approach will consider each section of the manual and infer what it tells you about the inner workings of the system.

## Taking a system analysis approach

The manual will describe the following:

- If and how the system can interact with the environment
- If and how the user can interact with the system
- How the system will inform the user about its internal status
- If (but usually not how) the system interacts with other system
- How the system is powered

The manual will inform us about the following:

- What sensors are present to sense the environment
- Where some sensors are (and sometimes which type) for user interaction
- What display block components are present
- Whether some networking capabilities are present

Now, let's look at our Furby manual.

## For our Furby manual

We will read the Furby's manual and infer some information from it:

| What is the manual saying? | What do we conclude? | What can we infer? |
| --- | --- | --- |
| You need 4x AA batteries. | The system runs on 6 V. | 5 V logic levels are used internally. |
| The toy will react to being petted on the fur on its belly and head. | At least two touch sensors are involved. | The MCU or a part will have touch sensing capabilities. |

| What is the manual saying? | What do we conclude? | What can we infer? |
| --- | --- | --- |
| The toy will react to having its tail pulled or its tongue pushed. | At least two micro switches are involved. | The MCU will be able to read pins (this is more than supposition...). |
| The toy will react to being pulled upside down or picked up. This is sensed by the inside sensor. | There will be a form, tilt, or acceleration sensor inside it. | |
| The toy will react to the light level (some versions of the manual explicitly mention a light sensor). | There is a light sensor. | |
| The toy will react to clapping, speech, or music. | There is a microphone. | |
| The toy will talk to other toys if they're facing them and they are within 4 feet. | There is a form of networking. | The networking is probably acoustic-based since it's directional and very range-limited when the microphone/speaker is in the front of the toy. |
| The toy can connect to a phone app (the manual indicates that the phone needs to be very close). | There is a form of networking. | It is probably acoustic since there is no mention of pairing (hence excluding Bluetooth) and the phone has to be really close to the toy. |
| The toy moves (body, eyelids, ears, and so on). | There are motors inside the toy. | |
| The toy's eyes illuminate and show patterns. | There are LCDs inside the toy. | |
| The toy "talks" gibberish and language-dependent sound samples. | There is a high speaker in the toy. | The sound samples are stored in the toy in a programmable way (since toys are sold in language-specific versions). |
| The toy will go through four stages of development. | The toy can store an internal stage. | There will probably be an EEPROM inside the toy. |

By simply going through the manual, we have been able to gather information about the system without opening it at all.

# Harvesting information — researching on the internet

Scour the internet for all the information you can find – anything that could be useful for your project.

The following information sources are of particular interest:

- Manuals for the main system or add-ons.

- Support/repair manuals for the main system or add-ons.

- Patents related to the system.

- Academic articles and known flaws and attacks on the technologies you know the system uses.

- User groups and wikis.

- Previous research that's been done regarding the system (existing vulnerabilities, articles, "Maker" analysis of the product, and more).

- Mobile phone application stores.

- If the system uses radio communication and is sold in the US, there will be a **Federal Communication Commission** (**FCC**) filing with an FCC number indicated on the system.

Now, let's look at what we'll need for the Furby.

## For the Furby

I have been able to find out the following information regarding the Furby:

- One patent directly linked to the toy, US6544098, which was filed in 1998 by David Mark Hampton and Caleb Chung.

- This patent covers an older version of the toy; some descriptions may not be extremely accurate regarding the current version:

| What is the document saying/showing? | What can we conclude? | What can we infer? |
| --- | --- | --- |
| Feedback about the motor movement being received by the IR sensors through a slotted wheel. | The system is aware of the motor's position. | The MCU will be able to read pins (this is more than supposition...). |
| US6544098: "As previously discussed, the toy includes sensors; for example, IR transmitters and receivers, which allow communication to occur between the toys." | | The inter-toy communication may be IR-based. |
| Multiple inter-toy communications are possible, and an IR emitter and receiver is described. | | There must be a toy-toy communication protocol, potentially over IR. |
| There is a tilt switch inside the toy. | | |
| *Figures 43* and *44* show the wiring of the MCU (very interesting) hinting at a SPC81A. | The original system may be based on a SPC81A (a 6502 derivative by Sunplus). | |
| US6544098: "The information processor is designed to work with a co-processor, which is provided for speech and infrared communications capabilities." [...] "herein a Texas Instruments speech synthesis processor, TSP50C04" ... "It will be easy for the child to learn and understand Furbish."[...]" Eventually, the toy plaything will be able to speak a native language in addition to its own unique language. Examples of native languages the toy 10 may be programmed with include English, Spanish, [...]". | The IR and sound synthesis is offloaded to a co-processor (TSP50C04). | There should be a language-specific (EEP)ROM for changing the language or taking control of it. |

| What is the document saying/showing? | What can we conclude? | What can we infer? |
|---|---|---|
| "Electrically programmable read-only memory (EEPROM), which provides 1 kilobit non-volatile memory for data storage with a 93LC46 type EEROM". | There is an EEPROM (93LC46). | |
| "An oscillator circuit that incorporates a cadmium sulfide, CdS LDR, photoconductive cell, which is provided as a resistant element in a feedback loop, along with a resistor". | This is the light detection circuit (so that it sleeps at night). | |

There are multiple user communities dedicated to getting the most out of their toys. From there, I retrieved the following information:

| What is the community saying? | What can we conclude? | What can we infer? |
|---|---|---|
| There is a personality reset action if you don't like the current one. | | It will erase/reset the personality-related sectors/chunks in the EEPROM. This is worth sniffing so that we can get the EEPROM write commands if we can't find out what the EEPROM is. |
| Some personalities are easier to implement using the app ("chatterbox"). | | The way we interact with the toy has an influence on its behavior. |
| The shapes the eyes can form and some eye patterns are personality-dependent. | | These should be stored in an EEPROM as changing them should be one of our goals. |
| A long description of what you can do in the app, depending on the edition of the toy. | Depending on the edition of the toy, you can do multiple things since the communication protocol is backward-compatible and extended for certain editions. | It could be possible to reverse the protocol and spoof a Furby to the app. |

Multiple teardown videos show the following:

| What the video shows | What can we conclude? | What can we infer? |
| --- | --- | --- |
| Internal construction of the toy | It will help us tear down the toy properly. | |
| There are multiple revisions of the hardware | We may acquire different revisions and have more or less luck with some having broken out buses. | |
| Different versions of the toy can interact with each other | The interaction protocol is backward-compatible. | |

There are three different versions for Android phone and a single one for iPhone:

- APKs for Android have been downloaded for further investigation

• The assembly source code for an older version of the toy has been leaked (this is very interesting, but since it is not entirely legal, I will not link it here):

- Downloaded for further investigation

# Starting the system diagram

The system diagram will be one of the main documents we will use to identify the various components and subsystems. I will be using LibreOffice Draw to do this (it's free and you can use it too if you so wish), but you can use whatever diagram software you like or even a whiteboard or pen and paper – it doesn't really matter.

In this schema, I have the seven blocks that were presented in *Chapter 1*, *Setting Up Your Pentesting Lab and Ensuring Lab Safety* (Power, Networking, Storage, CPU, Sensor, Actuator, and Interface).

You will be able to find a template and multiple versions in the repository for this book.

Before you get started, establish a convention for yourself. My personal convention is as follows:

• Empty rectangles for blocks.

• Ovals for components, with the background color indicating the level of confidence I have in the information.

• Arrows for buses or data paths.

• Lines for power control or analog connections.

I also color code the objects according to the confidence level I have in them:

- **Green**: It's certain at this point.
- **Yellow**: I am reasonably certain that it exists, but I have doubts about the details (such as the exact model).
- **Orange**: It should be there, but I have reasons to doubt its presence.
- **Red**: Changed my mind but not ready to delete it yet.

# For our Furby

You will be able to find the functional schema for this stage in the GitHub repository for this book, which can be found at ch3/functional_diagram_1.odg.

In the following diagram, we can see how the components have been ventilated between the different functional blocks:

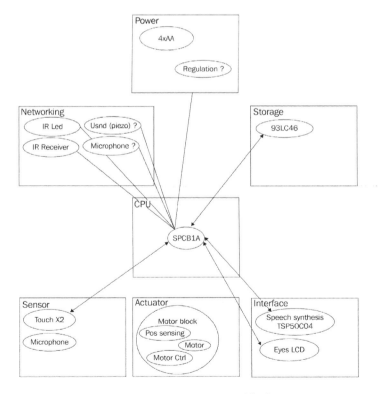

Figure 3.1 – Components in blocks

Now, let's explore the system in more detail.

# Continuing system exploration – identifying and putting components in the diagram

We will power on the system as described in the manual; that is, we'll insert the required number of batteries and boot the system.

Start interacting with it, learn where the sensors are, try to feel around to see where certain things are, look for where the screws are, and get a general feeling for the system.

## Opening the Furby

From now on, it is recommended that you do the following:

- Be smart and take precautions – you will be dealing with pointy, sharp, and other objects that can hurt you. At the end of the day, you will only be losing 30 seconds of your life and sparing yourself a trip to E.R.

- Take note of which screw goes where. Put **all** screws, bits, nuts, bolts, and pieces in a nice bowl, magnetic recipient, or sorting tray if available.

- Document as much as possible and take pictures of everything (the higher the definition, the better). You will forget things 3 or 4 days down the road (yes, this gray cable harness, the left one, was it for connector A or B?). Again, these 30 seconds feeling like a tourist and taking plenty of pictures *will* save you an afternoon trying to figure out whether the weird gray thing was holding piece X or Y in place.

## Manipulating the system

We will also be manipulating the system (in that we will be touching it with our hands, moving it while it's open, screwing it, unscrewing it, probing it, turning it, and more). Embedded systems are not engineered for this at all; they are made to sit firm while being held by screws, glue, and plastic supports. Out interference may actually damage the system, so we should take the following precautions to prevent this and to protect ourselves from accidents:

- Reread the safety directions provided in *Chapter 1, Setting Up Your Pentesting Lab and Ensuring Lab Safety*.

- Wires soldered to the PCB are not made to move a lot, be pulled, torn, and support all of the abuse that we will inevitably put on them. I like to put a blob of hot glue on the solder joint, which acts as a force relief and prevents the actual copper in the wire from moving (copper tends to break easily).

- Plastic connectors tend to easily rip from the PCBs, especially when they have plastic clasps that hold them securely and you unplug/plug them repeatedly. I like to remove the clasps with a scalpel blade and secure the connector to the PCB with a bit of cyanoacrylate glue.

- Some battery powered systems don't have an on/off switch and removing the batteries can be tiring. Get in there and add an on/off switch just next to the batteries. This will save you a lot of time (unless you're forced to do otherwise, add the switch to the wire connected to the positive side of the batteries and hot glue it securely in place).

- Probing and holding a PCB at the same time is hard, so get yourself a PCB vise or, even better, one of those PCB workstations with articulated arms that can be 3D printed or bought on eBay.

- Some systems don't have an on/off visual indicator. Most of the time, it's just a matter of adding a LED and a resistor.

- If the system is mains powered or connected to an equally dangerous power source (these 12 V/56 A server PSUs can grill meat just fine if you are unlucky enough for the current to start flowing), find a way to add a very visible, very obvious "**I AM PLUGGED IN TO DEADLY POWER**" indicator – it's not because the system is sleeping that the mains/high energy won't kill you. For this, I use a lamp with a red bulb, placed in parallel to the extension cord, for projects like this, as well as an isolation transformer.

# Dismantling the Furby

You will be able to find the dismantling picture in the GitHub repository for this book, in the `ch3/dismantling_pictures` folder.

# Identifying chips

Take pictures (as readable as possible) of every circuit board, in relationship to others and themselves.

Take closeups of every chip and module you find.

Identify the markings (if they have not been rubbed off or erased) and try to identify the package. The package is the name of the physical package the chip comes in. There are plenty of them – some standard, some not. Please refer to `https://en.wikipedia.org/wiki/List_of_integrated_circuit_packaging_types` as a basic way to identify them. There is no other means to memorize and recognize them but to see and use plenty of different ones.

# Chips in the Furby

We will now try to get a general sense of how to find more detailed information about chips. Since we found the chips in the Furby, we need to know what they are doing. We can learn about them by looking at the part numbers on the chips and identifying the package family.

## Main package families and markings

You should be able to identify the following packages:

| | | |
|---|---|---|
| TO – <br><br>*Transistor Outline* | This is a through-hole package. TO92s (pictured) are usually signal transistors or other devices that produce very little heat. This is a plastic package with usually two or three legs, with one side of the body being flat so that you can identify the different legs. Markings are on the flat side. There is also a variation of it for high-power applications that has a big tab for heat transfer (TO220). | |
| SOT – <br><br>*Small Outline Transistor* | This is a surface mount package and the surface mount adaptation of TO. This can vary a lot, from SOT23 (for small signal transistors without many heat transfer requirements) to SOT223 (for power management that can transfer a lot of heat to a copper pad thanks to a large metal tab). The markings are on top of it. | |
| SIL – <br><br>*Single In Line* | This is a through-hole package. It's usually used for through-hole power circuits and resistor networks. Its markings are on its side. | |

| DIP – Dual In Line | This is a through-hole package. It's what you usually think about in terms of integrated circuits. Its markings are on top of it. | |
| --- | --- | --- |
| SOIC – Small Outline Integrated Circuit | This is a surface mount package and an adaptation of DIP to surface mount. Its markings are on top of it. | |
| QFP – Quad Flat Pack | This is a surface mount package. It is a flat package with leads on its side. Its markings are on top of it. | |
| QFN – Quad Flat pack - No lead | This is a surface mount package. It is a flat package with "no leads" on the side. These contact areas do not protrude from the body and are meant to be wet by the solder during reflow. Its markings are on top of it. | |

On top of the chips, there are markings, which are usually as follows:

- Some kind of company logo
- A model reference number
- A lot number and/or fabrication date

Normally, the markings are written in white, but they can wear out. In this case, just a little bit of spit rubbed on it (or solvent if you are squeamish) may make them easier to see.

Sometimes, markings are lasered or sanded off. In this case, you can usually identify the chips by studying their function and pinout.

The best way to find out information about a chip is to do a quick internet search:

- On a general search engine: The markings we found and datasheet. This will (hopefully) give us a document that describes the chip's behavior and connections.

- On websites dedicated to electronic components (mouser, DigiKey, element14, arrow, and so on): The markings should link us to a page (if the site sells the component), along with a link to the datasheet.

Here, we can find the following information:

| Chip's marking | What is it? | What is it connected to? |
|---|---|---|
| ATMLH306 02CM | The internet states that it's a Chinese copy of an ATMEL EEPROM (24LC series). By digging deeper into the ATMEL datasheets, we can find that it is actually an old version of the marking for Atmel's 24LC series. This would be a good fit for our SPI EEPROM candidate (well, it's an i2c EEPROM, but the maker could easily have replaced one communication protocol with another). The 02CM is very small (256 bytes). | |
| Z100401K9 | This is a SOT89-3 package, but there's no obvious reference to be found on the internet. This is very common for China-only chips (that is, common/"jellybean" parts available in China for mass production). | To be investigated further by probing and looking into its relationship with other parts. |
| 3D3G | This is a SOT89-3 package, but there's no obvious reference to be found on the internet. This is very common for China-only chips (that is, common/"jellybean" parts available in China for mass production). | To be investigated further by probing and looking into its relationship with other parts. |
| AT5561S | This is an H-Bridge – an IC that is designed to make a DC motor change its direction of rotation (that is, turn clockwise or counterclockwise). This one provides integrated stop (that is, hold) and braking functions. The datasheet states "those features that are suitable for [a] toy". | |

| Chip's marking | What is it? | What is it connected to? |
|---|---|---|
| 74HC14M | The 74 series logic chips are ubiquitous chips, present everywhere as glue logic and produced by the millions by plenty of manufacturers. This one is a 6-channel (hex) inverting Schmitt trigger (`https://en.wikipedia.org/wiki/Schmitt_trigger`). Just think of it as having 6 NOT gates (output HIGH when input is LOW and vice versa). | |
| A green module with an epoxy blob | This is a proprietary module; the markings won't help. | This is connected to the high speaker. This is probably the speech synthesis chip. Probing will clarify this. |
| A blue module marked FR with an epoxy blob | This is a proprietary module; the markings won't help. | The toy I have is French speaking, so this is probably where the language-dependent data is stored. |
| An epoxy blob on the PCB side | This has no markings. | It is connected to a board-to-board connector marked as MISO, MOSI, SCK, and so on. This could be the main CPU or an IC dedicated to driving the motor so that it can sense movement. |
| A big epoxy blob behind the eyes' LCD | This has no markings. | This is connected to the big parallel connector of the LCD and the test points are marked with an SPI-related signal (data in, data out clock). It is connected to the FR module and the green module. This could be the main CPU or used for voice synthesis. |

Now, let's learn how to identify unmarked/mysterious chips.

# Identifying unmarked/mysterious chips

This is a trickier activity; it is not uncommon for a vendor to erase markings/use an unmarked chip (or even have their own marking put on the chip) in order to impede their products from being analyzed or replicated.

Identifying an unknown chip boils down to performing an investigation:

- The environment:

  - What other chips did you identify that are connected to it?

  - What are its suspected functions? (Is it connected to a storage chip, an MCU, or an analog sensor? Does it act as glue logic between an MCU and a peripheral?)

- The chip itself:

  - What package is the chip using? Is it through-hole or surface mount? How many legs (leads) does it have?

  - Can we identify pin functions? (Are some pin(s) connected to the ground? Are they connected to the power rails? Are they used as an **analog to digital** (ADC) converter or **digital to analog** (DAC) converter? Are they connected to actuators?)

  - Once powered, what voltage is it powered with?

  - Is it using an external oscillator (a crystal or another form of oscillator)?

With this information in mind, you can then go to a chip vendor website. These websites (DigiKey, Mouser, Keil, and so on) usually propose a parametric search engine where you can input your data. You will generally end up with a handful of candidates across websites (not every vendor sells chips from all chip makers). Harvest the datasheets for the aforementioned candidates and match your chip's connections with the pin-out of the adequate footprint/package.

## Epoxy blobs

Epoxy blobs (they look like black epoxy resin blobs) are very common in high-volume products (that is, systems that are produced in very high numbers for which every tenth of a cent saved counts). They are usually hiding one or more die.

---

**Information Box**

A die is the actual piece of silicon for the chip. Typically, when you picture a chip in your mind, you think of a more or less square, black plastic object. This is actually what is called a package; that is, a die enclosed in an epoxy package with its electric contacts (the pads) wired to "legs" (the leads).

---

Often, packaging a die (that is, putting it in a plastic case, adding the lead, bonding the pads to the lead with gold wire, and so on) can cost a fair amount of money with respect to the cost of the die itself. So, if the product is made in large numbers, if the die is very cheap or if the die is custom-made for the application, it can make economic sense to directly wire the pads to the traces on the **printed circuit board** (**PCB**). Epoxy blobs can prove difficult to work with since the tricks used to identify chips (using the pinout of the package and so on) don't really make sense anymore. Looking into the signals that get in and out of the blob can help in identifying these functions. It is possible to remove the epoxy using dangerous chemicals and inspecting the exposed die with a microscope, but this is an advanced technique that requires significant know-how and that goes beyond the scope of an introductory book.

# Furby — the mystery meat

In this section, we will look at the components we had trouble identifying. Here, the goal is either to identify them formally or get the best idea possible about their functionality/roles.

## Z100401K9 and 3D3G

We were unable to find references for Z100401K9 and 3D3G. These chips are on a daughterboard, where we suspect the main MCU is located. Let's start probing around with our multimeter.

Please read your multimeter's manual and familiarize yourself with operating it (the same applies to all your tools, actually). We will be using two of its most common modes of operation:

- Direct current voltage reading (also known as DC, as in the kind you find across a battery where the voltage stays the same, as opposed to AC, which is the kind you find in the wall plug where the voltage varies periodically between two voltages). This DC voltage reading tells you the voltage (the difference of potential) between your two probes. Since voltage only has a difference between TWO points, the usual point of reference is called ground (also marked as GND for short). The usual ground is (for DC circuits) the negative pole of your batteries, but (and I must really insist this because it confuses a lot of people when they are starting) this is just a way to call a shared reference point. Measuring this only makes sense when the toy is turned on.

- A continuity test, which tells you if there is a direct path (that is, a simple wire) between your two probes. Do this with the tool turned off completely (that is, batteries removed). When you place your probes between two points that are connected, your multimeter will beep.

By probing around the two chips, we can identify the following connections:

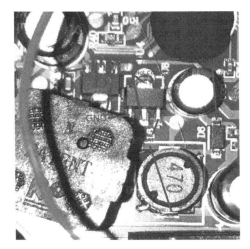

Figure 3.2 – Probing the power section chips

The round component marked 470 with a PCB reference of L6 is an inductor (that is, a coil), D6 is a diode, and C58 (to the right of D6) is a capacitor.

They are arranged as follows:

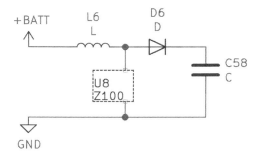

Figure 3.3 – Equivalent schematic for the Z100

This is a very typical step-up transformer. This is used to maintain a high enough voltage for the rest of the circuit to function properly when the battery voltage starts to decrease (batteries have a discharge curve where the voltage goes down with the charge). I strongly encourage you to have a look at the different types of topology available. You don't need to learn them off by heart (unless you are an electrical engineer, in which can you probably know them already) – knowing what they are and how to find their references is much more important.

3D3G is a typical 3.3 V LDO that's used to provide the circuit with the 3.3 V needed by the components. There are a few voltages (called logic levels) that are very typical for chips to be powered with or to communicate over. The most classic is 5 V (called TTL), which is still present today mainly for compatibility reasons. 3.3 V is the most common as of today, but lower voltages are becoming more and more common (1.8 V, 1.2 V, 0.95 V) to limit consumption and heat dissipation while having faster clocks.

Both of these components can be found in the power block.

## The green module with an epoxy blob

First, with your multimeter in continuity mode, you can find out which pin is the ground pin. Weirdly, I didn't find a pin connected to neither the batteries (we will call this VBAT), the boosted output of the batteries (we will call this VBATB), or the 3.3 V rail. Maybe this IC is only provided with power when consumption needs to be reduced (this will later prove to be right)? By probing around, we can find out that the two pins are connected to the High Speaker. One is indeed switching to 3.3V shortly before the toy "speaks," and two pins read varying voltage levels (this can be a sign that these can actually be digital buses).

Let's take note of the pinouts:

Figure 3.4 – Pinout of the green module

We can confirm if the pins are digital buses or not by looking at the signal using either a logic analyzer or an oscilloscope (two really useful tools you will really, really want to have in your toolbox).

An oscilloscope is, simply put, a very fast multimeter that regularly reads the voltages between the probe point and a reference point (usually an alligator clip attached to the probe) and shows you the value of these samples as a function of time.

By looking at the signal on a scope, we will no signal structure that actually looks like a digital signal (digital signals usually toggle between a high and a low state in quite clear states and don't linger somewhere in the middle). It is more likely that this module is actually just acting as an (inverting) audio amplifier, as shown in the following image:

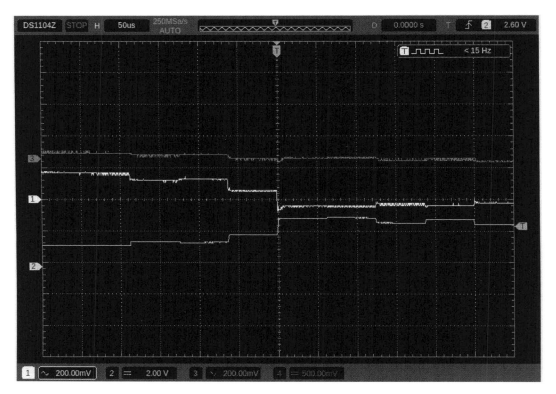

Figure 3.5 – Traces of the signals on the oscilloscope

The preceding image was extracted from my oscilloscope through a dedicated vendor utility. When you look at the dynamics of the signal, signal 1 (the middle line) has a very low amplitude (the scale is 200 mV/Div) that matches the behavior of the signal that is going through the speaker (signal 2, the lower line, with a scale of 2 V/Div).

This module goes into the interface block.

## The blue module with an epoxy blob

This module is marked FR and all my test toys are French-speaking, which means this may be responsible for speech synthesis. Let's probe around and identify the pins:

Figure 3.6 – The SPI blue module

From our naming convention, we can expect a **Serial-Parallel Interface (SPI)** style communication. SPI will be covered in *Chapter 6, Sniffing and Attacking the Most Common Protocols*. Let's probe these pins while they're functioning to verify if there's correlation with the sounds:

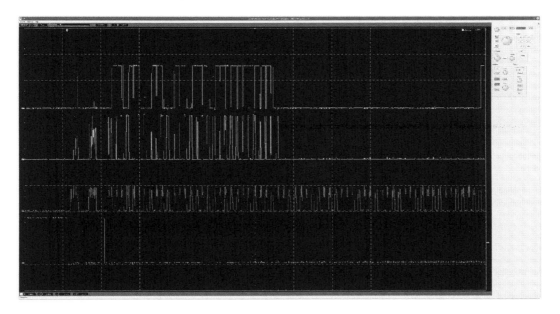

Figure 3.7 – Traces of the SPI signal on the oscilloscope

The following is an zoomed-in image showing the start of the signal:

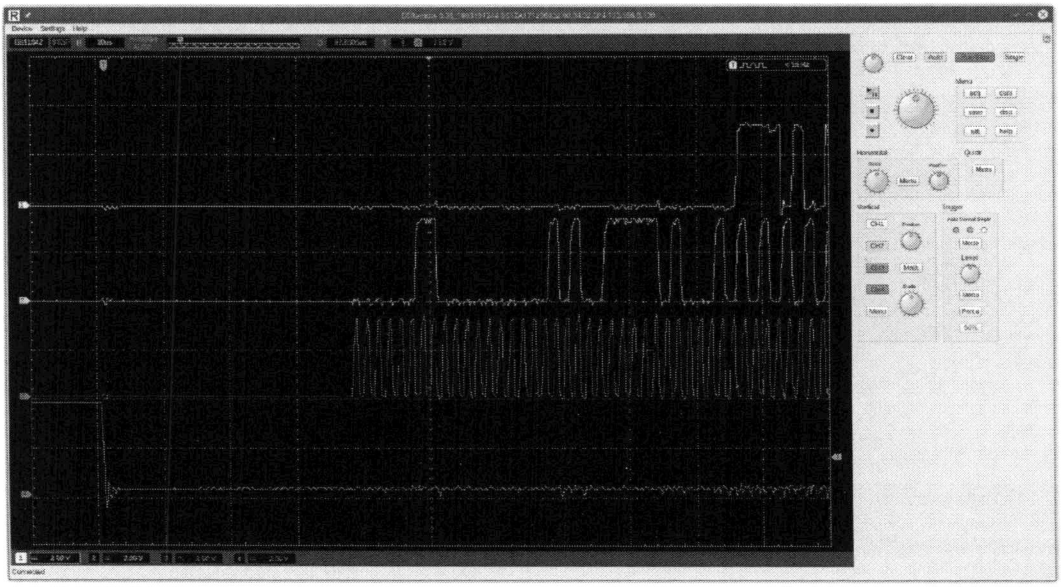

Figure 3.8 – Zoomed-in version of the start of the signal

Indeed, these signals (one clock, one data in, one data out, and a chip enabled) are very typical of SPI (I will go through the typical protocols used for chip-to-chip communication in *Chapter 6, Sniffing and Attacking the Most Common Protocols*). The `sip_wp` (typos on PCB silkscreens are not uncommon; the engineer typed `sip` instead of `spi` – `wp` is a very common shorthand in datasheets for write protection) test pad connected to the pin between the ground and power (3.3v pin) hints at a SPI EEPROM. Maybe the data for speech synthesis is stored here. At this point, we may not want to be too destructive, so we should lift the module and try to dump and reprogram it at a later stage. We can note that down on our functional diagram. This could actually be the SPI EEPROM, as discussed in the patent, and the ATMLH306 may be used for something else (storing the general status of the "learning" of the toy, maybe?).

This module probably goes in the storage block.

## A big epoxy blob behind the eyes' LCD

This is a contender for hiding the main MCU (and possibly other dies).

This blob has a very large number of traces exiting from it since it is directly driving an LCD with a fair number of pixels in it. It is possible that there is a dedicated LCD driver die hidden under the epoxy.

By following traces with our multimeter (and with the help of a very fine needle to follow vias from side to side of the PCB (a via is a hole in the fiberglass that is plated with a conductive material to allow a trace to jump from one side to the other or a layer to another, so when you see a trace ending on a hole or with a hole in it, that's a via), we can see (by probing with our multimeter in continuity mode) that it is connected to the following:

- The LCD's zebra strips (a zebra strip, also known as an elastomeric connector, is a flexible piece of foam that has conductive zones).

- A 32,768 Hz crystal (this is commonly used for RTCs, though it is better for time stability for the driver of communication protocols).

- The piezo element we suspect is the emitter for networking (it's in parallel with a 3.3 mH inductor and driven through a transistor, but it could also be driven from the IR output of the TSP50C04).

- The electret microphone that is acting as the receiver for ultrasound networking. The TSP50C04 is not acting as a receiver, so this module isn't hosting only this die (or the die that performs voice synthesis).

- The SPI EEPROM.

- The ATMLH308 i2C EEPROM.

- The movement sensor on the green daughter board.

The variety of protocols, buses, and peripherals it is connected to doesn't leave any room for doubt: this is where the MCU die is hosted. We can also reasonably assume that the speech synthesis die is also hosted under the same epoxy blob. This blob is not a single component and will not appear in the functional diagram as such, but this investigation allowed us to locate two very important components (the MCU and screen driver).

## An epoxy blob on the side PCB

This module is actually a "daughterboard" that's connected perpendicularly to the main PCB. There is a soldered bus toward the main blue PCB that has 17 connections toward it. We have already seen that the main power regulation, as well as the motor driving and sensing, happens on this daughterboard. This board also hosts a sensor that is probably acting as a position sensor (a black box that makes spring/rattling noises when tapped, probably an archaic multi-axis vibration/acceleration sensor that the toy uses to sense when it is being shaken).

The blob is connected to the following:

- The aluminum sticky tapes, which are used as touch sensors
- The AT5561S (H bridge/motor driver).
- The SPI bus (marked on the connector).

This is probably a cheap general-purpose MCU acting as a slave for motor driving and touch sensing.

# The borders of functional blocks

As we have seen from our example systems, a component can sometimes fulfill functions in multiple blocks (for example, our side MCU). In this case, I like to split the component into two sub-components that I can put in their respective blocks.

Sometimes, this can be a little bit tricky since, for example, some components are powered from their communication interface (look into the Dallas 1-wire interface) or use a sensor for communication (in our example system, the microphone is used as a sensor for loud sound detection and as a communication receiver for receiving ultrasound). In such cases, the selected block will be to a judgment call. Do not let the functional diagram become a problem for you – it is there to assist you, so just add plenty of annotations and continue your investigation.

# Summary

In this chapter, we have learned how to harvest data on a system without having to open it. This process included collecting documentations and pieces that will feed our investigation and reflection process.

We then learned how to open a system and the necessary precautions that we must take when doing so in order to protect our test system and ourselves. This primary approach to the system will feed our ongoing analysis and will allow us to understand how the system will actually implement the functionality it provides to the user.

In the next chapter, we will go through a methodology that will help you assess where the important bits of information are in a system, as well as how to assess how they should be protected.

# Questions

The following questions have not necessarily been answered in this chapter, so you may need to do some research on your own. The first part of this chapter was about searching for information on an unknown system. Use your head or your keyboard!

1. When you are arranging the contractual framework for pentesting with your client, how many test systems should you request?

2. Can you formally guarantee your client that all the test systems that they provided will be returned to them in a full functioning and undamaged state?

3. When I was inspecting the green amplifier module, I looked into the pins that were varying to check if these were digital buses or not. Look at the signal from the oscilloscope for these pins and at the signal for actual digital buses for the blue FR module. Do you have any idea why an oscillating signal such as a digital bus can be read as a floating-point value by your multimeter?

4. Using a chip vendor website, have a look at the 74HC14 and compare the price of the through-hole package and the surface mount package for the same chip maker. The die inside is exactly the same. What does this tell you?

5. The 74HC14 is a member of a logic family called the 74 family. Can you find a another very common logic family? If so, what are the main differences between them?

6. What is FCC? What type of system should you try to look for in the FCC database?

7. The patent hinted at a 6502-based architecture, but it is not clear if this is still the case in the real system. Is 6502 a Harvard or Von Neumann architecture?

# 4
# Approaching and Planning the Test

In this chapter, we will go through the security properties that are necessary to ensure that a system (an alarm, a connected doorbell, and so on) is secure enough. Not every property will exist in every system since they may not be relevant to particular systems. This chapter will also introduce the STRIDE methodology, which allows you to map threats that are relevant to the system. In a real-world test, this can be used to build the attack scenarios that your client will want you to execute.

The following topics will be covered in this chapter:

- The STRIDE methodology
- Applying the methodology to the example system
- Basic security properties
- Planning the test

Let's get started!

# The STRIDE methodology

This methodology was built to evaluate the threats that can be applied to a system (this is called **threat modeling**). This was devised by Praerit Garg and Loren Kohnfelder at Microsoft. STRIDE is an acronym for the six main avenues of attacks used to compromise a system:

| Domain | Definition |
| --- | --- |
| Spoofing | To successfully identify a person or a program trying to gain an illegitimate advantage by falsifying data. |
| Tampering | Intentionally modifying products in a way that would make them harmful to the consumer. |
| Repudiation | A statement's author being unable to successfully dispute the authority or validity of an associated action. |
| Information disclosure | A privacy break or data leak. |
| Denial of service | Makes a machine or network resource unavailable to its intended users by temporarily or indefinitely disrupting services. |
| Escalation of privileges | Used to gain elevated access to resources that are normally protected from an application or user. |

These domains are as follows:

| Domain | My actions are in this domain if I can... |
| --- | --- |
| Spoofing | Pose as someone/something that I am not. |
| Tampering | Change something I am not supposed to. |
| Repudiation | Do something without the owner being able to prove I did it. |
| Information disclosure | Get access to data or information while I am not supposed to. |
| Denial of service | Keep it from working (via continuous interaction or a one-shot operation). |
| Escalation of privileges | Do things I am not supposed to without the privileges they normally require. |

The goal of the methodology is to ensure that you will go through all of these threats for the components and the systems at play. This is sometimes a little bit tedious, depending on the granularity level you choose to place yourself at. With experience, you will learn to dynamically adapt at the granularity level to target common problems (from a component level up to a functional block or a whole system level). There are no one-size-fits-all answers, but often, your own experience and understanding of the system (and hence the risks linked with them) will make you avoid questions that make little sense for a specific system or context.

> **Tip**
>
> Microsoft provides a tool (`https://www.microsoft.com/en-us/securityengineering/sdl/threatmodeling`) that supports the methodology and a deck of cards that supports the scenario definition workshops with the clients.

For example, the goal of this methodology is to end up with certain conclusions, such as the following:

- If a piece of local storage contains temperature data in a consumer weather station, it would not make a lot of sense to protect it against tampering/reading by ciphering its content.
- Protecting the piece of storage, this time used to store encryption keys for a police **TErrestrial TRunked RAdio** (**TETRA**) radio that could be recovered from a trash container or stolen, would totally make sense.

Now, let's consider the following questions:

- How can we find what is worth protecting?
- Is the necessary protection already in place?
- Can we compromise the existing protection?

Let's use the following diagram to understand this better:

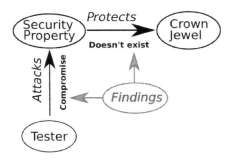

Figure 4.1 – A link between the security functions, the crown jewels, and how the findings are related

We have findings if we manage to compromise an existing security property OR if a security property should be there but isn't.

We will answer these questions in the following sections.

## Finding the crown jewels in the assessed system

In every system, there are "crown jewels" – the crispy, fat, tasty morsels an attacker will have as an **ultimate** target. Losing these (or one of these) is generally the client's worst nightmare. If the client has a mature risk management process, these crown jewels are usually ranked high on the business risk scale. If it doesn't, then you have to speak with your client to point this out.

Successful attacks on the crown jewels can lead to different impacts for the company that produces the system. These impacts can be varied (such as legal implications, loss of business, damage to the company's reputation (usually referred to as image risk), loss of human life, and so on).

Depending on the system, these are the crown jewels that have to be determined with the client. They can be very diverse and are usually very specific to the system.

Here are a few examples of systems that have potential crown jewels (and their related security properties) for different systems:

| Example System | Crown Jewel(s) | Security properties: What we expect Possible impacts |
|---|---|---|
| A game console | <ul><li>Bypassing protection and running a pirated game.</li><li>The ability to leverage the console to attack or pivot to the dedicated gaming network.</li><li>The ability to extract new versions of HDCP keys from secure key storage.</li></ul> | <ul><li>Loss of money</li><li>Loss of integrity or availability for the gaming network</li><li>Fines</li></ul> |
| A secure phone | <ul><li>The ability to run unsigned code.</li><li>Being able to fake a legitimate code signature or to piggyback on legitimately signed code execution.</li><li>The ability to load unsigned kernel extensions.</li><li>Running a customized kernel.</li><li>Extracting stored/protected cryptographic keys.</li><li>Remotely spying on user activity.</li></ul> | <ul><li>Damaging the product image by making the phone less secure for the user</li></ul> |
| A baby monitor | <ul><li>The ability to listen/view security footage without the proper credentials.</li><li>Starting the camera while it is supposed to be off.</li><li>Using the monitor for unintended activities (Mirai style).</li></ul> | <ul><li>Possible litigation around privacy; the impact on the product and company image</li></ul> |

| Example System | Crown Jewel(s) | Security properties: What we expect Possible impacts |
|---|---|---|
| A remote-controlled power plug | • The ability to repeatedly turn the plug on and off in order to start a fire or damage the connected appliance. | • Possible material damages or loss of life, resulting in legal actions against the company<br>• Product and company image can be damaged |
| A smart electricity meter | • The ability to steal energy without being detected.<br>• Remotely turning off the breaker and bricking the meter for one meter, in a city, a region, a country.<br>• Remotely monitoring electricity usage and deducing the presence of the user at home or to profile users that are candidates for a provider change (by a competitor provider). | • Financial loss for the client company that could legally turn against the provider<br>• Product and company image can be damaged |
| A medical device | • The ability to remotely trigger defibrillation in a pacemaker.<br>• Emptying the whole syringe in an infusion pump.<br>• Remotely stealing analysis records in an automated bloodwork automaton. | • Possible litigation around privacy<br>• Possible loss of life, resulting in legal actions against the company<br>• Product and company image can be damaged<br>• Security properties: What do we expect |
| An industrial PLC | • The ability to steal a recipe or a secret process.<br>• Paralyzing a plant production.<br>• Sabotaging production. | • Copied product, triggering loss of money<br>• Nonproductive plant, triggering loss of money<br>• Reduced quality of the product or damage to the consumer's health, triggering damages to the company image |

These crown jewels are the ultimate goal of your test. They are the things you are trying to reach. Compromising these jewels is the goal you reach when you're trying to compromise different security mechanisms. Compromising these mechanisms is what you test inside the defined scenarios. Usually, your scenarios are chained to reach the crown jewel(s).

Each of these crown jewel defense mechanisms should be the subject of at least one scenario. Some of these scenarios are defined as a high-level story, as follows:

- An attacker manages to run a pirated game on our console by bypassing the media authentication mechanism.

- An attacker manages to run a pirated game on our console by disabling the authentication code in the firmware.

- An attacker manages to steal a user's private data by inserting unsigned code into the phone's kernel.

- An attacker manages to use our phone as a zombie by forcing an un-validated app to be downloaded.

- An attacker manages to steal our recipe by reading the ingredient dosage on the PLC interface.

- An attacker manages to steal our recipe by reading the ingredient dosage in the PLC cyphered network traffic.

- An attacker manages to crash our stock and damage our reputation by triggering a heart attack in the patients sporting our pacemaker.

We will now look into what the usual security mechanisms are and what properties they should have.

# Security properties – what do we expect?

We are now going to look into an embedded system. But what do we want to find in there? What do we want to test and why do we want to verify that it is done properly?

Not every system will require each of these functions (communication, maintenance, self-test, and so on), but these functions should at least have been considered by the client in their security requirements. From there, either the security properties are integrated as risk mitigation or the linked risk has been formally accepted within their risk management process – that is, if these risk management steps were followed in the product design.

Very often, these steps (establishing formal security requirements and integrating the unfulfilled mitigations in the risk management process) are overlooked. This is bad for the product, but this is very common. These are two findings for your report right here!

Now, let's look at the usual functions of a system and what the security trinity (confidentiality, integrity, and availability) of security properties (and trust, when applicable) mean for the different aspects of the system.

# Communication

The communication security properties ensure that the system can communicate securely with other systems over unsecured communication channels. Let's take a look at this in more detail:

- **Confidentiality**: Communications should be ciphered so that eavesdropping is impossible (or very hard).

- **Integrity**: Any form of disturbance in the communication should be (at least) detected and remediated (at any layer) to make the system able to detect tampering or errors in the communication.

- **Trust**: The parties involved, and their communication, should be authenticated adequately.

- **Availability**: Communication should be available (if it makes sense for the system).

# Maintenance

The goal of the maintenance function is to ensure that the system can be securely updated and maintained. This is very common for a system with external libraries (that can be vulnerable) or one that should have vulnerabilities of its own. The ability to securely fix these problems should be present and should not be leveraged as an attack path easily. Let's take a look at this in more detail:

- **Confidentiality**: The updates should be ciphered (or at least happen over a ciphered channel).

- **Integrity**: The integrity of the updates should be verified (through signature or hash verification).

- **Trust**: The origin of the updates should be verified (through signature verification).

- **Availability**: Unless very specific circumstances have been outlined, a way to update the system must be foreseen and must be available.

# System integrity and self-testing

The system will be outside the control of the client, and there is no way to guarantee who has control of the physical environment on the consumer's premises, nor the security of the supply chain. For example, some US three-letter agencies have been known to alter the firmware of a major networking equipment vendor for the final clients of interest. The system should be able to verify that it is running in a trusted way when possible. Let's take a look at this in more detail:

- **Integrity**: The system should be able to verify it is running without modifications.

- **Trust**: The system should be able to verify that every element in the trust chain involved in its final running state is safe and trusted (look into the concept of trusted boot chain, trusted computing platforms, and more).

- **Availability**: The system should be able to verify it is running code that can be trusted and that can be traced back to a trusted source of code.

# Protection of secrets or security elements

The things that ensure security (embedded certificates, keys, and so on) should be properly protected. Storing them within an un-ciphered, easily accessible external chip or making them easy to dump from an MCU can easily lead to the whole edifice being compromised. Let's look at this in more detail:

- **Confidentiality**: Secrets should be kept secret.

- **Integrity**: If a secret is changed, the system must be able to detect the change.

- **Trust**: The origin of the secrets should be verifiable.

- **Availability**: The secrets should be available, and the system should fail graciously if they are not.

Depending on the system, other aspects could be taken into account (since some systems may have other critical aspects to them), but the principles should stay the same. Now that we have looked into the desired properties, let's look at how we can leverage deficiencies.

# Reaching the crown jewels – how do we create impacts?

The means to achieving these target goals will involve using STRIDE to evaluate the components of the system. We will try to reason about the system to see how we can reach those crown jewels (usually by weakening or compromising security properties). During the evaluation process, we will look at the system within its ecosystem (as a functional part of a whole process) and try to understand how we can reach the crown jewels by compromising it.

Once the crown jewels have been identified, we will evaluate the components in terms of STRIDE to understand how they can allow us to reach the crown jewels.

## STRIDE through the components to compromise properties

> **Tip**
>
> Some other methodologies exist to take care of this, but they are far beyond the scope of this book. If you are interested, you can refer to EBIOS (`https://www.ssi.gouv.fr/en/guide/ebios-risk-manager-the-method/`) or ISO/IEC 13335-2 (`https://www.iso.org/standard/21755.html`).

The first step is to make or acquire an overview of the general architecture of both your components and flows:

- The architecture of the system itself
- The architecture of the ecosystem

Once this has been established or acquired, you will go through each of these "actors" (the components) and relationships (the data flow). Then, you must consider the possibilities of the methodologies approaches (spoofing, tampering, repudiation, information leak, denial of service, and escalation of privileges) for each of them. Do this in the light of your best knowledge regarding the technology in use (and research about it if you don't really know enough).

This may be the port that reaches more into your imagination. For each component, ask yourself "what if ?" regarding the following:

- **Spoofing**: Can I pose as this chip (for example, a chip on a board, or a sub-processor that is doing DSP)? Can I send fake messages on a communication bus? Can I pretend to be the backend or the DNS server?

- **Tampering**: Can I change the data in that flash? Can I change or replace the code that runs on the MCU?

- **Repudiation**: Can I access the circuitry of a tamper-evident device without leaving any trace of this?

- **Information leak**: Can I read the network traffic? Can I steal keys that are stored in an EEPROM?

- **Denial of service**: Can I make the device crash by sending data or pressing buttons randomly?

- **Escalation of privileges**: Can I access the management menu? Can I change settings without being authorized to?

Once you've done this, you have to agree on the test approach you wish to use with your client. This approach type depends on the type of scenario they want to look into (malicious internal personnel, external attacker, and so on).

## The test approach

In pentesting, there are three classical approaches: white box, gray box, and black box. These three approaches represent three types of attackers, and each has its own pros and cons.

### Black box

The attacker is given the exact same level of information as a user, a few systems to test, and then they are sent on their merry way:

- **Pros**: This approach generally mimics an external attacker that has no internal knowledge about the system. It is very representative of the majority of attacks that the client's system will endure in real life.

- **Cons**: This is long and expensive for the client. There is no guarantee that even the simplest flaws are going to be exposed. Even wrongly implemented security features or properties relying on security by obscurity could stay undiscovered, hence providing a very low level of assurance to the client.

## Gray box

The tester is given some general but internal information about the system architecture, the protocols used for communication, and the security requirements used for system design:

- **Pros**: This is a good balance between information and test efficiency/speed. It can be a good representation of an attacker with internal knowledge (a disgruntled employee, for example).

- **Cons**: Establishing the **Non-Disclosure Agreement** (**NDA**) to cover the documentation can go beyond the standard NDA, and the client may not like the idea of sharing documentation.

## White box

The tester is given full access to the internal documentation, the source code, and all schematics. These are potentially given to developers of the system so that they can ask questions:

- **Pros**: This gives the best assurance level to the client.

- **Cons**: It requires having good knowledge of the technology stack being used by the system.

# For the example system – the Furby

In this section, we will look into finding the crown jewels and applying the STRIDE methodology to the Furby toy.

As you may recall (*Chapter 2, Understanding Your Target*, and *Chapter 3, Identifying the Components of Your Target*), the "ecosystem" of the toy can be seen as follows:

- The toy is becoming mature by the user taking care of it physically.
- The toy is becoming mature by the user taking care of it via the app.
- The toy can switch its personality, depending on the way it is taken care of.
- The toy can talk to other toys.
- The toy can talk with the app (and have eggs in the app).

Since we don't have a real client, let's give ourselves some "crown jewels" targets:

- Make the toy quote Shakespeare instead of saying gibberish sentences (a malicious mind would have it say inappropriate things to a child, and that wouldn't be very good for the image of a toy vendor).

- Change the evolution state of the toy at will by manipulating its storage.

- Change what is displayed by the eyes of the Furby at will.

- Harvest all the goodies and objects in the app.

- Have control of the eggs in the app.

- Make the toy crash or execute code remotely.

We will stay away from reversing the Android application in the testing phases as much as possible since that is outside the scope of this book. If you are interested in this subject, please refer to the *Learning Android Forensics* book from Packt.

In the following subsections, we will go through the STRIDE methodology for the toy's components and ask ourselves the questions our test should answer.

## Spoofing

I don't appreciate when conference talks start with a dictionary definition – I feel that it just underlines the inability of the speaker to explain things with simple words. Spoofing is simple: it means posing as someone or something you are not (and misbehaving). These questions, if answered with yes, all fall into the spoofing domain:

- Can we pose as the app to the toy?

- Can we pose as the toy to the app?

- Can we pose as a toy to another toy?

- The app has a version dedicated to collectors called "war in-between stars" that provides specific character versions of the toy. Can we fake having one while we don't own a real one?

- Can we pose as a legitimate user and fake taking care of it?

## Tampering

Tampering: Noun. "Tampering is the action"... Just joking. To tamper with something means to change it maliciously. These questions, if answered with yes, all fall into the tampering domain:

- Can we change the settings and characteristics that are stored in the Furby?
- Can we change the stored sounds/speech synthesis settings?
- Can we change the Furby's eye patterns?
- Can we make it fully grown/evolved in one go?

## Repudiation

To repudiate means to deny being responsible for an action. Since the toy has no concept of identity, this does not apply in this context.

## Information disclosure

Let's see if we can find out information that we are not supposed to have access to:

- Can we dump internal EEPROMS and find out what information they are storing and how?
- Can we abuse the MCU to dump its program?
- Can we sniff ultrasound communication and understand how it works?

## Denial of service

Let's see if we can make things unresponsive:

- Can we make the toy crash remotely for good (that is, to manually restart the device) or if we sustain our attack?

## Escalation of privileges

Let's see if we can do things we are not supposed to be doing:

- Can we run code on the toy MCU?
- Can we run code on the user's phone?
- Can we trigger behaviors we are not supposed to be triggering (for instance, laying hundreds of eggs, creating bugged objects, and so on)?

With all of these questions in our mind, let's see how they link to our scenarios by learning how to plan the test and discuss its budget with our client.

# Planning the test

After some workshops with your client and gaining more information about the target system, you should have identified the following:

- The crown jewels and their security functions
- The testing scenarios and questions (and validated them with your client)
- Identified a global "difficulty level" for your scenarios (depending on the "box color", you may already know if a certain component or security function is more or less well-protected)

Now, the question is, *How do we allocate time to which scenario?* This is a difficult question, especially when you're utilizing a black box approach (since you have no details about the system architecture). Let's talk more about this balancing act.

## Balancing your scenarios

Typically, your scenarios will have an associated impact and difficulty. Let's be realistic: at this point, these impacts and difficulties are mainly "gut feelings" since we haven't done any exploratory surgery yet and the client may not be very forthcoming about the internals.

I usually define these difficulties as follows:

| Score | Type of actor | Means |
|-------|---------------|-------|
| 1 | Kid with an Arduino and a soldering iron | Well, it's a 14-year-old with an Arduino – the attacks will be very simple things such as dumping a storage chip, reading and writing from/to a slow bus, and so on. |
| 2 | Amateur | Here, we assume the attacker has a basic understanding of electronics and can crack simple "historic" ciphers (Cesar's, Vigenere, and so on) and has access to a basic electronics lab (can remove non-**ball grid array** (**BGA**) parts, the slow logic analyzer, and so on) with a limited amount of time to implement them (since the attacker will only spend the evenings and weekends doing this). |

| Score | Type of actor | Means |
| --- | --- | --- |
| 3 | Security researcher | Here, we assume the attacker has a good understanding of electronics and can crack weak/broken ciphers (RC4 with weak initialization, linear feedback registers with known plain text, and so on) and has access to a good electronic lab (chip-off and reading BGA flash, reaching buried traces, and so on), with a somewhat limited time to implement them (2-3 days a week for a month, for example). |
| 4 | Criminal group | Here, we assume there's a team of 2-3 people with a good understanding of electronics that can crack old or badly handled (but not necessarily weak) ciphers/hashes (DES brute-force, 3-DES with the same keys, MD5 collisions, and so on), have access to a very good electronic lab (chip-off and re-soldering of big BGAs, big FPGA projects, and so on), and have a decent amount of time to carry out the attacks (a full month for the team, for example). |
| 5 | State actor or electronics company | The attackers can deploy very advanced attacks. They can do things that require a lot of money, very advanced equipment, and knowledge of decapping and actively probing chips silicon, focused ion beam reworking of silicon, breaking state of the art ciphers such as AES, how to generate trusted certificates by court order, and so on. |

Now, we must classify the impact of these scenarios:

| Scenario Score | Hypothetical impact from STRIDE by domain | Impact on the crown jewels |
|---|---|---|
| 1 | • **Spoofing**: Pose as the update provider (or a security-critical external information source), such as a mission-critical sensor or as another system than the one that's tested toward the backend.<br>• **Tampering**: Change the code running on the system, change security-critical data, or change data in tamper-proof elements or in tamper-evident elements without evidence.<br>• **Repudiation**: Proceed with any of these level 1 S, T, I, D, or E actions without leaving adequate traces (according to the 5W criteria for traces: Who, What, Where, Why, and How) or being able to pin level 4 or 5 actions on someone else.<br>• **Information Leak**: Stealing root or intermediary certificates and private keys, dumping security-critical or intellectual property code, and stealing highly critical data (health data, ITAR data, and so on).<br>• **Denial of Service**: Definitively bricking the device (that is, just a reset isn't enough) intentionally and remotely with a one-shot action (that is, without maintaining the action to keep the device unavailable).<br>• **Escalation of Privilege:** Being able to trigger a critical administrative action as an unprivileged user. | Total compromise |

| Scenario Score | Hypothetical impact from STRIDE by domain | Impact on the crown jewels |
|---|---|---|
| 2 | • **Spoofing**: Pose as a non-secure but mission-critical external information source.<br>• **Tampering**: Change mission-critical data stored in the system (that you shouldn't be able to change) and change data in tamper-proof elements with evidence.<br>• **Repudiation**: Proceed with any of these level 2 S, T, I, D, or E actions without leaving adequate traces (according to the 5W criteria for traces: Who, What, Where, Why, and How) or being able to pin a level 3 action on someone else.<br>• **Information Leak**: Stealing personal or regulated information (credit card numbers and personally identifiable information). Stealing security-relevant but not critical data (that is, function addresses, pointers, and so on).<br>• **Denial of Service**: Preventing the device service with a low volume but continuous action (for example, one packet or request every 10 seconds) or impeding it (that is, degraded performance) with a one-shot action.<br>• **Escalation of privilege**: Being able to trigger a non-critical administrative action as an unprivileged user. | Partial compromise |
| 3 | • **Spoofing**: Pose as a nonsecure, non-mission-critical external information source without leaving any traces.<br>• **Tampering**: Change important but non-mission-critical data stored in the system (that you shouldn't be able to change).<br>• **Repudiation**: Proceed with any of these level 3 S, T, I, D, or E actions without leaving adequate traces (according to the 5W criteria for traces: Who, What, Where, Why, and How) or being able to pin a level 2 action on someone else.<br>• **Information Leak**: Steal information about the current security state of the system (for example, the exact version of the operating system or libraries).<br>• **Denial of Service**: Preventing the device service with a medium volume but continuous action (for example, one packet or request every second) or impeding it with a low volume, continuous action.<br>• **Escalation of privilege**: Being able to trigger a critical user action as another unprivileged user. | Lowering of the security posture |

| Scenario Score | Hypothetical impact from STRIDE by domain | Impact on the crown jewels |
|---|---|---|
| 4 | • **Spoofing**: Pose as a nonsecure, non-mission-critical external information source without leaving any traces.<br>• **Tampering**: Change unimportant but non-mission-critical data stored in the system (that you shouldn't be able to change).<br>• **Repudiation**: Proceed with any of these level 4 S, T, I, D, or E actions without leaving adequate traces (according to the 5W criteria for traces: Who, What, Where, Why, and How) or being able to pin a level 1 action on someone else.<br>• **Information Leak**: Steal information about the current state of the system (for example, its uptime, precise local time, and so on).<br>• **Denial of Service**: Preventing the device service with a high volume but continuous action (for example, multiple packets or requests every second) or impeding it with a medium volume, continuous action.<br>• **Escalation of privilege**: Being able to trigger a non-critical user action as another unprivileged user or a guest user. | A slight lowering of the security stance |
| 5 | • **Spoofing**: Being able to pose as an information source that is inconsequential for the system's functionality or security stance (for example, displaying the temperature in Tokyo).<br>• **Tampering**: Change unimportant but non-mission-critical data stored in the system (that you shouldn't be able to change).<br>• **Repudiation**: Proceed with any of these level 5 S, T, I, D, or E actions without leaving adequate traces (according to the 5W criteria for traces: Who, What, Where, Why, and How).<br>• **Information Leak**: Stealing minor pieces of information (for example, major versions, CPU load, and so on).<br>• **Denial of Service**: Preventing the device service with a continuous flooding action (for example, a packet or request as fast as a modern PC can) or impeding it with a high volume, continuous action.<br>• **Escalation of privilege**: Being able to trigger a non-critical user action as another unprivileged user or a guest user. | None |

Once you have done this scoring exercise for each scenario, multiply the impact and difficulties score to get a priority ranking for your different scenarios. At this point, all you need to do is negotiate a time budget affectation for each scenario with your client.

Doing a time budget negotiation is always the hardest part (as always, having people part with their money is not the easiest):

- Factor in the price of the equipment you will need to acquire. Some companies will accept to reimburse you with an equipment bill, some will accept an equipment budget being in the contract, while others won't want to hear about it. If they don't want to hear about it, just "sprinkle" in additional days so that they can pay for the necessary equipment.

- For each scenario, add a day where you will consume upfront to get to know the system, explore the functionalities that you may not be aware of (for example, storing games on a hard drive, how the application store works, how things are connected, and so on), and perform external research (some people may have published articles, for example).

- Get to know yourself. Maybe you are a beginner and you need 2 days for a difficulty 1 scenario. You may have a colleague in your company that works abroad who is an expert on the specific CPU architecture you will be using, but they may have a high day rate. If you are a beginner, I would advise the following:

| Scenario complexity | Time |
|---|---|
| 1 | 2 days |
| 2 | 4 days |
| 3 | 10 days |
| 4 | 30 days and up or not possible to execute |
| 5 | Not possible to execute |

Add a little bit of "time fat" for unexpected circumstances and external research.

- Do not forget the reporting and report proofing time.

# Summary

In this chapter, we learned about the STRIDE methodology and understood how to use it to define various attack scenarios. You then learned how to use the methodology efficiently by using it again and again against real-world devices. When you start out, you will probably sit for hours thinking about "Is this possible?", "How can I do this?", and reading about the components and attack methods that are available to use. This is absolutely normal and should not make you feel discouraged.

In the next chapter, we will become familiar with the attack tool we will be using throughout this book and also (finally!) start with practical assignments.

# Questions

1.  What does STRIDE stand for?

2.  What is the goal of the methodology, from a risk and practical standpoint?

3.  What are the 5W criteria for traces?

4.  Can you actually test for a scenario where the state actor operates above your level (that is, you have an amateur lab and the putative actor is a criminal group)?

5.  Why is a system being able to update itself very important?

6.  What is a black box test? What are its advantages for the client?

7.  What is a crown jewel?

# Further reading

To learn more about the topics that were covered in this chapter, please refer to the following link:

*   The starting article for STRIDE: `https://www.microsoft.com/security/blog/2009/08/27/the-threats-to-our-products/`

# Section 2: Attacking the Hardware

In this section, you will get up close and personal with hardware, using off-the-shelf tools and a very cheap, but quite capable, hardware platform (a cheap development board) to analyze and attack in-circuit protocols. You will also become more familiar with common wireless protocols and how to use them to attack hardware devices.

This section comprises the following chapters:

- *Chapter 5, Our Main Attack Platform*

- *Chapter 6, Sniffing and Attacking the Most Common Protocols*

- *Chapter 7, Extracting and Manipulating Onboard Storage*

- *Chapter 8, Attacking Wi-Fi, Bluetooth, and BLE*

- *Chapter 9, Software-Defined Radio Attacks*

# 5
# Our Main Attack Platform

We cannot interact physically with the systems (humans are not very well equipped to see and produce precise and fast electrical signals, are they?) and we may not want to risk our main computer platform by connecting it directly to a **device under test** (**DUT**). We will need a specialized tool for this.

In this chapter, we will look at the main tool we will use to actively attack our targets. The bluepill board we are going to use is very cheap, accessible, and can be programmed with an entirely open source toolchain. We will review what it is exactly, its hardware, its variants, and how to program it (with a little introduction to C) before actually using it to attack protocols and chips in the next chapters.

In this chapter, we will cover the following topics:

- Introduction to the bluepill board

- Why C and not Arduino?

- The toolchain

- Introduction to C

# Technical requirements

In order to be able to program and use the bluepill, it is essential to have the following:

- A bluepill board (I'd advise you to buy a few, as they are always useful; search for `bluepill stm32f103` on any bidding site).

- A breadboard.

- An STLINK USB stick: This looks like a USB stick with pins on the side opposite to the USB connector.

- A few wires for connections.

For the examples, you will require the following:

- Protocol: I2C: Chip: A PDIP 24LC I2C EEPROM

- Protocol: SPI: Chip: An MX25L8008 flash on a DIP breakout

- Protocol: UART: Any USB-to-serial adapter (the cheap ones based on CP2102 will do the job perfectly and they are useful tools too. Ordering more than one is a great idea; you need at least two)

- Protocol: Dallas 1-Wire: Chip: A DS18B20 (a temperature sensor)

You may want to also buy or find components that are using the same protocol but that are slightly different, so as to train yourself in adapting the examples.

In terms of the compilation of programs and flashing, install the following (for a Debian-based system):

- `gcc-arm-none-eabi`

- `libnewlib-arm-none-eabi`

- `binutils-arm-none-eabi`

- `gdb-multiarch`

- `openocd`

- `make`

- `texane st-link` (`https://github.com/texane/stlink`)

> **Note**
> Please be aware that the version that your distribution sports may not be sufficiently new. If this is the case, it could have a problem with the cheaper clones (in that case, install from source by following the instructions here: `https://github.com/texane/stlink/blob/master/doc/compiling.md`).

You can refer to the code used in this chapter at the following link:

`https://github.com/PacktPublishing/Practical-Hardware-Pentesting`

Check out the following link to see the Code in Action video:

`https://bit.ly/307nM2u`

# Introduction to the bluepill board

A board to do what? What is the board? What can it do? How much does it cost? Why this one? Where is the documentation? Yes, you surely have plenty of questions! You will sometimes need a reminder while testing or doing the exercises, so I will also point to the chip's documentation. These questions are exactly what we are going to be talking about in the following sub-headings.

## A board to do what?

Well, we will need to interface the board with the circuit we will want to attack. Since a general-usage PC doesn't really have a readily accessible interface board to connect with the most common protocols, we will use a bluepill to do so.

## What is it?

The bluepill is a colloquial name for many different boards that have the following characteristics:

- Are cheaply available on bidding or Chinese goods sites such as eBay, Taobao, and AliExpress (in the €1.5 range at the time of writing this book)

- Host an STM32F103C8T6 (or drop-in replacement parts from Chinese chip manufacturers) and its basic power circuity

- Break out most of the interesting pins in a format that can be plugged into a breadboard

The STM32F103C8T6 is a quite capable (32 bits, 72 MHz) microcontroller produced by STMicroelectronics that comes with a wide range of typical general-use peripherals:

- Two 12-bit ADCs
- Two I2Cs
- Two SPIs
- Three USARTs
- A USB
- A CAN
- GPIOs

We can now use these to interface with our target systems. Also, in quite practical terms, it is possible to program it directly in C (which we will use in the book) or use the Arduino IDE and API to program.

> **Important note**
> Some vendors are selling boards that have a clone of the STM32F103C8T6 on it. These should be fine, but the programming software may complain about it.

# Why C and not Arduino?

The C programming language has a reputation for being hard to use and complex. Trust me, it is not. This reputation comes from the fact it doesn't come with a lot of the convenience functions of more modern languages. The simplicity that comes with this language makes it shine when the resources are constrained and when the execution needs to be really efficient, like on a microcontroller!

While I am quite sure that most of the examples in the book could be written using the Arduino IDE and API, it would do the following:

- Hide too much of the compilation chain and the programming process from you
- Prevent you from actually understanding the capabilities of the chip
- Make it difficult for you to actually know what is happening on the chip (since it uses some of the chip capabilities to provide you with convenience functions)
- Actually consume quite a bit of storage space to provide you with these convenience functions

All of this (unless you actually have a degree in electrical engineering or experience in programming embedded systems) would hinder your ability to understand your actual targets! It would do so because you will understand some fundamental concepts about the way in which microcontrollers work and are used on your targets!

Aside from that, you definitely should buy an Arduino and play around with it, but I will not focus on that here. You can even use the STM32duino libraries on this platform!

# The documentation

The datasheet has a scope that is restricted to the model itself. Like most of the chip manufacturers, their chips are named in a nomenclature that allows us to decipher the capabilities of the chip that is soldered on the bluepill. For example, let's look at the nomenclature for STM32F103C8T6:

- STM32: The family; a line of 32-bit cortex M-based MCUs.

- F1: This is a general-purpose, medium-density chip (F0s are even cheaper, L0s are energy-efficient chips, F3s are used for digital signal processing, and so on).

- F103: This is a 73 MHz chip with a CAN and USB.

- C: This is the pin count (48 for C).

- 8: This tells us that the chip has 64 KB of Flash and 20 KB of RAM.

- T: This is the package (the dimensions of the plastic capsule that encloses the silicon). T is LQFP (low-profile quad flat package).

- 6: This chip is designed to work in a "normal" range of temperature and not be exposed to too much heat or humidity, and so on.

In STMicro vocabulary, the document that will provide you with the detailed information of the family is a "reference manual." It will give you the addresses of the different memory-projected registers. It also explains the way in which the peripherals are programmed and all the things that are shared across the family members, irrespective of how much memory they have, how many leads are available on this package or that package, and so on.

---

**Tip**

The datasheet can be found here: https://www.st.com/resource/en/datasheet/stm32f103c8.pdf. The reference manual can be found here: https://www.st.com/resource/en/reference_manual/cd00171190.pdf.

## Reading the documentation

In the reference manual, you will find a description of all the peripherals that are on the chip. While reading the documentation for a peripheral, you should expect to always find the same following sequence:

- **Functional description of the peripheral**:

    - How the peripheral type behaves in general

    - What the available functionalities of the peripheral type are

    - How to initialize and configure the peripheral type

    - How to use the internal peripheral behavior (what the interrupts are, how they play out together, which bit is flipped by which events, and so on)

- **Configuration of the registers for the peripheral**: A description of all the registers (their addresses and all of their bits) that manage the peripherals, and for each instance of the same peripheral type

- **A register map**: A brief overview of all the registers described in the configuration

# Memory-projected registers

Like most (if not all) programming languages, the main thing C does is make the CPU core move values from memory locations to other memory locations. In order to react to the programming, the chip has special memory regions where memory locations are actually special storage units ("the registers," as opposed to generic storage locations) that react to the stored value by altering the chip behavior. At some of these special addresses (that is, some registers), it is the behavior of the chip itself (such as its clock and turning peripherals on and off) that is set, and for others, it is the behavior of peripherals around the CPU that is altered. This concept is called **memory-projected register** and is the basis of the operation of MCUs and CPUs. Let's now dive into how this is translated in a binary that defines the MCU's behavior.

# The toolchain

We will use a set of tools to transform a high-level language (yes, I wrote that, C is a high-level language) into the binary code that the chip understands and is laid out in a file that it can execute. To make it short, it's called **compilation** (compilation is actually one step of it, but it is a quite easy shorthand). We will push this file to the chip and have it run our code. In order to do that, we will have to use a set of tools and I will describe these in the following sections.

# The compilation process

Under the generic compilation concept, the way it is understood by most people, we turn the code into something that can be executed by a computer. From the push of a button or a sternly typed command line, we see a file appear that we can run (a .exe file, a .elf file, or other formats). In reality, this is (of course) a little bit more complicated.

## The compilation in itself

The goal of the compilation process is to turn a human-readable language (C, C++, assembly opcodes, Java, and so on) into a sequence of instructions that the decoding unit in the CPU can understand.

For the bluepill, we will use the **GNU Compiler Collection** (**GCC**) and, more specifically, a flavor (gcc-am-none-eabi) that is geared toward our architecture (arm) without any specific operating system (none-eabi).

In order to be able to understand the process, we will perform this operation on our local machine since it is easier to see the result than on the bluepill, and the process is essentially the same.

First, let's compile a simple hello world code:

```
$ cat hello.c
#include <stdio.h>
int main(){printf("hello world!");}
$ gcc -c hello.c
$ file hello.o
hello.o: ELF 64-bit LSB relocatable, x86-64, version 1 (SYSV),
not stripped
$ chmod u+x hello.o
$ ./hello.o
bash: ./hello.o: cannot execute binary file: Exec format error
```

Here, gcc -c means compile only. When we try to execute hello.o, the error tells us that this is not a binary file that our computer knows how to execute. This is because we need to put it in a format it understands.

If you need to include header files (header files described by the functions provided by a library or another .o file), use -I to provide the path to the header directory and use the #include directive in the source file.

## The linking

The linking turns object files into an understandable format for the operating system. In our example, the `printf()` function is provided by an external library (the description of what the library provides comes from the `#include <stdio.h>` line), but the operating system has no clue as to which library just by looking at the object file. This is the linker's job (we will use `gcc` to call the linker) to link it (and put the relevant information) into a file format that the operating system will understand:

```
$ gcc -o hello.elf hello.o
$ ./hello.elf
hello world!
```

This process (since it is not very clear in our very small example) is very important as soon as a project is divided into multiple source files. Each will become a `.o` object file and will be linked together as something that is usable.

# Driving the compilation

Of course, a project can do the following:

- Encompass dozens of files.
- Need to be compiled in a debug version.
- Search for the location of libraries.
- ... and a myriad of other tasks that it would not be very practical to do by hand each time.

That is why there are tools to drive the compilation process. The simplest and most ubiquitous one is Make. Make is driven by a description file called a **Makefile**.

## Anatomy of a Makefile

A Makefile can be complex (if you look at a big file for a complex project) but is composed of very simple elements:

- **Variables**: These are usually used to store things that you can use later. It is very common to put the name of the compiler, options, and path in variables. The affectation is done with the `VARIABLENAME=` value outside of targets and the evaluation with `$(VARIABLENAME)`.

- **Targets**: The things make must do in order to achieve the goal (the goal in question is usually a file). Targets can be described with dependencies in order to take care of the tasks required by the current target (again, usually a file). The file's dependencies follow a : after a target name. make looks at the change date of the files listed in the dependencies and only launches the tasks for the dependency files that are more recent than the target.

Let's have a look at a very simple Makefile to compile our hello world example:

```
CC=arm-none-eabi-gcc
hello : hello.o
    $(CC) -o hello hello.o
hello.o : hello.c
    $(CC) -c -o hello.o hello.c
```

Let's discuss a few terms from this Makefile:

- CC: A variable that contains the name of the compiler executable

- hello: Our main target, which requires hello.o in order to be started

- hello.o: A requirement target for hello

> **Important note**
>
> In Makefiles, before a list of tasks (such as the $(CC) directive (the tasks for the target)), there must be a **tabulation** (\t) and not just a space. If the make command tells you a separator is missing, this means that your editor transformed the tab into multiple spaces, and this will not work.

To illustrate the dependencies system, let's try a number of things:

```
$ make # (1)
make: 'hello' is up to date.
$ rm hello # (2)
$ make
gcc -o hello hello.o
$ touch hello.c # (3)
$ make
gcc -c -o hello.o hello.c
gcc -o hello hello.o
```

Let's understand this code:

- First, we see that everything is up to date (1).

- If we remove the executable file (the hello file), make will rebuild just that (2).

- If we make the source file more recent than the outputs produced (3), make rebuilds everything.

Make is very powerful and allows much more than this simple example. I strongly encourage you to read some Makefiles to get used to its possibilities and, of course, read the documentation on Make's website:

https://www.gnu.org/software/make/

Now we can build code, let's see how we can push it to the chip.

## Flashing the chip

The easiest and most versatile software for STM32 chips on Linux is an open source implementation of ST's programming protocol. This software is available in the most modern distribution in a packaged format as the stlink-tools package.

> **Information box**
> For more information on the stlink-tools package, you can refer to the following link: https://github.com/texane/stlink.

It comes with different tools:

- st-flash: The basic tool to read from and write to the embedded Flash of an STM32.

- st-info: This tool gives you information regarding the connected chip.

Now, enough with the examples, let's do the real thing.

## Putting it into practice for the bluepill

In order to make our first program for our chips, we will need to do the following:

1. First, we will need to write a simple C program that will initialize the chip and blink the onboard LED.

2.  In the second step, we will use a linker script that will tell our compiler how to arrange the executable format in a way that is understood by our STM32.

3.  Finally, we will flash it to the chip.

## Using libopencm3

Before we start coding, we will need a corpus of information that will help us with providing all of the addresses of the different registers and constants that will help set them up without constantly doing (usually quite error-prone) bitwise arithmetic with raw values. Additionally, the opencm3 library comes with convenience functions to set up and use peripherals that we will use later on.

Here is how to get the library:

```
$ git clone https://github.com/libopencm3/libopencm3.git
...
$ cd libopencm3
$ make
...
$cd ..
```

At this point, the library is ready to be used.

## The code

The chip needs to be initialized for the following purposes:

*   To tell the chip which clock source to use (its internal oscillator or a more precise external crystal)

*   To know what to do with the clock source in order to clock itself (via an internal component called a PLL, it can multiply or divide the clock source to feed the different clock signals it needs)

*   To determine what peripherals to initialize in order to use the general-purpose input/output to which the LED is attached

*   To toggle the pin that commands the LED wait a bit, toggle the pin that commands the LED ... and repeat infinitely

The entire code and Makefile can be found in the book's Git repository in bluepill/ ch5/blink (do not forget to clone it and its submodules with --recursive).

Try to read the Makefile and understand what it does, as well as what the different targets do:

- Connect your STLINK stick to the bluepill and flash the code to it (with `make flash`). Connect the GND on the STLINK to the GND on the bluepill, 3V3 to 3V3, SWD to SWD, and SWCLK to SWCLK).

- Try to change the value in the second `while` loop to make it blink slower.

- Try to change the value in the second `while` loop to make it blink faster.

- Search the `libopencm3` documentation to see how you could replace the `rcc_clock_setup_in_hse_8mhz_out_72mhz` function.

- Read the function code and the reference manual to understand how it works (in the RCC chapter of the reference manual).

- Make the MCU run at 48 MHz from the HSI through the PLL (there is an already made function in libopencm3 for that) and see how it influences the blinking speed.

- Download ST STM32Cube software, start a new project with the STM32F130C8, and then go to the clock management tab and look at how the different peripheral buses are clocked.

Now that we've seen how code is transformed into a binary that can be transferred to the chip, let's look a bit more into the code and how it works.

# Introduction to C

C will be your bread and butter for developing your attacks. Yes, there are easier, more modern, less cumbersome languages, but the following is true:

- The abstraction level prevents you from understanding what is happening on the hardware.

- Most of your reversing targets will be C-based.

So, pony up, and learn the language that makes the hardware run!

This is really intended as a crash course that will just allow you to understand the code that comes with this book. There are plenty of resources on C on the internet if you want to dig deeper (and trust me, you will want to).

# Operators

C comes with most of the operators you are expecting:

| | |
|---|---|
| + | Addition |
| - | Subtraction |
| * | Multiplication |
| / | Division |
| >> and << | Bit shift (right and left) |
| \| | Binary OR (the bits at 1 in the first or second operands will be at 1 in the result); widely used to set binary flags |
| & | Binary AND (the bits at 1 in the first and second operands will be at 1 in the result); widely used to mask or unset binary flags |
| ^ | Exclusive binary OR (the bits at 1 in the first and second (but not in both) operands will be at 1 in the result); widely used to toggle binary flags |
| % | Modulo (remainder of the division) |
| && | Logical AND |
| \|\| | Logical OR |
| == | Test for equality |
| < (and <=), > (and >=) | Test for is smaller than (and is smaller than or equal to), and is greater than (and is greater than or equal to) |
| ! (and !=) | Logical NOT and test for "is different" |
| var++ and var-- | Increment and decrement a variable (+1 and -1) |
| a ^= b | Shorthand a = a ^ b |
| a \|= b | Shorthand for a = a \| b |
| a &= b | Shorthand for a = a & b |
| test ? if_true : if_false | The ? operator (known as the ternary operator is a shorthand for if; it is equivalent to<br>if (test) { if_true } else {if_false} |

You may already be familiar with the majority of the statements:

| | |
|---|---|
| `if(test){block}` | Executes the lines in a block if the test is `true`. |
| `if(test){block1}` `else{block2}` | Executes the lines in `block1` if the test is `true`, otherwise the lines in `block2`. |
| `while(test){block}` | Executes the lines in a block while the test is `true`. |
| `for(pre_ action;test;post_ action){block}` | Executes the lines in a block while the test is `true`, but executes `pre_action` once before the block and `post_action` after every block. Usually, `pre_action` initializes a counter, while `post_action` changes the counter. |

The comments can come in two forms:

| | |
|---|---|
| `// comments` | A single-line comment |
| `/* comments */` | A multi-line comment |

Numeral bases as literals are also very straightforward:

| | |
|---|---|
| `1234` | Base 10; decimal number |
| `0x321b8f1` | Base 16; hexadecimal |
| `0b101` | Base 2; binary |
| `010` | Base 8; octal; this is rarely used, but since it starts with a 0, it can pretty easily look like a decimal number! |

# Types

Variables have a type. This is so that the compiler knows what kind of operation to apply to the variable.

The main types in C are as follows:

```
int: an integer value, usually 4 bytes
short : a short integer, usually 2 bytes
char : enough to hold a character, usually a byte
float : a representation of a real (floating point) value,
usually 4 bytes. Attention, the precision is limited !
```

That's it. There are no evolved types such as strings, lists, and hash maps out of the box. This is a very concise language where you have to create the evolved types you may need from the basic types. But don't underestimate C. The chances are that it is still the language that created the code managing the hardware in most of the devices you own. The majority of the kernels, the low-level libraries, are written in C because it is extremely efficient, both for size and for pure code performance.

## The dreaded pointer

Pointers are making people afraid of C, and this is somewhat ridiculous. Pointers, just by themselves, are making people afraid of this language. Generations of students have been frustrated by the dreaded and mystical beast called "segmentation fault" (the error that usually comes from flawed pointer operations).

It is true that people are scared of pointers, and I cannot fathom why. They are easy.

A variable is held at a memory location. The pointer is the address of this location. Done ... finished. It is no more complicated than that. Of course, our systems hold this address in a location in memory.

The notation for pointers is * (a pointer is a type and it points to a value with a type so that the compiler can perform a size calculation). The notation of "get address of" is &, while, within an expression, * is used as a dereference (that is, "this thing that is at the address I am applying the * to"):

```
int a = 5; // a holds 5, for example at address 632
int b = 8;
int * a_ptr = & a; // a_ptr, a pointer to an int, holds the
value 632
*a_ptr = 6; // the address 632 now hold the value 6, and so
does a (cause it is at address 632)
b    = b + *a_ptr; // b holds 14
* a_ptr = b + *a_ptr;//a holds 20,a_ptr still holds 632
```

In C, pointers are the way in which arrays are managed, either with dynamic allocation (almost never used in MCUs), or statically with the [] shorthand syntax:

```
int a[4];
for(int i=0;i<4;i++){ a[i]= i}; // we initialize the array with
0,1,2,3
```

```
a[0] = 1; // arrays are 0 based since the address of the array
holds the first value
*(a+0) == a[1]; // is now true, a+0 actually holds the address
of the first value
```

Since the array is so easy to use, it is also used to hold strings:

```
char * s1  = "hello reader !"; // s holds the address of the
first character,
                              //"" tells the compiler that the
initial value it is a 0
                              //terminated array of characters
char   s2[15];                // declare a new array
char * s1_ptr = s1;           // s1_ptr holds the address of
the first character of s1
char * s2_ptr = s2;           // s2_ptr holds the address of
the first character of s2
while(*s1_ptr != 0){*s2_ptr++ = *s1_ptr++; };
                              /* string are 0(null character)
terminated, and we use this to
                                 copy to the target array, i
used the ++ shorthand to do all
                                 of this in one statement */
*s2_ptr = 0;                  //We 0 terminate our target
string since the while didn't
                              //execute for the last 0
s2[0]='H'; // Change the first value of s2 to the character H,
it is now "Hello reader !"
s1[0]='H'; // This will crash ! (we will see why in the static
reverse engineering chapter)
```

Like I said before, this is just a crash course, but for now, you are able to code for the bluepill, push code onto it, and start having fun!

# Preprocessor directives

Preprocessor directives are directives that a special piece of code in the compiler (the preprocessor) understands. They begin with # and are used by the preprocessor to do text replacement or file inclusion.

The most frequently used directives are the following:

| | |
|---|---|
| `#include <filename>` | This directive pastes the content of the file "filename" (in the search path of the preprocessor) into the processed file. Two forms exist: `<filename>` means in the search path, and "filename" means relative to this file. |
| `#define text replacement_ text` | This directive replaces `'text'` with `'replacement text'`. This is usually done to define file-wide constants and text replacement variables and macros. It is possible to define replacements with variables like so: <br><br>`#define min(X, Y)  ((X) < (Y) ? (X) : (Y))` <br><br>For example, most of the register addresses in `libopencm3` are defined this way. |
| `#ifdef ...` <br><br> `#endif` | This directive is used to test for the definition of a text replacement variable. The negative form (`#ifndef`) is commonly used to avoid the inclusion of a header file multiple times, like this: <br><br>`#ifndef __MY_VARIABLE_THAT_PREVENTS_THIS_ HEADER_MULTIPLE_INCLUSION` <br><br>`#define __MY_VARIABLE_THAT_PREVENTS_THIS_ HEADER_MULTIPLE_INCLUSION` <br><br>`...header content...` <br><br>`#endif` |

Multiple other directives exist including #undef, #else, and more besides.

# Functions

Declaring a function in C is very easy:

```
function_return_type function_name(type_arg1 arg1, type_arg2
arg2){
body of function
}
```

Then, the function_name variable simply holds a pointer to the assembly code that implements the function. One consequence of this is that it is possible to use function pointers as variables that hold a reference to a function that you can change and call dynamically.

# Summary

In this chapter, we have programmed our main attack platform for the first time and then installed and compiled the library that will help us interact with its peripheral. We also had a brief introduction to the language we are going to use to program it – C.

In the next chapter, we will go through the most common protocols used in embedded systems, and learn how to find them, sniff them, and then attack them with our bluepills.

# Questions

1.  What is the GPIOC_ODR register that I XOR in the blinking example? Can you achieve the same effect by using other registers?

2.  Is it possible to have the MCU run at 72 MHz for the HSI? Why or how? What is to be expected then?

3.  What are the premade frequency assignment functions available in libopencm3?

4.  XOR each character of the string Z9kvzrj8 with 0x19 in a C program. What does this mean?

5.  What is the address of the GPIOC_ODR register? How can we find that easily?

# Further reading

Read more about the C language:

- The seminal C book: *The C Programming Language*, by Brian Kernighan and Dennis Ritchie; ISBN 978-0131103627

- *21st Century C*, by Ben Klemens; ISBN 978-1449327149, because just because the language is 40 years old, doesn't mean you have to write it like it was 40 years ago

Read more about GNU Make:

- *Managing Projects with GNU Make*, by Robert Mecklenburg, Andy Oram, and Steve Talbott; ISBN 978-0596006105

# 6
# Sniffing and Attacking the Most Common Protocols

Now that we've seen how to program the chip, let's apply it to an application and use it to actually start attacking systems. We will do that by looking into a number of standard protocols that are used to communicate between chips and the outside world. They usually define only the physical layer for chip-to-chip communication and (almost) never go into higher levels of abstractions. In this chapter, we will learn how to operate, sniff, and attack I2C, SPI, UART, and **Dallas 1-Wire (D1W)**.

In this chapter, we will cover the following topics:

- Understanding I2C
- Understanding, sniffing, and attacking SPI
- Understanding, sniffing, and attacking UART
- Understanding, sniffing, and attacking D1W

# Technical requirements

In this chapter, we will look into, sniff, inject, and man-in-the-middle the most common hardware protocols. There are a small number of things that you can get for yourself if you want to replicate the practical demonstrations. (These are not absolutely necessary but there is both a theoretical and a practical know-how aspect to what is covered in this chapter. I warmly recommend that you actually replicate the exercises.)

## Hardware

In order to be able to follow along, get yourself the following:

- A breadboard
- Two blue pills (very cheap Chinese STM32 boards; see `https://stm32duinoforum.com/forum/wiki_subdomain/index_title_Blue_Pill.html`)
- An STLink to program them (sometimes the UART bootloaders are not wired correctly)
- Jumper wires
- Any logic analyzer (we will use an open bench analyzer)

The following peripherals are required:

- **I2C**: A PDIP 24LC I2C EEPROM
- **SPI**: An MX25L8008 flash on a DIP breakout
- **UART**: Any USB-to-serial adapter (The cheap ones based on CP2102 will do the job perfectly, as they are useful tools. Ordering more than one is a great idea.)
- **D1W**: A DS18B20 (a temperature sensor)

The software needed for Linux is as follows:

- `arm-gcc-eabi-none`
- `stlink`
- `sigrok`
- Fritzing (to see the breadboard implementation of the components)

In this chapter, there are a few schemas that show how to connect components to a breadboard. Since the book is printed in grayscale, it may not always be very easy to differentiate the wires. If it is not clear enough for you, please download Fritzing, a software that can show (in color) the breadboard schematic files that are in the GitHub repository: `https://github.com/PacktPublishing/Practical-Hardware-Pentesting/tree/main/bluepill/ch6`.

The GitHub repository also contains all of the example code.

Let's start with I2C.

Check out the following link to see the Code in Action video:

`https://bit.ly/3q2TkRK`

# Understanding I2C

**I2C** (pronounced as *I-two-see*, or *I-square-see*), short for **Inter-Integrated Circuit**, is a protocol that was invented by Phillips in the early 80s to be used in televisions. Due to its easy topology and low part count, it is now widely adopted.

## Mode of operation

I2C connects chips with two wires: one is data (bidirectional) and the other is clock (of course, with a shared ground). On the bus, one chip acts as the master and the others as slaves (but they can exchange this role if this functionality is foreseen).

### Physical layer

A very important feature on the I2C bus is that both lines (classically called **Serial Data** (**SDA**) for the data line and **Serial Clock** (**SCL**) for the clock line) are pulled up. This means they both have a resistor to the logical positive rail (also called VCC or VDD) in order to guarantee that the bus is high when no chip is pulling it to ground level (low). The bus normally uses a bus topology, but at low speeds, it is possible to use a star topology. Both the bus master and slaves can (and will) clock the bus.

The bus classically looks like this:

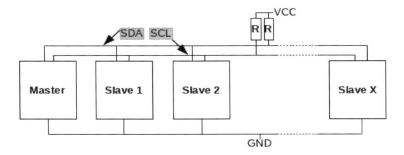

Figure 6.1 – General I2C architecture

Speed is very important regarding the physical layer (and will have an impact when you want to impersonate a chip, for example).

I2C comes in multiple speed grades, as shown in the following table:

| Mode | Abbreviation | Frequency | Min. charge current (Imin, typical) |
| --- | --- | --- | --- |
| Standard | Sm | $f \le 100$ KHz | 2 mA |
| Fast | Fm | $100$ KHz $< f \le 400$ KHz | 2 mA |
| Fast plus | Fm+ | $400$ KHz $< f \le 1$ MHz | 3 mA |
| High speed | HSm | $1$ MHz $< f \le 3.4$ MHz | 6 mA |
| Ultra-fast | UFm | $3.4$ MHz $< f \le 5$ MHz | 20 mA |

The speed mainly has an impact on the values of the pullup resistor for the following reasons:

- Everything on a board (traces, components, and more) has parasitic values (that is, the values that come from the environment, the package itself, and a plethora of other factors).

- The traces of the bus have a parasitic capacitance (but also their own resistance, inductance, and more); it is possible that the traces and the pullup resistor act as resistance that is charging a capacitor.

While the impact of this is very limited at slower speeds, it can be measurable and even disturbing at higher frequencies (this is the reason behind not using a breadboard at fast speed in *Chapter 1, Setting Up Your Pentesting Lab and Ensuring Lab Safety*).

> **Information box**
>
> The rule of thumb is, the higher the speed, the lower the resistance (lower resistance implies more current, which implies faster response – this is a rule of thumb; the capacitance of the circuit has an impact but you can't change it).

To calculate the needed resistance, the following formula can be applied. This is a simplified version; there is a formula that takes the parasitic capacitance of the traces into account, but it is hard to measure. Typical capacitance is taken into account in the *Imin* values indicated in the following formula:

$$Rpull = \frac{VCC - min(0.4, (0.1 * VCC))}{Imin}$$

Here is a table of resistance for common logic-level values (in reality, select the closest smallest standard value in the resistors you have available):

| Mode | VCC: logic level | | | | | | |
|---|---|---|---|---|---|---|---|
| | 5 V | 3 V | 2.5 V | 1.8 V | 1.5 V | 1.2 V | 1 V |
| Standard | 2300 | 1350 | 1125 | 810 | 675 | 540 | 450 |
| Fast | 2300 | 1350 | 1125 | 810 | 675 | 540 | 450 |
| Fast plus | 1533 | 900 | 750 | 540 | 450 | 360 | 300 |
| High speed | 766 | 450 | 375 | 270 | 225 | 180 | 150 |
| Ultra-fast | 230 | 135 | 1125 | 81 | 67.5 | 54 | 45 |

> **Important note**
>
> Not every MCU can sink this much current easily! If you don't pay attention, you can easily burn your pin (or your MCU). Some additional transistors can solve this problem. Selecting a value too low for the pullup resistor will lower the state change time but can also change the minimal voltage and make it not close enough to GND. This can prevent the system from working.

## Logic levels and voltage translation

*This logic translation is mainly used for I2C but can also be applied to other protocols.*

I2C doesn't really force a specific value for the logic levels, and both the slaves and the master can pull the SDA low. However, it is then necessary to use a bidirectional voltage-level translation that is able to cope with this. Dedicated chips exist but they tend to be expensive. Thankfully, an engineer for Philips has provided us with a clever trick to do this using just two MOSFETs. The arrangement is shown in the following diagram:

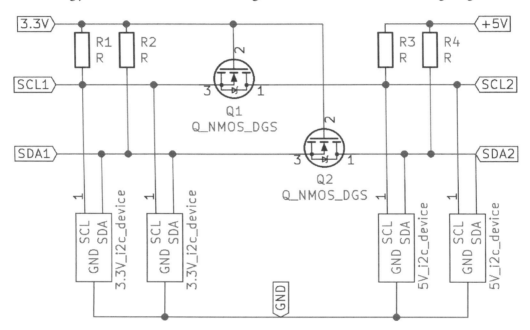

Figure 6.2 – Bidirectional voltage translation

The original author (Herman Schutte) suggests using BSS138 MOSFETs for 5 V<>3.3 V translation. This MOSFET typically drives with a gate voltage of 1.3 V (refer to the datasheet). So, you will need to find replacements if your logic levels are lower (than 1.8 V to be on the safe side). You may need to find a MOSFET with a lower gate threshold. Some vendors offer BSS138 with a very low minimal gate threshold. You may need to buy a few dozen, find the ones that are more on the lower end of the spectrum, and select those specific ones in the lot for your voltage translation. I found BSS138 with a Vgs as low as 700 mV in a lot from Diode Incorporated.

## The physical format of the bits

The bits are transferred by encoding them in the way SDA and SCL behave relative to one another.

The bits are transmitted as shown:

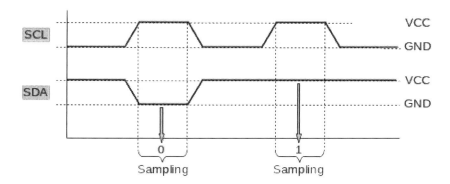

Figure 6.3 – I2C sampling

The sampling is typically done around the middle of the active clock cycle (that is, SCL is high, as shown in the preceding figure) or on an SCL raising edge. The sampling reads the state of SDA to get a 0 or 1 from the signal.

A few special conditions that are not following the normal bit encoding or behavior rules are used to support additional signaling between the devices:

- **Start condition**: To start communication on the bus, the bus master pulls SDA low while SCL is kept high:

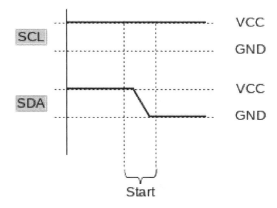

Figure 6.4 – I2C start condition

- **Stop condition**: To stop communication on the bus, the bus master pulls SDA high while SCL is kept high:

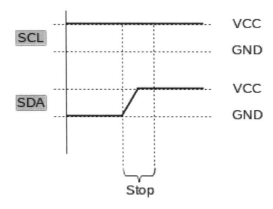

Figure 6.5 – I2C stop condition

- **Restart condition**: This is similar to the start condition. During a transaction, SDA goes low while SCL is kept high:

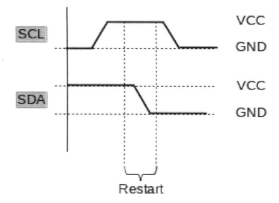

Figure 6.6 – I2C restart condition

- **Pause**: The slave keeps SCL low, preventing the master from clocking SCL (the master detects it and pauses the transmission) and frees up SCL for the master when it is done:

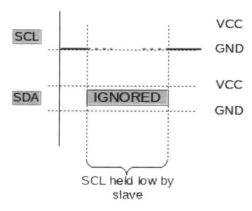

Figure 6.7 – I2C pause

We have covered the physical layer, so let's have a look at the logical layer now.

## Logical layer

I2C supports an addressing system over 7 bits (or 10 bits with an extension but this is not supported by all devices). This means that the theoretical maximum number of devices is 126 (the zero address is supposed to be a broadcast, but this is not actually implemented in all chips).

Every device has a 7-bit address and the last bit of the byte is used to indicate whether this is a read or write request:

| Bit READ | Emitter WRITE | Bit signification WRITE | | Bit WRITE | Emitter READ | Bit signification READ | |
|---|---|---|---|---|---|---|---|
| | Master | Start | | | Master | (Re)start | |
| 0 | Master | Address bit 1 | | 0 | Master | Address bit 1 | |
| 1 | Master | Address bit 2 | | 1 | Master | Address bit 2 | |
| 2 | Master | Address bit 3 | | 2 | Master | Address bit 3 | |
| 3 | Master | Address bit 4 | | 3 | Master | Address bit 4 | |
| 4 | Master | Address bit 5 | | 4 | Master | Address bit 5 | |
| 5 | Master | Address bit 6 | | 5 | Master | Address bit 6 | |
| 6 | Master | Address bit 7 | | 6 | Master | Address bit 7 | |
| 7 | Master | Write: 0 | | 7 | Master | Read: 1 | |
| 8 | Slave | Acknowledgment | | 8 | Slave | Data bit 1 | |
| 9 | Slave | (Optional) Pause | | 9 | Slave | Data bit 2 | |
| 10 | Master | Command bit 1 | | 10 | Slave | Data bit 3 | |

| Bit READ | Emitter WRITE | Bit signification WRITE | | Bit WRITE | Emitter READ | Bit signification READ | |
|---|---|---|---|---|---|---|---|
| 11 | Master | Command bit 2 | | 11 | Slave | Data bit 4 | |
| 12 | Master | Command bit 3 | | 12 | Slave | Data bit 5 | |
| 13 | Master | Command bit 4 | | 13 | Slave | Data bit 6 | |
| 14 | Master | Command bit 5 | | 14 | Slave | Data bit 7 | |
| 15 | Master | Command bit 6 | | 15 | Slave | Data bit 8 | |
| 16 | Master | Command bit 7 | | 16 | Master | Acknowledgment | |
| 17 | Master | Command bit 8 | | | Slave | (Optional) Pause | |
| 18 | Slave | Acknowledgment | | 17 | Slave | Data bit 1 | Repeat as needed |
| | Slave | (Optional) Pause | Repeat as needed | 18 | Slave | Data bit 2 | |
| | Master | (Re)start | | 19 | Slave | Data bit 3 | |
| 0 | Master | Address bit 1 | | 20 | Slave | Data bit 4 | |
| 1 | Master | Address bit 2 | | 21 | Slave | Data bit 5 | |
| 2 | Master | Address bit 3 | | 22 | Slave | Data bit 6 | |
| 3 | Master | Address bit 4 | | 23 | Slave | Data bit 7 | |
| 4 | Master | Address bit 5 | | 24 | Slave | Data bit 8 | |
| 5 | Master | Address bit 6 | | 25 | Master | Acknowledgment | |
| 6 | Master | Address bit 7 | | | Slave | (Optional) Pause | |
| 7 | Master | Write: 0 | | | | | |
| 8 | Slave | Acknowledgment | | | | | |
| 9 | Slave | (Optional) Pause | | | | | |
| 10 | Master | Command bit 1 | | | | | |
| 11 | Master | Command bit 2 | | | | | |
| 12 | Master | Command bit 3 | | | | | |
| 13 | Master | Command bit 4 | | | | | |
| 14 | Master | Command bit 5 | | | | | |
| 15 | Master | Command bit 6 | | | | | |
| 16 | Master | Command bit 7 | | | | | |
| 17 | Master | Command bit 8 | | | | | |
| 18 | Slave | Acknowledgment | | | | | |
| | Slave | (Optional) Pause | | | | | |

This is a complete description of an I2C transaction between a master and slave. Now that we know this, let's sniff a communication and see how the protocol is used in the communication.

# Sniffing I2C

There are at least two ways to sniff I2C: the generic way (with any logic analyzer) or by using the Bus Pirate.

The target circuit we use as an example is any micro-controller (a blue pill for us) connected to an I2C chip (PCF8574P for me).

> **Information box**
>
> Since it will probably be the first time you interact with your USB devices, don't forget to set up `udev` rules (for Linux) in order to be able to interact with them without needing superuser privileges.

Look into your system log (`dmesg` for Linux) after plugging in the device and note down the `vendorid` and product ID values. For example, this is what `dmesg` says for my logic sniffer:

```
[xxx.xx] usb xxx: New USB device found, idVendor=04d8,
idProduct=fc92, bcdDevice= 1.00
```

```
[xxx.xx] usb xxx: New USB device strings: Mfr=1, Product=2,
SerialNumber=0
```

```
[xxx.xx] usb xxx: Product: Logic Sniffer CDC-232
```

Create a file for `udev` (usually in `/etc/udev/rules.d/`) with a line like this:

```
SUBSYSTEMS=="usb", ATTRS{idVendor}=="[vendor id you noted
down]", ATTRS{idProduct}=="[product id you noted down]",
MODE:="0666"
```

Reload the rules with the following (as `root`/`sudo`):

```
#udevadm control --reload-rules
```

Now that we have seen how the protocol is behaving, let's have a look at how we can read it.

## Using a generic logic analyzer

*While we're using the logic analyzer for the first time for I2C, it is of course also usable for the other protocols.*

We will use an open bench logic analyzer and `sigrok` (the open bench logic analyzer is open source hardware and `sigrok` is open source software).

We will need to connect the following.

The blue pill, the EEPROM, the two pullup resistors, and the serial adapter need to be connected like so:

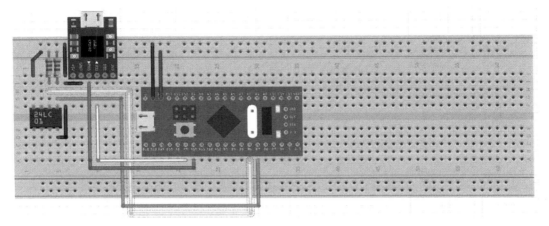

Figure 6.8 – I2C usage connection

Open the Fritzing schematic (`https://github.com/PacktPublishing/ Practical-Hardware-Pentesting/tree/main/bluepill/ch6/fritzing_ Schematics`) to identify the components.

To connect the analyzer to the circuit, do the following:

1. Connect the ground together.

2. Connect pin 0 of the analyzer to the SCL line.

3. Connect pin 1 of the analyzer to the SDA line.

4. Connect the analyzer to USB.

5. Launch PulseView (`sigrok`'s GUI) and connect it to the logic analyzer.

6. Click on the **Connect device** button and set up the analyzer as shown:

Figure 6.9 – Connecting the logic analyzer

7.  Select the logic analyzer pins you used from the menu with this icon: 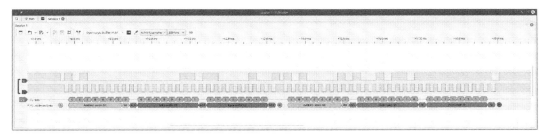. Click on the sniffing button until you see a waveform that looks like this:

Figure 6.10 – Adding a decoder

8.  Add a decoder (I2C) by clicking on the yellow-and-green button on the top bar.

9.  Click on the I2C decoder to select which line is SCL and which is SDA (in my sniff, I used pins 6 and 7: 7 as SCL and 6 as SDA).

Now we can see on the decoder line what the values that transited on the I2C bus are!

Now you can sniff I2C with a logic analyzer.

## Using the Bus Pirate

*This is also applicable to other protocols.*

The Bus Pirate offers multiple easy ways to interact with I2C but has the downside of coming without a GUI. It is available as a serial device on your computer and you can interact with it on the command line. It can sniff I2C up to 100 KHz.

All the commands related to I2C are documented here: `http://dangerousprototypes.com/docs/Bus_Pirate_I2C` (the commands for the other protocols have their own pages).

The Bus Pirate can sniff (relatively) low-speed I2C and render the traffic in the same syntax it would use to emit the I2C traffic. You will then be able to replay the traffic really easily. Just connect the Bus Pirate pins to the previous breadboard.

Let's give this a try:

1.  Connect to the command-line interface of the Bus Pirate (screen or minicom, whichever is your favorite serial client; for me, it is screen). Don't forget the `udev` rules; you can even give a cool persistent name such as `/dev/buspirate` with the SYMLINK directive. I'll let you search how to use `udev` directives by yourself; maybe there will be questions on this at the end of the chapter!:

```
$screen /dev/ttyUSB0 115200
```

2.  Put it in I2C mode in the terminal (4) and launch the `snif` macro (2).

3.  Power the circuit.

    You should see something like this:

```
[0xa0+0x00+0x01+[0xa1+0xXX-0xff]
```

`0xXX` is dependent on the content of your EEPROM. If it has never been written to, it will be a random value.

Let's look into the datasheet for the EEPROM and make sense of this traffic:

- [: The start condition

- 0xa0: But the device address was 0x50 in the sigrok sniff! Remember how the address is on 7 bits and uses the eighth bit of the byte to indicate read or write? 0x50 << 1   = 0xa0  = is the write address of the peripheral at 0x50.

> **Information box**
>
> << means shift to the right.
>
> We need to be familiar with the following.
>
> The C notation for bit-wise and Boolean operators (as these operations are extensively used in embedded systems) is really important. Please refer to the GNU C manual: https://www.gnu.org/software/gnu-c-manual/gnu-c-manual.html#Bitwise-Logical-Operators.
>
> Memory representation of various types (that is, how an integer, a float, or a long long is represented in memory and what this representation entails in term of limitations) is also very important to know; you don't really need to know the details intimately but knowing they exist and how to find out how they work will sometimes open interesting doors for you.

- +: The address is ACKed by the EEPROM.

- 0x00: First bit of the address...

- + is ACKed.

- 0x01: Second bit of the address...

- + is ACKed.

- [: We restart.

- 0xa1: 0xa0 | 1 = 0xa1 – the last bit is 1, so we want to read.

- 0xXX: We read a byte that we NACK (since it is the last byte we want).

- And the state machine of the MCU just clocks in a byte anyway (because that is how it works) and stops.

# Injecting I2C

Injecting I2C can be really tricky for two reasons:

- Not all masters on an I2C bus are able to follow the multi-master arbitration protocol. In order to be able to inject I2C on a live bus, if the multi-master is not supported, we will need to get crafty (either by studying the period at which the master is transmitting and leverage pauses or by actually doing a man in the middle).

- Remember how I2C is an open collector bus with pullup resistors? This means that you have to pull down the bus (actually do a bus stretching like you were a slave) and use its pullups. Sometimes, this makes the bus masters that don't support the multi-master functionality behave really weirdly and sometimes crash (that can also be interesting but, in my experience, not very useful).

Otherwise, injecting I2C is just a matter of connecting another master on the bus without a pullup resistor (it is using the existing ones) and avoiding collisions.

## Exercise

1.  Connect one blue pill and flash the code for the I2C sniffing example.

2.  Do the same for the second blue pill without dedicated pullup resistors (there shouldn't be any collision unless you are really, really, really unlucky).

3.  What do you see on both serial outputs?

4.  What do you conclude?

# I2C man in the middle

By using a micro-controller with two I2C peripherals (such as the blue pills), we can put ourselves physically in between the master and slaves, acting as a slave to the master and as a master to the slaves. For this, we just have to know the expected address of the slave.

Here is how to put the components on a breadboard:

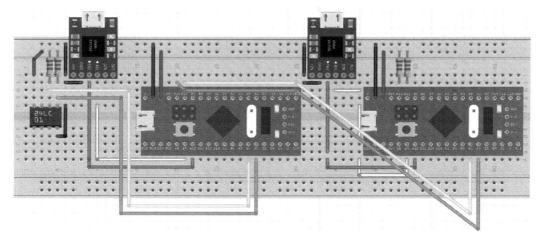

Figure 6.11 – I2C man-in-the-middle connection

We will alter the traffic to have the master read p-e-n-t-e-s-t every 100 bytes.

The code is in this chapter's folder in the cloned directory. Compare it to the reading code, play with the interrupts, and try to understand it.

# Understanding SPI

**SPI**, or **serial-to-parallel interface**, is a (usually minimum) three-wire bus. One acts as the clock (CLK), one as **Master Out Slave In** (**MOSI**), and one as **Master In Slave Out** (**MISO**). If multiple slaves are present in the bus, there is also an additional wire per slave called **CS** or **SS** (**Chip Select** or **Slave Select**, usually active low).

Here is how multiple slaves are connected:

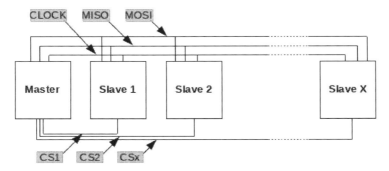

Figure 6.12 – SPI general architecture

SPI only manages how the bits are transferred on the line; there is no logical layer in the protocol (like I2C has).

On systems where the speed of transfer is important, SPI can come in the **QSPI** flavor (**queued SPI/quad SPI**) where there are four data lines. You should note that some chips support both modes and can switch between them with internal commands (that is, commands in the data that are transported by SPI, not commands determined by the SPI protocol itself).

Now that we have seen how the chips are connected, let's see how it works.

# Mode of operation

First things first, SPI has a frequency. This frequency is determined by the master (which is pulsing the clock) and must fall within the max frequency that the currently selected peripheral (with a CS wire) supports.

The second thing to take into account with SPI is two parameters called CPOL and CPHA. These parameters manage the clock polarity and clock phase:

- **Clock Polarity** (**CPOL**) governs the fact that the clock wire is considered active high or low.

- **Clock Phase** (**CPHA**) governs the timing at which the data will be sampled on the adequate wire in respect to the clock cycles.

This creates four "modes" (CPOL and CPHA names are inherited from PIC MCUs but this became a de facto standard).

## SPI mode 0

In this mode, the clock is active high. Data is sampled on the leading edge of the clock cycle and changed on the trailing edge:

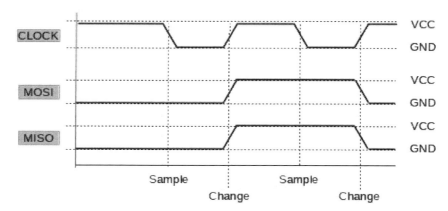

Figure 6.13 – SPI mode 0 timing

## SPI mode 1

In this mode, the clock is active high. Data is sampled on the trailing edge of the clock cycle and changed on the leading edge of the following clock cycle:

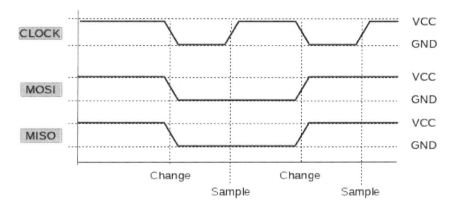

Figure 6.14 – SPI mode 1 timing

## SPI mode 2

In this mode, the clock is active low. Data is sampled on the leading edge of the clock cycle and changed on the trailing edge:

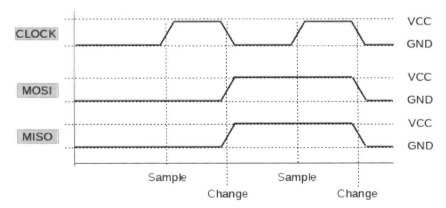

Figure 6.15 – SPI mode 2 timing

## SPI mode 3

In this mode, the clock is active low. Data is sampled on the trailing edge of the clock cycle and changed on the leading edge of the following clock cycle:

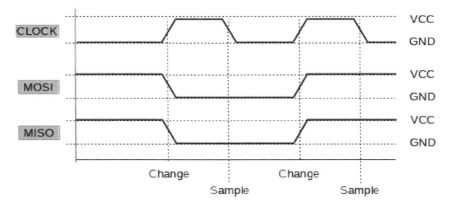

Figure 6.16 – SPI mode 3 timing

Now that we know what SPI is supposed to look like, let's have a look at it.

# Sniffing SPI

Like we did for I2C, we will now sniff SPI.

The sniffing protocols are largely the same for all of them: put the circuit using the protocol in place, connect your logic analyzer to the appropriate pins, and launch PulseView. Refer to the *Sniffing I2C* section if you have forgotten.

Build up the circuit as shown here:

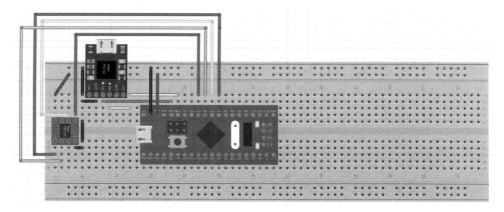

Figure 6.17 – SPI usage connection

This is basically the same deal as for I2C: just connect the ground together, then connect pin 0 to CLK, pin 1 to MISO, pin 2 to MOSI, and pin 3 to CS.

Launch PulseView and add an SPI decoder.

The code for the blue pill is here: `https://github.com/PacktPublishing/Practical-Hardware-Pentesting/tree/main/bluepill/ch6/spi_client`.

We will follow the same pattern and now inject data on an SPI bus.

## Injecting SPI

To inject SPI, just add your master to the bus, the MOSI to the MOSI line, the MISO to the MISO line, CS to CS, and CLK to CLK, and listen to the CLK line to establish a pattern and avoid collisions.

If multiple peripherals are present, you will also have to manage the CS line.

## SPI – man in the middle

Put yourself between the master and the slaves; act as a slave to the master and as a master to the slave. An (easily worked around) problem is that most of the hardware peripherals included in the MCUs need an external CS/SS. Just connect to the ground so that the peripheral believes it is always selected if the MCU you use needs it.

> **Important note**
>
> Depending on the speed of the communication between the original master and the original slave (and the speeds supported by the original slave), it is not always possible to man-in-the-middle SPI with a micro-controller. Especially with SPI EEPROMs, the communication is not transactional (that is, the MCU finishes asking its questions and then the EEPROM answers). For some EEPROMs, the EEPROM starts to send back data while the MCU is still sending commands. If you have to face this kind of situation, look into SPI Spy (`https://github.com/osresearch/spispy`), an FPGA-based tool that can solve this.

Here is the connection schema in the Fritzing folder. Open the Fritzing document here to better see the components and connection points as shown in the following figure:

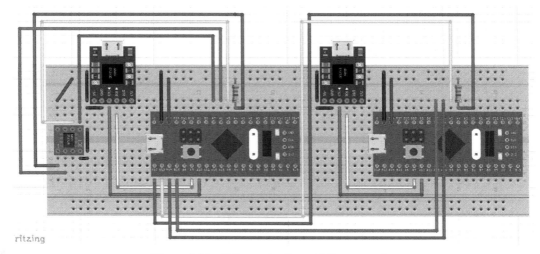

Figure 6.18 – SPI man-in-the-middle connection

The code is here: `https://github.com/PacktPublishing/Practical-Hardware-Pentesting/tree/main/bluepill/ch6/spi_mitm`.

Now we are going to look into UART (serial link).

# Understanding UART

UART (otherwise known as RS232 or serial) is a time-based protocol. The data travels on two wires.

From the MCU point of view, they are named as follows:

- **RX (Receive)**: The wire on which data comes from the peripheral
- **TX (Transmit)**: The wire on which data goes to the peripheral

The flow control can come in two main flavors:

- **With hardware flow control**: Two additional control wires control the flow of the data. This hardware flow control itself can come in two flavors: either with control from the master, **CTS (Clear To Send)**, or from the slave, **DTR (Data Terminal Ready)**.

- **Without hardware flow control**: UART without hardware flow control only takes care of "transporting the bits." There is no logic layer to it.

Error detection is also possible in the form of a parity bit added at the end of the transmission.

It can connect multiple devices but is not taking care of the addressing (the payload will have to take care of this). It also serves as a base of multiple "flavors" of communication (IrDA, smartcard communication, and more).

Here are the different signals:

| Pin name | Description |
|---|---|
| TX | Transmission wire. |
| RX | Reception wire. |
| CTS/DTR | This signal gives the name to the "style" of the flow control: either Clear To Send or Data Terminal Ready. |
| RTS/DSR | Ready To Send (RTS) or Data Set Ready (DSR). |

Now that we have seen the different signals, let's see how they are used to send data.

## Mode of operation

In the UART schema, idle lines are high, and the signal is sent by pulling it low.

This is assured by a pullup resistor that is normally taken care of on the TX line (meaning the MCU takes care of the pullup resistor on its TX and the peripheral on its own TX (which is the MCU's RX)). But why is it important, you ask? In the end, there is a pullup on each line. True, but these resistors can be internal to both the MCU and the peripheral and as we will need to put ourselves on these lines, we will need to pay attention that we don't disturb this mechanism too much.

The first parameter to know is called the baud rate, which is the number of bits sent by second. This is a critical parameter since the protocol is time-based. This determines the time of the transmission for one bit.

There is a list of "usual" baud rates and their corresponding symbol times. The symbol time is very practical to determine the correct baud rate to set on your devices:

| Baud rate (bps) | Symbol time |
|---|---|
| 110 | 0.009090909 |
| 300 | 0.003333333 |
| 600 | 0.001666667 |
| 1200 | 0.000833333 |
| 2400 | 0.000416667 |
| 4800 | 0.000208333 |
| 9600 | 0.000104167 |
| 14400 | 6.94E-05 |
| 19200 | 5.21E-05 |
| 38400 | 2.60E-05 |
| 57600 | 1.74E-05 |
| 115200 | 8.68E-06 |
| 128000 | 7.81E-06 |
| 256000 | 3.91E-06 |

> **Tip**
> UART operations are very sensitive to the precision of the clock. Try to always use a crystal oscillator as the clock source since internal RC oscillators (build with resistors and capacitors) tend to be less precise and drift more.

UART transmissions always start with a start bit (to signal the line is not idle and a finish with one or more stop bit). The transmission can be of any number of bits (but is usually 7 or 8 bits long). The transmission can also contain a parity bit to allow for error detection (this bit is optional).

A very common way to describe the settings of serial communication is a string that goes: *Baud rate/number of bits – Presence of the parity bit (Yes/No) – Number of stop bits.*

For example, 9600/8-N-1 is a very common configuration (9,600 bps/8 bits – No parity – 1 stop bit).

# Sniffing UART

Sniffing UART with a logic analyzer is very straightforward. Connect the ground together and your analyzer in the usual way: PIN 0 to the RX and PIN 1 to the TX. Then sniff and add a UART decoder in PulseView. You can also just connect the ground of a USB-to-serial adapter to the circuit ground and its RX pin to the direction you want to sniff (do not connect its TX pin as it could disturb the communication).

# Injecting UART

The simplest way is to connect the TX pin of a USB-to-serial adapter to the line you want to inject traffic in. This does not always work because your TX pin could pull the line too high for the original sender to transmit.

Here is an example situation:

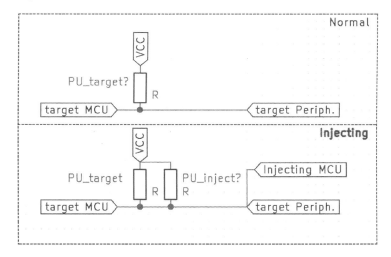

Figure 6.19 – The problem with UART injection

In a normal situation, the MCU pin pulls the pin to ground with a given strength (usually it is quite "strong," with very low resistance). This changes the voltage on the line to be very low (*not* null, since there is still a little bit of resistance; the pullup and the resistance act as a voltage divider), low enough to be under the threshold that the peripheral pin detected as 0/LOW.

When we add our pullup in parallel to the normal pullup, we actually lower the resulting resistance (resistors in series = sum of resistances. Resistors in parallel = sum of the inverse). This means that it is possible that we (or the original MCU) aren't able to pull the line low enough for the MCU to detect a LOW (this also means that too much current can flow through the MCU's or your UART adapter's pin, damaging it in the process).

In this case, do the following:

- Remove the pullup on your adapter if possible or change the value of your pullup resistor (to a higher one; the already-present pullup of the peripheral TX will act as a divider).

- If this doesn't work, go in the man-in-the-middle direction.

### Exercise

Adapt the code of the UART script of the I2C example to inject your UART traffic instead of showing the I2C traffic (get inspiration from the bit of script in the next section).

## UART – man in the middle

You can use two USB-to-serial adapters on your computer and use a simple Python program to alter the content of the communication (do not forget to cut or disconnect the original connections).

For example, the following code adds 1 to every byte received on ttyUSB0 and sends it to ttyUSB1:

```python
#! /usr/bin/python
import serial
#imports the serial module
serin = serial.Serial('/dev/ttyUSB0', 115200)
#opens serial adapter one
serout = serial.Serial('/dev/ttyUSB1', 115200)
#opens serial adapter two
while(True):
    c = serin.read()
#read one char on adapter 1
    c = chr(ord(c)+1)
#add one
    serout.write(c)
#prints on adapter 2
```

Now we are looking into a protocol that we have to bit-bang since there is no hardware peripheral for it. D1W is a pretty nifty protocol that is used for simple applications such as ensuring that a guard did their rounds. With what I will show you in the next section, you will be able to take a guard job and stay in your sentry box during cold winter nights...

# Understanding D1W

D1W is a one-wire bus. It is usually used for simple sensors (temperature or humidity) and has "buttons" that just show a unique identifier. This is an interesting bus where the power of the device can also come from the wire that is used to transmit data. This is usually not supported by hardware peripherals in MCUs; you need to bit-bang the protocol. Bit-banging a protocol means that we will implement the protocol manually by using the GPIOs of the blue pill. 1-Wire is an open-drain bus (like I2C or UART) and hence needs an external pullup resistor (usually of 5k ohms) to set the voltage to a known state when the MCU disconnects the pin (also called floating as in the code).

## Mode of operation

The communication on the D1W is time-based and is initialized by sending a reset pulse that the slave will answer to (the presence pulse).

### The reset pulse

The reset pulse is initialized by the master pulling low the data line for at least 480 μS.

So, the first challenge is to set up the GPIO. For this, we will use and have a precise enough time source to measure the 480 μS. So, we will need to use a timer. Please have a look at the **client** (since the man-in-the-middle code is event-driven, it is better to start with a more sequential program) code for this in the GitHub repository here: `https://github.com/PacktPublishing/Practical-Hardware-Pentesting/tree/main/bluepill/ch6/1w_client`. The setup code is in `libLHP`.

### The presence pulse

Now the master listens on the bus for at least 480 μS and each device will pull down the line for 80 to 240 μs as shown in the following figure:

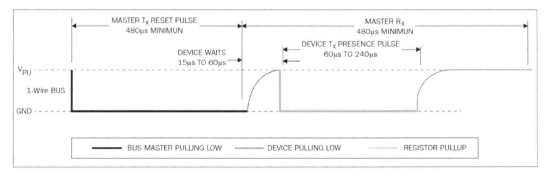

Figure 6.20 – D1W timing diagram

Now that we have seen what the presence pulse is, let's look at the other operations.

## Reading and writing

Basically, all reads and writes are started by the master. To write a 0, the master pulls down the line for 80 to 120 μs and to write a 1, it pulls down the line very shortly (1 μS) and lets the resistor pull up the bus.

To read, the master pulls the line low and measures whether the bus goes high in the next 15 μs. If it does it is a 1 and if it's doesn't it's a 0. All the timings are described in the MAX31820 datasheet (`https://github.com/PacktPublishing/Practical-Hardware-Pentesting/tree/main/datasheets`) on *page 17*:

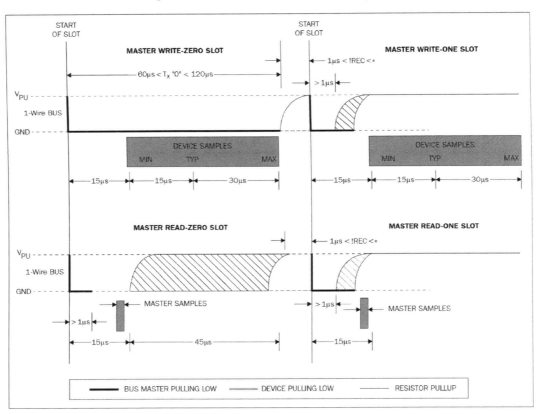

Figure 6.21 – D1W timing diagram, READ and WRITE

D1W also uses a **Cyclic Redundancy Check** (**CRC**) to enable the detection of errors. Please refer to the D1W documentation to learn how to use it (this will have an impact on the man in the middle since the CRC has to be corrected if we change data).

## Sniffing D1W

Here is the connection schema: `https://github.com/PacktPublishing/ Practical-Hardware-Pentesting/tree/main/bluepill/ch6/fritzing_ Schematics`. Open the Fritzing document here to better see the components and connection points as shown in the following figure:

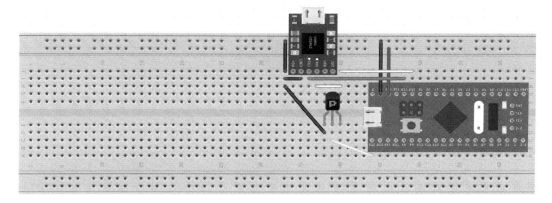

Figure 6.22 – D1W connection

As usual, connect the ground together, connect pin 0 to the data line, and sniff and add the D1W analyzer.

## Injecting D1W

Connect a master to the data line and just act as the master (sending requests and reading answers).

The communication on the D1W bus is (in the vast majority of cases) very spaced out. The chances of collision are very low but if you get a CRC error, just wait for a few ms before retrying).

## D1W – man in the middle

Open the Fritzing document to better see the components and connection points as shown in the following figure:

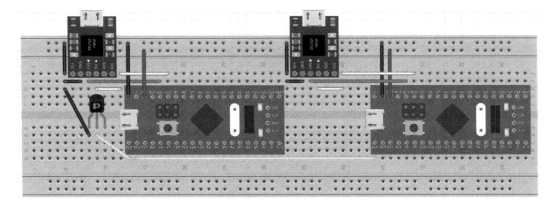

Figure 6.23 – D1W man in the middle

This is basically the same deal as usual: act as a slave to the master and as a master to the slave. Here we are modifying the temperature readout and the CRC.

# Summary

In this chapter, we have seen the most common of circuit protocols, how to sniff them, and how to man-in-the-middle them. This will allow you to take control of most of the slower-speed protocols and will provide you with the necessary tools and approaches to alter the behavior of a system and find secrets that are exchanged on the wires.

In the next chapter, we will learn how to identify the access points to these signals and, if necessary, how to create our own access points.

# Questions

1.  You are visualizing something and you are pretty sure there is some UART traffic on your scope. You see the following waveform. What is the baud rate?

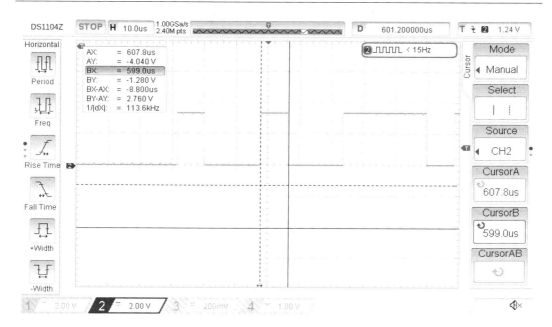

Figure 6.24 – UART oscilloscope signal: what is the baudrate?

2.  What is QSPI?

3.  What is the usage of the parity byte in UART?

4.  Who invented the I2C protocol?

5.  How can you use multiple 24LC EEPROMs on the same I2C bus?

6.  You have to man in the middle an I2C bus with two different devices and a master. Sadly, the hardware peripheral on the blue pill can only have a single address and you can't think of a way to have it alternate between the addresses (the master apparently talks randomly to the devices). What would be your approach?

7.  `0x41 0x20 0x76 0x65 0x72 0x79 0x20 0x76 0x65 0x72 0x79`
    `0x20 0x73 0x65 0x72 0x69 0x6f 0x75 0x73 0x20 0x6b 0x65`
    `0x79 0x21`

    ^

    `0x08 0x00 0x1a 0x0a 0x04 0x1c 0x00 0x14 0x0c 0x1c 0x18`
    `0x52 0x0a 0x45 0x1d 0x19 0x0a 0x07 0x12 0x54 0x04 0x17`
    `0x0a 0x00?`

# 7
# Extracting and Manipulating Onboard Storage

Embedded systems store their data and sometimes their code on media that can take multiple forms on the board (chips, external storage such as SD cards, and so on). Getting access to this storage is crucial to be able to analyze the code and get access to security-relevant elements. In this chapter, we will go through multiple components that can hold this data, how to extract data from the component, how to understand how it is stored, and lastly, how to peruse and change the data (in raw form or with a filesystem).

The following topics will be covered in this chapter:

- Finding the data
- Extracting the data
- Understanding unknown storage structures
- Mounting filesystems
- Repacking

# Technical requirements

The software required is as follows:

- Binwalk
- A Linux machine

The hardware required (to repeat the examples) is as follows:

- The Bus Pirate
- An I2C or SPI EEPROM (you should already have this from the previous chapter)

Check out the following link to see the Code in Action video:
`https://bit.ly/383OzkJ`

# Finding the data

Before parsing the data, we have to find it. In addition to classical storage media (hard drives, **Solid State Drive (SSDs)**, onboard USB storage, and more), embedded systems use more specific chips and systems to store data, and some of them are listed as follows:

- EEPROMs
- EMMC and NAND/NOR Flash
- Static RAM, and so on...

Let's look at each of them in the following sections.

## EEPROMs

**EEPROM (Electrically Erasable Programmable Read-Only Memory**) and flash memory are "one-chip" storage solutions that keep the data even when the power is off. They are available on pretty much every existing protocol (I2C, (Q)SPI, 1-Wire, and more). Locating these chips is not always easy (especially if they are unmarked or rebranded) but (as already discussed in the component identification section in the previous chapter), it is possible to identify them by elimination or by sniffing the protocol on the board. Typically, the storage capacity is small, and the storage structure is custom made for the system (that is, it does not embed a typical, well-known filesystem like bigger storage mediums).

# EMMC and NAND/NOR Flash

EMMC is a physical variant of **MMC** (**MultiMediaCard**) in which the chip is soldered on the board instead of being removable. It is entirely possible to remove the chip (doing so is called chip-off) and use an adapter to read it as a classical MMC (with a USB adapter), basically transforming it into a USB thumb drive.

NAND and NOR Flash are also soldered directly on the board but don't really offer a "standard" protocol to talk to the chip and need a lower-level approach (such as programming the adequate protocol on a micro-controller) or a specific adapter/programmer.

These chips come with multiple "standard" footprints (EMMC: BGA221, BGA162, BHA186, and more; NAND/NOR: BGA137, BGA63, and more) that all require a different adapter (to accommodate the footprint). These adapters can be found on auction sites or from Chinese retail sites (AliExpress, TaoBao, and so on). Single-use adapters are reasonably priced but require a reflowing phase (that is, resoldering the chip on the adapter, for which you will very probably need a paste application stencil), which can be tricky to master and comes with a risk of damaging the chip (it is pretty common to short pins while manually reflowing a BGA chip).

Reusable ones (with a clamshell adapter) are more expensive but (if you are doing this often) are worth the price since you will bypass the reflowing step and the risks that come with it.

# Hard drives, SSDs, and other storage mediums

While less common on simple systems (such as systems running from simple micro-controllers), it is pretty common to find systems that are running a full-fledged OS (that is, the same kind that runs on a laptop or desktop computer) for the simple reason that the system is a computer in the commonly understood sense of the term.

For example, anything running Android (such as a Linux kernel) is a complete computer and comes with high-speed data interfaces (PATA/SATA, M.2, PCI-E/X, and more). It is then pretty tempting for a system constructor to leverage the relatively cheap storage price by using commonly available interfaces, especially given the small form factors currently available. M.2 sticks or 1.8" SSD drives are very small and provide huge capacities compared to the usual specific embedded solutions.

Some older styles of storage are also found on more legacy/industrial systems (for example, CompactFlash/Microdrive) that need specific adapters. USB adapters for these styles of storage are quite commonplace on auction sites.

# Extracting the data

For cases where we don't have the data already (that is, we did not succeed in getting updates), we need to extract the data from its storage place to our computer. Being able to process and modify the data on a computer will allow us to use higher-level programming languages and tools.

Let's have a look at the most common things we have to extract.

## On-chip firmware

Most micro-controllers will embed their programs (that is, their firmware), at least partially, on on-chip (or on-module) flash or other forms of storage, such as EEPROM. The worst-case scenario for us is cases where programs are stored in **One-Time Programmable** (OTP) memory, such as the MCU used in the Furby toy (in a masked ROM) or a lot of very cheap MCUs.

For example, most ARM chips come with on-chip flash. The ESP family of chips has a flash storage chip on the module from where the chip retrieves its program. These can usually store long-term variables (across reboots). It is very important for us to be able to retrieve this data if we want to be able to reverse-engineer the program behavior.

An essential step in acquiring the firmware is to find an adequate hardware programmer and the associated software. Most chips will use some form or variation of the JTAG interface (we will talk in more detail about JTAG in *Chapter 10*, *Accessing the Debug Interfaces*). In modern chips, it is very common to find the correct hardware programmer (bundled with the software) integrated into the development kit for the target chip. This programmer usually allows us to read back the binary form of the program that is stored in the onboard flash. Some commercial products implement protection against reading back this data, but they can sometimes be bypassed. Bypassing these protections usually requires some more advanced and specific attacks (such as finding bugs in bootloaders or glitching), but these attacks are usually complex and fall out of the scope of this introductory book.

Depending on the complexity of the device, it is also possible that a bootloader (for example, U-Boot) will be present on the device. If this is the case and you manage to get access to it (from a debug serial console, for example), it should be possible to extract the storage via the serial cable; for example, U-Boot's md or **nand** commands can help:

- `https://www.denx.de/wiki/view/DULG/UBootCmdGroupNand`
- `https://www.denx.de/wiki/view/DULG/UBootCmdGroupMemory`

# Onboard storage – specific interfaces

Unless the device is supported by mainstream tools (such as flashrom), you will have to implement a specific dumping tool on a micro-controller or use a tool such as the Bus Pirate to access the content. Flashrom is usually used for BIOS flash chips but also supports many other flash chips, for example, the Macronix 25L8008 SPI flash we used in the previous chapter.

The details of the behavior can be found by reading the datasheet. To dump the content to your computer, you will have to implement this behavior. This is usually implemented on a micro-controller and the data is transferred over serial. This transfer is achieved using a USB-to-serial device and a variant of the script we used to man-in-the-middle UART. The exercise to modify the script to write to a file instead of writing to the other UART serial bridge is left to you.

# Onboard storage – common interfaces

If the device uses a standard interface (SATA, MMC, SD card, or others), it should be recognized (at least as a device) by your computer. It should show up in your logs (you can display your log with the dmesg command) as being available as a device (in the /dev directory).

For example, my USB adapter connects and detects an 8 GB micro SD card as /dev/sdg (this specific adapter is based on a Realtek RTS5169 chip and supports multiple media, CompactFlash, SD card, memory sticks, and more):

```
$dmesg|tail
[112959.731873] usb 2-1: new high-speed USB device number 8
using xhci_hcd
[112959.930354] usb 2-1: New USB device found, idVendor=0bda,
idProduct=0161, bcdDevice=61.23
[112959.930357] usb 2-1: New USB device strings: Mfr=1,
Product=2, SerialNumber=3
[...]
[112959.933071] usb-storage 2-1:1.1: USB Mass Storage device
detected
[112959.933314] scsi host8: usb-storage 2-1:1.1
[112960.955475] scsi 8:0:0:0: Direct-Access Generic- Compact
Flash 1.00 PQ: 0 ANSI: 0 CCS
[...]
[...]
[112961.001598] scsi 8:0:0:3: Direct-Access Generic- MS/MS-Pro
```

```
1.00 PQ: 0 ANSI: 0 CCS
[...]
[113022.188644] sd 8:0:0:2: [sdg] 15564800 512-byte logical
blocks: (7.97 GB/7.42 GiB)
[113022.191353] sdg: sdg1 sdg2
```

If your media is recognized like this (here, it shows sdg: sdg1 sdg2), the best tool to image it is dd. dd is a part of coreutils (and is most probably installed by default on your Linux box).

dd has a peculiar syntax for a Linux command-line utility, without the usual - or -- as a flag indicator. The options you will want to use are as follows:

- if=<path to the input file>: This can be /dev/ device (in the end, you are using a Unix box, where everything is a file).
- of=<path to the outputfile>.
- bs=<block size>: This support k, M, and G shorthands; usually 1M will do.
- oflag=<a comma separated list of flags for output>: I personally like to use the sync flag here, especially when writing to flash devices, in order to ensure that the data doesn't end up in a kernel buffer, which makes dd quit while the kernel is actually still writing.
- status=progress: (Only available in recent versions of dd.) This will show you a progress indication (older versions of dd will only print this when they receive a USR1 signal; use kill -USR1 <dd process id> if you have an older version).

Take the following example:

1. To dump an SD card to a file, use the following:

```
dd if=/dev/sdg1 of=./dump.bin bs=1k status=progress
```

2. To put the modified data on an SD card, use the following:

```
dd if=./dump_modified.bin of=/dev/sdg1 bs=1k oflag=sync
status=progress
```

Now that we have saved the storage to our machine, let's look into it.

# Understanding unknown storage structures

More often than not, light systems (those not embedding a full-fledged OS such as Linux) will have a pretty well-documented way of storing their firmware internally (since this storage form is crucial for the target MCU to function properly, it is well described in the target MCU datasheet). On the other hand, the way the data is stored by the firmware itself is very much left to the firmware developer device.

## Unknown storage formats

There is no definitive way to reverse engineer the way data is stored, as for most reverse engineering, it is as much an art as it is a science. The only way to get a good knack for it is, just like soldering, doing it again and again, but having spent a fair share of my time reversing a lot of different things, such as network protocols, storage structures, and more, I can give you some pointers.

Understanding the way the data is organized for storage depends on multiple factors. There are some general hints that can help you along the way.

Note the following about the data itself:

- Will the data change a lot in terms of content (such as settings or readings) or is it "mostly static" (such as firmware and executable code)?

- Will the data change a lot in terms of size (such as strings or structure data with members that are optional) or is it mostly static (such as binary readings, binary fields, and so on)?

- Will the changing data be of variable size or is it well organized? Will it be of fixed-size chunks?

Consider the following data processing commonalities:

- The developers will tend to store similar data together (images next to images, text together, and so on).

- Code reuse. For example, when you look at compression, the same algorithm will be reused multiple times, and hence block and code structure will be repeated, and so on.

- Storage optimization. For example, data that would be relevant on a per-file storage basis on a computer wouldn't make sense on a space-constrained system (why keep image data headers if I am guaranteed by construction that I will only store 64x64, 24-bit, per-pixel color image information?).

Consider the following for the storage media:

- How is the storage media itself organized?

  - Is the chip organized in blocks, pages, or sectors?

  - Is it easy to make random, relatively small accesses or does the MCU have to read "big chunks" of data?

- How is the storage media behaving regarding large numbers or write cycles? (For example, flash only supports a given number of write cycles before dying. If the chip controller is not implementing wear leveling (to spread data in order to avoid killing blocks prematurely), the firmware author may have been tempted to implement a home-made system for that.)

Consider the following for a classical storage scheme:

- **FAT**: FAT is well known as a filesystem, but this filesystem actually gets its name from the concept of **file allocation tables**. It is very common to put a "table of contents" in front of your storage, with the start address and size of your storage item (possibly with a filename and other attributes such as timestamps of modification, and so on).

- Size and value pairs, the same way it is used in a lot of network protocols.

- Fixed-size "blocks," for example, 100 bytes for preference, then 2 KB for static strings, then 5 KB for pictures, and so on.

So, understanding the way storage is organized requires some detective work and does not necessarily involve well-known structures and mechanisms.

## Well-known storage formats

Sometimes, the storage format is well known (because someone reversed and documented it before or because it uses well-known mechanisms) and tools are available to extract it. One of the best known and most extensive in terms of support of different packing mechanisms is Binwalk (`https://github.com/ReFirmLabs/binwalk`).

Binwalk will search the target file for well-known headers and try to extract them for you (with `-e`).

Binwalk is Python-based and is a very useful tool to analyze firmware and storage images (even if the format is not a well-known one, as it contains tools to help you analyze it). You really should read the documentation (`https://github.com/ReFirmLabs/binwalk/wiki`) and train yourself on multiple firmware images (router updates are really ideal for that).

Binwalk will be able to find the following:

- General compression formats (`.gz`, `.lzma`, `.xz`, and so on)
- Linux kernels and images
- Filesystems (SquashFS, JFFS2, and so on)

# Let's look for storage in our Furby

Let's look into the EEPROM and the SPI blob. We will dump them and look at their content in order to guide you through an example of the tools and processes used for it.

## First candidate – the ATMLH306 I2C EEPROM

The first data store we identify is an I2C EEPROM. Let's dump it to a file.

Extract it from the **Printed Circuit Board** (**PCB**), mount it on a breakout, and connect it to our Bus Pirate as shown in the following photo:

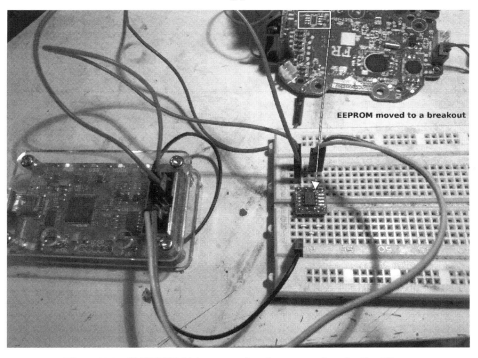

Figure 7.1 – I2C EEPROM extracted and connected to the Bus Pirate

Once the Bus Pirate has connected successfully (it will show in the output of `dmesg`), we can go on.

Let's verify that our connection works by scanning the I2C bus with the following actions in the Bus Pirate text menu:

```
$screen /dev/ttyACM0 115200
HiZ>m
[...]
4. I2C
[...]
x. exit(without change)
(1)>4
I2C mode:
 1. Software
 2. Hardware
(1)>2
Set speed:
 1. 100KHz
 2. 400KHz
 3. 1MHz
(1)>1
Clutch disengaged!!!
To finish setup, start up the power supplies with command
'W'
Ready
I2C>W
POWER SUPPLIES ON
Clutch engaged!!!
I2C>P
Pull-up resistors ON
I2C>(1)
Searching I2C address space. Found devices at:
0xA0(0x50 W) 0xA1(0x50 R)
```

Depending on your version, the Bus Pirate output can be slightly different. Now we will connect to the Bus Pirate in binary mode using a Python script and save the EEPROM to a file. You will be able to find the script and the dumped data on the GitHub repository in the ch7 directory to output the content to a file (and the output if you can't find a Furby).

Now let's look into this file:

```
$hexdump output_eeprom_file
00000000    00 03 00 00 00 cc 00 00    00 03 00 00 00 cc 00 00
|................|
00000010    00 00 00 00 00 00 00 00    00 00 00 00 00 00 00 01
|................|
00000020    00 00 2c 01 00 ec b2 01    00 00 2c 01 00 ec b2 64
|..,.........,...d|
00000030    00 00 00 00 00 a0 f5 64    00 00 00 00 00 a0 f5 00
|.......d........|
00000040    00 00 00 00 00 00 00 00    00 00 00 00 00 00 00 07
|................|
00000050    00 00 00 00 00 58 0d 07    00 00 00 00 00 58 0d 00
|.....X.......X..|
00000060    00 00 00 00 00 00 00 00    00 00 00 00 00 00 00 00
|................|
*
000000f0    00 00 00 00 00 00 00 00    00 00 00 00 00 00 f8 00
|................|
00000100
```

We are starting by just doing a hex dump to look at the general content (Is there a lot of data? A lot of 0s? What does it look like?).

This EEPROM is very small, but looking at the content, we can already see some kind of structure emerge. There is a lot of symmetry between the left side (the first 8 bytes) and the right side (the next 8 bytes). We don't have a lot of data to start a static analysis (and certainly not to launch Binwalk on) but this is promising for the dynamic analysis (that is, changing the EEPROM content and seeing what happens). We can deduce from the size of the storage that the sounds and the eye pictures are not stored here (too small).

Let's now look at the second storage chip.

## Second candidate – the FR-marked SPI blob

The SPI chips are a little more complicated and contain more data, and we will approach it in two steps (dump and analysis). By covering I2C and SPI, you will be ready to face most on-board storage for systems that use bare-metal MCUs. More complex systems (such as ones that embed a full-fledged Linux system) will usually use parallel flash chips that require more advanced soldering skills and equipment to dump (but are largely within your reach with training).

## Dumping it

We know this is an SPI chip, so let's remove it from the board and put it on a breadboard. Doing this, we find a footprint under the mouse bite daughter board.

When we sniffed the SPI chip traffic, the MCU was using a `0xAB` instruction to wake the SPI chip up and a `0x3` instruction for reads. I first suspected a 25LC SPI EEPROM from Atmel (there was already an I2C from this vendor on the board).

Looking further into the format of the communication, I found a document where somebody had already dumped this EEPROM (so I happened to be wrong; it is an MX23L3254 from its JDEC identifier) and partially reverse-engineered the storage format of the SPI chip (Michael Coppola, ReCON 2014: `https://mncoppola.files.wordpress.com/2014/07/performing-open-heart-surgery-on-a-furby-recon-2014.pdf`).

Let's use the (correct) RDID instruction and check whether it is the case in our hardware version:

```
$./dump_25lc_BP.py
b'\xc2\x05\x16'
```

Indeed, it is the case.

Apparently, we should be able to easily dump it with flashrom. It failed with my Bus Pirate v4 (due to some firmware differences, but it worked on my Bus Pirate v3). Let's use flashrom to dump the SPI flash:

```
$sudo flashrom -V -c MX23L3254 -p busp
rate_spi:dev=/dev/ttyUSB0 -r out.bin
flashrom v1.1-rc1-28-g712ba3a0 on Linux 5.1.3 (x86_64)
flashrom is free software, get the source code at https://
flashrom.org
flashrom was built with libpci 3.5.2, GCC 8.3.0, little endian
Command line (7 args): flashrom -V -c MX23L3254 -p buspirate_
spi:dev=/dev/ttyUSB0 -r out.bin
Using clock_gettime for delay loops (clk_id: 1, resolution:
1ns).
Initializing buspirate_spi programmer
Detected Bus Pirate hardware 3.5
...
The following protocols are supported: SPI.
Probing for Macronix MX23L3254, 4096 kB:
```

```
probe_spi_rdid_generic: id1 0xc2, id2 0x516
Found Macronix flash chip "MX23L3254" (4096 kB, SPI) on
buspirate_spi.
This chip's main memory can not be erased/written by design.
Reading flash... done.
Raw bitbang mode version 1
Bus Pirate shutdown completed.
```

The original chip is a mask ROM, so we cannot change the content.

The MX25L8008E we used in *Chapter 6, Sniffing and Attacking the Most Common Protocols*, is a perfect, writable drop-in replacement (honestly out of sheer luck!).

Having a well-stocked component stock and keeping a decent amount of questionable e-waste around will both (and just as often!) create routine "is it really useful?" discussions with your significant other and save your buttocks during engagements.

## Unpacking it

We know from the presentation that Binwalk and strings will not yield results. But let's try anyway.

### Dealing with strings

There are two command-line tools of interest:

- *Strings* well... looks for strings in a file and dumps them to `stdout`. Something a lot of people overlook is trying all the different possible encodings (depending on what you are analyzing, this can be relevant, especially if you are dealing with Windows executables and DLLs or non-Latin alphabets; you will find a script in this chapter's folder do automate this: `string_all_enc.sh`).

- *iconv* converts between different encodings. This is especially useful for "weird" characters, such as é, ñ, and so on.

### Dealing with packed data

Binwalk will try to peruse a file for known formats but will also allow us to have an overview of the entropy in a file (look into `https://en.wikipedia.org/wiki/Entropy_(information_theory)`). Entropy is roughly the measure of how random data looks. Measuring the entropy is a good way to get an idea of whether the data you are looking at is cyphered or compressed and the global layout of a file.

Launch this command:

```
$binwalk -E out.bin
```

The following figure shows the entropy in the file:

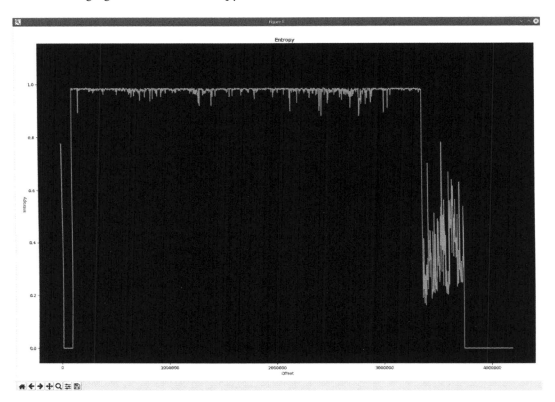

Figure 7.2 – Entropy in a file

We can clearly see four zones:

- The header zone, which should contain information about the organization of the file
- A big, very entropic zone
- A medium zone with widely varying entropy
- An anentropic zone

These are probably the following:

- The zone with the offsets
- Image or sound data (we remember from the patent that the sound may be voice-synthesized, taking up much less space than actually digitized sound)
- Image or sound data (well, the other type compared to the previous section)
- Padding (the data is actually full of `0x01` at the end)
- Michael's parser works on our data and can extract pictures, great!

We can see that the data Michael found and ours differ:

```
$md5sum hisdata.bin
4c0955f8623ac9380296d41edf7817d3 hisdata.bin
$md5sum out.bin
e91fadd53a0ddd44fe7d335a5f92a904 out.bin
```

His data has 2,806 pieces of data and ours has 2,820. Even if it is the same version of the toy (2012), we may have another firmware version.

I'll leave it as an exercise to you to write a small script to identify the zones with the two entropies:

- The first zone (with the entropy's "plateau") is the sound data.
- The second is the images.

When we look at the organization of the storage in the header of the EEPROM, we see that it is based on the concept of FAT, with the number of "files," and the offsets to the different files with their size stored in front of their content. This is a very classical organization scheme.

# Mounting filesystems

The `mount` command (you have to be privileged to use it; use `sudo`) is the main tool for this.

Modern versions of the command recognize the filesystem automatically. If the detection is not working but you know the filesystem in use, the `-t` option will allow you to force the filesystem format to be used.

To list the filesystems your kernel is currently supporting, look into the `/proc/filesystems` file (as a side note, not all modules can be mounted; to get a list of what it does support, look into the `/lib/modules/$(uname -r)/kernel/fs` directory).

Some filesystems used in embedded systems may not be supported in some usual distribution kernels and so you may need to do the following:

- Recompile your kernel with more filesystems.

- Compile additional modules for your kernel.

- Use userspace filesystem management (such as FUSE).

Since most of the firmware or storage images we get are in the form of a file instead of a block device, some options are useful for managing this specific case. They are managed through the `-o` command-line switch. This switch uses a comma-separated list to manage multiple options (whether the options are global or filesystem-specific):

- `loop`: Makes `mount` use a file as a block device

- `offset=xxx`: Skips xxx bytes in the target block device

# Repacking

The repacking process is mainly taking the reverse path we took for packing, recreating a consistent image with the modifications we want.

I would strongly encourage you to look into the firmware modkit if you need to repack routers and other xx-WRT-based firmware (`https://code.google.com/archive/p/firmware-mod-kit/`).

Since most of the standard filesystems that are mounted from a file with a `-o loop` option will be read-only, a common approach is to work on the files on a normal directory on your computer, create an empty image of the necessary size, recreate an empty filesystem, and copy the files onto it.

Some systems may not implement the filesystems completely and you may need to tailor the filesystem creation (or use specific versions) for it to work with the final target system.

# Summary

In this chapter, we saw the different media that can be used in embedded systems and the tools we need to approach them, extract them, understand their structures, and modify them. Since the ways to store data are very variable from one system to another, it is not possible to go through every possible variation but, after reading this chapter, you will know (at least partially) the possible tools that you can use, how things are generally organized, and some concepts you could think about when reverse-engineering storage schemes. These tools are very powerful but, like any tool, are limited by the skill of the person that uses them. That's why you should practice and read the documentation of the tools as much as possible.

In the next chapter, we will look into how to modify the stored elements and, from the changes in the system behavior, better understand the structure of the stored data.

# Questions

1.  What tool can you use to take an image of a peripheral that is recognized by your Linux machine?

2.  What is the use of the -o loop command-line switch for mount?

3.  Why are the lists in cat /proc/filesystems and /lib/modules/xxx/ kernel/fs/ different?

4.  You found a module marked eUSB on a device you are testing. What is it? How would you read it?

5.  What is the eMMC standard? How would you read it?

6.  What is FUSE? What is user space? How can you use it?

# Further reading

Read the mount, iconv, dd, and Binwalk documentation (use the man command). Look at the firmware modkit wiki, and check how to recompile a kernel or modules for your distribution.

# 8
# Attacking Wi-Fi, Bluetooth, and BLE

In this chapter, we will learn how to peek and poke into the network connection of an embedded system. Embedded systems use more diverse network types and media in addition to their usual IP/Ethernet/Wi-Fi. We will peek into the most usual types (Ethernet, TCP/IP, HTTPS, Bluetooth, Wi-Fi, and USB) and look into the solutions available for the more custom types, such as unknown radio links, sound, and so on. Networking is usually a very interesting field to look into since developers tend to make mistakes here too, which allows us to peek into the internal workings of the systems and their relationship with the digital world.

In this chapter, we will cover the following topics:

- Basics of networking
- Networking in embedded systems using Wi-Fi
- Networking in embedded systems using Bluetooth

Let's get started!

# Technical requirements

For this chapter, we will need the following:

- A Linux laptop with a Wi-Fi card and an Ethernet card to act as a Wi-Fi gateway. Depending on your requirements, it is possible that the Wi-Fi card that is embedded in your laptop has not been adapted for the test. You need a card that supports raw injection (for example, based on an Atheros AR9271, Ralink RT3070, or Realtek 8187L, though you will have to search on your own to find an adequate one. Alfacards sell adapters that are usually targeted at injection).

- Hardware capable of sniffing Bluetooth traffic (I use an Ubertooth One), with a Bluetooth 4.0 capable dongle and BBlueZ installed.

Check out the following link to see the Code in Action video:
`https://bit.ly/3b5LkuT`

# Basics of networking

Networking relies on a few basic concepts:

- **Encapsulation**: Just like a matryoshka doll, network packets behave like a box in a box in a box in a... you get the point. The OSI model describes the seven classics layers of encapsulation that are potentially present in all communications. For example, it is possible to change the physical layer of a packer without impacting the upper layer (that is what happens when you send an ethernet frame over Wi-Fi, for example).

- **Routing**: Routing allows a packet to reach its destination without the sender knowing exactly how to get to it or the destination knowing exactly how to send the response to the sender. This boils down, in a very oversimplified fashion, to each machine knowing how to reach a given number of networks (or groups of networks) and having a machine to give packets to when it doesn't know how to reach the destination network.

- **Connection**: A connection is a logical link that's established between two devices, where both are aware of the other system being connected to another and of the state of data transfer between the two. A well-known protocol that behaves in a connected way is TCP (as opposed to UDP, where the connection state is not kept by the systems).

Now, let's look at networking in embedded systems using Wi-Fi.

# Networking in embedded systems using Wi-Fi

Wi-Fi is a well-known radio network that is used by a lot of embedded systems. We will learn how to intercept traffic by mounting our own access point and listening and changing the traffic that goes through it. The methodology we will use is common to most Wi-Fi traffic analysis (phone apps, connected devices, and so on).

## Selecting Wi-Fi hardware

Just like for Wi-Fi attacks, not every Wi-Fi chipset is capable of doing everything we need. Depending on your device requirements, it is possible that you may have to buy some specific hardware:

- Check that your hardware is compatible with the Wi-Fi band used by your device (a/b/g/n).
- Check that your device supports injection: `https://www.aircrack-ng.org/doku.php?id=compatible_cards`.
- Check that your hardware driver supports **Access Point (AP)** mode. You can check if the following command outputs something:

```
$sudo iw list|sed -n -r '/ace modes/,/^\t[^\t]/p'
```

If the output is empty, you should get another device that supports injection:

```
$airmon-ng start wlan0 # sets it in monitor mode
$aireplay-ng --test wlan0mon
```

If the output say `0%`, you should get another device.

## Creating our access point

We will create an access point for the device to connect to.

In terms of Wi-Fi, the device must want/offer the following:

- The device offers a Wi-Fi network of its own
- The device joins a network that we can control
- The device looks for a specific network to join

In terms of functionality, the device needs, at the very least, the following:

- DHCP
- DNS
- Routing

Some other services may be needed, depending on the specific device.

### Control on the joined network

To create our access point, we will use `hostapd` (a piece of software that will allow us to easily create and manage the access point). Before we create our network, we will need to know which cipher the device supports (WEP or the WPA family) in order to create a network it can connect to. Depending on the country the system comes from and your country of residence, you may have to tweak the country code of your Wi-Fi for it to work.

## Creating the access point and the basic network services

First, set up your machine's own local network and routing. Then, create your `hostapd` configuration file like so (you should adapt it to your needs; that is, change your country, the needed cipher family, and so on. Type `man 5 hostpad.conf` into a Terminal to get an explanation of the different directives):

```
#Wifi interface, the names appears in the command : ip addr
interface=wlx00c0ca1a03ef
#Name of the AP
ssid=hostile_wifi_do_not_connect
#Channel
channel=8
#mode (g is 2.4GHz, 54Mbps)
hw_mode=g
driver=nl80211
#where you live
country_code=BE
# 3 is wep and wpa
auth_algs=3
#wpa2
```

```
wpa=2
#preshared keys
wpa_key_mgmt=WPA-PSK
rsn_pairwise=CCMP
#the password
wpa_passphrase=TestPass
```

Now, we are going to create the configuration file for dnsmasq. This will allow us to provide DNS and DHCP services to the newly created network (type man 8 dnsmasq for the details of the configuration. There is a lot there, but you should only need to change non-obvious values). The following is the contents of the dnsmasq.conf file:

```
#dhcp
#listen on the wifi interface, the names appears in the command
: ip addr
interface=wlx00c0ca1a03ef
dhcp-authoritative
#we will give adresses in this range, for 24 hours
dhcp-range=192.168.254.2,192.168.254.3,24h
# Log DHCP transactions.
log-dhcp
#dhcp add services
#gateway
dhcp-option=option:router,192.168.254.1
#subnet
dhcp-option=option:netmask,255.255.255.252
#dns server
dhcp-option=option:dns-server,192.168.254.1
#dns
listen-address=192.168.254.1
#spoofed DNS entries
addn-hosts=./spoof.hosts
# log dns
log-queries
```

Let's create a shell script that launches the access point, gives it an IP, launches dnsmasq, and tells our machine to act as an IPV4 NATting router. The following is the code from the ap.sh file:

```
#! /bin/bash
#change to the name of your device
WIFIIFACE=wlx00c0ca1a03ef
#change to the name of your output interface
OUTIFACE=eth0
#enables ipv4 routing
echo 1 > /proc/sys/net/ipv4/ip_forward
hostapd ./hostapd.conf &
ip addr flush dev $WIFIIFACE
ip addr add 192.168.254.1/24 dev $WIFIIFACE
dnsmasq --no-daemon --log-queries -C dnsmasq.conf
iptables -t nat -A POSTROUTING -o $OUTIFACE -j MASQUERADE
```

At this point, when you launch this script, a Wi-Fi AP with the name hostile_wifi_do_ not_connect should appear. You should be able to connect to it and navigate normally.

However, at this point, we cannot access the traffic with an attack proxy (for example, ZAP from OWASP) or by redirecting the traffic to our custom services. We can achieve this by having the attack proxy listening on a reachable interface (here, 192.168.0.2 is on the eth0 side of the capturing access point, on ports 8080 and 8443) and modifying our script so that it redirects all the traffic over ports 80 and 443 to the proxy with firewall rules (or by providing a proxy in the DHCP settings (for more information, read about the **Web Proxy Auto-Discovery (WPAD)** protocol and pac files; you can add it to the dnsmasq configuration file with dhcp-option 252)):

```
ATK_PROXY_IP=192.168.0.2
iptables -t nat -A PREROUTING -i $WIFIIFACE -j DNAT -p tcp
--dport 80 --to-destination $ATK_PROXY_IP:8080
iptables -t nat -A PREROUTING -i $WIFIIFACE -j DNAT -p tcp
--dport 443 --to-destination $ATK_PROXY_IP:8443
```

You can redirect any connection like this – just change the ports to a server that's adequate for the protocol (ZAP will work for HTTP/S, but you may need to write your own for more specific services).

At this point, you should be able to log all the traffic from the device and tamper with it with "normal" network tools (`ettercap`, ZAP proxy, `nmap`, and so on) that are very well-documented all over the internet.

### Other Wi-Fi attacks

Some other attacks exists, but they usually target the Wi-Fi infrastructure, not the device. An excellent introduction book is Vivek Ramachandran's *Wireless Penetration Testing Beginner's Guide*.

# Networking in embedded systems using Bluetooth

Many devices have Bluetooth connectivity available, from phones to headsets to input devices. Let's see what we can look at with this interface.

## Bluetooth basics

Bluetooth is a radio protocol that operates between 2.4 and 2.48 GHz. It is not easy to sniff because it is transmitted by hopping on multiple frequencies pseudorandomly (depending on the address of the master device) and has several variants:

- **BT/1.x (2000), also known as the ancestor**: This has not been deployed in new products for a long time. It had privacy problems since it was sending a unique ID over the air.

- **BT/2.x (2004), also known as classic Bluetooth**: This has been around for years and is "kind of" kept in the hands of the big players of the market. This is the doing of Apple since, to be able to be used by iPhones, you have to send an entry ticket to them (called the MFi). It is faster than BT1 and introduces a better pairing system and effort in terms of energy consumption.

- **BT/3.x (2009), also known as "high speed" (HS)**: This comes with some (optional) hi-speed transfers over Wi-Fi and introduces connection less low latency data transfer and some more effort in terms of consumption.

- **BTLE/4.x (2010), also known as "Low Energy" or "smart"**: This actually adds a **Bluetooth Low Energy (BLE)** on top of classic and HS, with a very large reduction in terms of power consumption for the BLE part.

- **BT5.x (2018)**: This is the latest version, but it is only supported by some flagship phones and a few devices at the moment. Adoption will probably be larger in the future.

Bluetooth, of course, supports addressing, and the addresses look like ethernet MAC addresses:

- 6 bytes

- 2 vendor IEEE-assigned OUI bytes (NAP)

- 1 IEEE-assigned **Upper Address Part (UAP)**, not directly present in the traffic but deductible from the data

- 3 **Lower address parts (LAPs)** in the sent packets

If we can find the full address, we can deduce the channel hopping sequence and sniff the communication (more on that later).

Bluetooth, in addition to a **physical (PHY)** layer that acts as the radio link, implements other layers in the protocol. Each layer is managed by a different part of the protocol and managed by the layer above it (from the IEEE Bluetooth proposal):

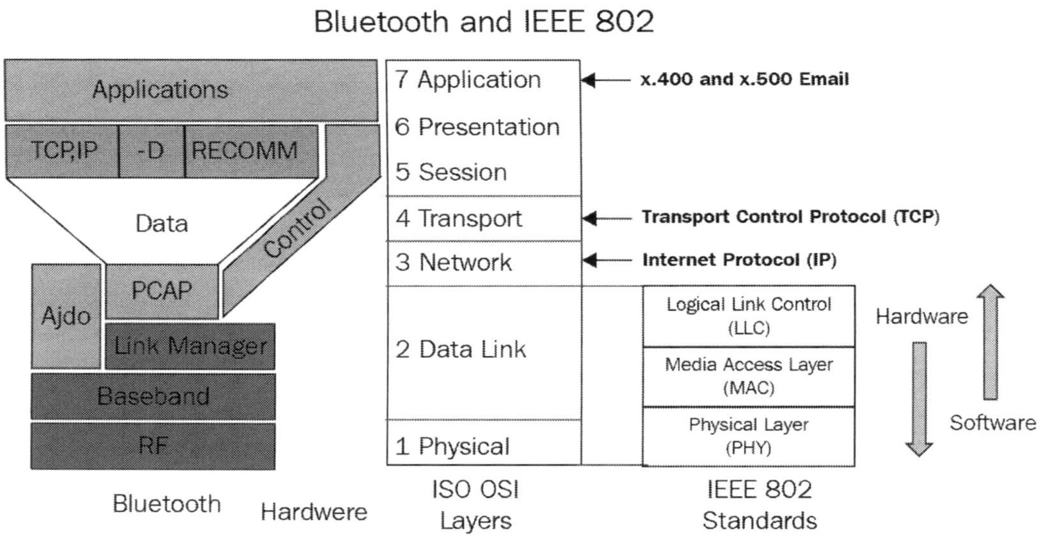

## Bluetooth and IEEE 802

Figure 8.1 – Bluetooth protocol stack model

Now that we've looked into the protocol stack, let's get familiar with the tools we will be using.

# Discovering Bluetooth

In this section, we will learn how to discover Bluetooth devices and work with them. First, find out the name of your Bluetooth device by using the following command:

```
$hcitool dev
Devices:
        hci0 00:1A:7D:DA:71:13
```

My Bluetooth device is hci0 with a hardware address of 00:11:67:2E:B3:5D.

Let's find out what it can do:

```
$hciconfig hci0 -a
hci0:   Type: Primary   Bus: USB
        BD Address: 00:1A:7D:DA:71:13   ACL MTU: 310:10   SCO
MTU: 64:8
        UP RUNNING
        RX bytes:304197 acl:0 sco:0 events:867 errors:0
        TX bytes:16504 acl:0 sco:0 commands:369 errors:0
        Features: 0xff 0xff 0x8f 0xfe 0xdb 0xff 0x5b 0x87
        Packet type: DM1 DM3 DM5 DH1 DH3 DH5 HV1 HV2 HV3
        Link policy: RSWITCH HOLD SNIFF PARK                   *
can "sniff",i means receive only
        Link mode: SLAVE ACCEPT
        Name: 'xxx'
        Class: 0x100104
        Service Classes: Object Transfer
        Device Class: Computer, Desktop workstation
        HCI Version: 4.0 (0x6)   Revision: 0x22bb              *<
accepts BT4.0
        LMP Version: 4.0 (0x6)   Subversion: 0x22bb
        Manufacturer: Cambridge Silicon Radio (10)            *
manufacturer of the radio
```

BlueZ (the official Linux BT stack) can provide you with a lot of information, such as the following:

- The `hciconfig hci0` commands list supported commands.

- `sudo bccmd -d hci0 pslist` lists adapter settings (`psread` will dump them, `psget` will get one, and `psset` will change one).

- `bt-adapter -i` lists more general adapter information but shows the BLE GATT characteristics of our adapter.

I usually have five Bluetooth devices around my desk:

- A headset

- A joystick

- My work phone (a fruity, expensive device that has been forced on me)

- My testing phone (which I use for security things, a bit "saltier")

- My watch (which doesn't have a discoverable mode; I have to use the Wear OS application to connect my phone to it)

Let's put them all into discoverable mode and scan for discoverable devices:

```
$hcitool scan
Scanning ...
        70:26:05:AC:09:37       WH-1000XM2              * This is
my bluetooth headset
        D5:24:02:10:01:17       MOCUTE-032S_A02-24D5 * This is a
Bluetooth joystick
        14:C2:13:D6:95:EF       Fruity                  * The
fruity one
        C0:EE:FB:21:9B:2D       Salty                   * My
testing phone
```

`bt-adapter -d` provides more information when scanning, such as the device class.

As expected, the watch is missing. Also, we had to put everything in discoverable mode manually. Using the BlueZ tool can help with "normally" manipulating the devices (associating with them, forgetting them, and so on) but not discovering devices that are not advertising themselves. Now, let's learn how to get to know a BT classic device better:

```
$sudo hcitool -i hci0 info C0:EE:FB:21:9B:2D
Requesting information ...
```

BD Address:   C0:EE:FB:21:9B:2D

OUI Company: OnePlus Tech (Shenzhen) Ltd (C0-EE-FB)

Device Name: Salty

LMP Version: 4.0 (0x6) LMP Subversion: 0x7d3

Manufacturer: Qualcomm (29)

Features page 0: 0xff 0xfe 0x8f 0xfe 0xd8 0x3f 0x5b 0x87

    <3-slot packets> <5-slot packets> <encryption> <slot offset>

    <timing accuracy> <role switch> <hold mode> <sniff mode>

    <RSSI> <channel quality> <SCO link> <HV2 packets>

    <HV3 packets> <u-law log> <A-law log> <CVSD> <paging scheme>

    <power control> <transparent SCO> <broadcast encrypt>

    <EDR ACL 2 Mbps> <EDR ACL 3 Mbps> <enhanced iscan>

    <interlaced iscan> <interlaced pscan> <inquiry with RSSI>

    <extended SCO> <AFH cap. slave> <AFH class. slave>

    <LE support> <3-slot EDR ACL> <5-slot EDR ACL>

    <sniff subrating> <pause encryption> <AFH cap. master>

    <AFH class. master> <EDR eSCO 2 Mbps> <extended inquiry>

    <LE and BR/EDR> <simple pairing> <encapsulated PDU>

    <non-flush flag> <LSTO> <inquiry TX power> <EPC>

    <extended features>

Features page 1: 0x07 0x00 0x00 0x00 0x00 0x00 0x00 0x00

So, this phone supports encryption, RSSI (the quality of the radio link), and simple pairing (it can work in different modes, depending on the other party, in terms of comparing numbers or PIN mode). Let's compare it to fruity:

```
$sudo hcitool -i hci0 info C0:EE:FB:21:9B:2D >
hci_tool_info_salty
$ sudo hcitool -i hci0 info 14:C2:13:D6:95:EF >
hci_tool_info_fruity
$ comm -3 <(cat hci_tool_info_salty |grep -P '^\t\t'|tr -d
'\t\n' |sed 's/> />\n/g'|sort) <(cat hci_tool_info_fruity |grep
-P '^\t\t'|tr -d '\t\n' |sed 's/> />\n/g'|sort)
        <3-slot EDR eSCO>
        <EDR eSCO 3 Mbps>
        <err. data report>
        <EV4 packets>
        <EV5 packets>
<hold mode>
```

Salty supports hold mode (while fruity does not), while fruity supports EDR, EV4, and EV5 (when it comes to voice packets, fruity is a bit more modern). This tidbit is useful for comparing new versions of a device, for example.

Let's see how we can enumerate the services available on a device. Let's use our joystick, which should be presented as an HID device:

```
$ sdptool -i hci0 browse D5:24:02:10:01:17
Browsing D5:24:02:10:01:17 ...
Service Name: Gamepad
Service Description: Bluetooth KB
Service Provider: MOCUTE
Service RecHandle: 0x10002
Service Class ID List:
  "Human Interface Device" (0x1124)
Protocol Descriptor List:
  "L2CAP" (0x0100)
    PSM: 17
  "HIDP" (0x0011)
Language Base Attr List:
  code_ISO639: 0x656e
```

```
encoding: 0x6a
base_offset: 0x100
Profile Descriptor List:
  "Human Interface Device" (0x1124)
    Version: 0x0100
Browsing D5:24:02:10:01:17 ...
Service Search failed: Connection timed out
Service Name: Port
Service RecHandle: 0x10001
Service Class ID List:
  "Serial Port" (0x1101)
Protocol Descriptor List:
  "L2CAP" (0x0100)
  "RFCOMM" (0x0003)
    Channel: 1
```

Here, we can see that the joystick times out when we browse the services and actually crashes.

# Native Linux Bluetooth tools – looking into the joystick crash

This crash is a perfect example of something that happens when devices are not very well-programmed. Normal Bluetooth activity such as browsing the service should never crash the joystick (you have to press the reset button to make it react again). This will be the perfect opportunity for us to look into the core of the Linux Bluetooth userland tool.

Let's see exactly when it crashes.

## Investigating the crash with a high-level interface to BlueZ/libbluetooth

Let's start by installing pyBlueZ. You can do this by running the following command on a Linux Terminal:

```
sudo pip3 install pyBlueZ
```

pyBlueZ is a very quick way to interact with `libbluetooth` and offers very nice, high-level access to the library. It will allow you to find devices and services, explore devices, connect to services, and so on. I strongly encourage you to read the documentation (`https://github.com/pyBlueZ/pyBlueZ`) and try out the examples provided.

Let's scan the visible devices in Python with the `pyBlueZ` example:

```
ipython3
Python 3.7.3 (default, Apr  3 2019, 05:39:12)
[snip]
In [1]: import bluetooth
   ...:
   ...: nearby_devices = bluetooth.discover_devices(lookup_
names=True)
   ...: print("found %d devices" % len(nearby_devices))
   ...:
   ...: for addr, name in nearby_devices:
   ...:        print("  %s - %s" % (addr, name))
   ...:
found 3 devices
  FC:45:96:C1:4C:99 - Grayson 9915
  C0:EE:FB:21:9B:2D - Salty
  D5:24:02:10:01:17 - MOCUTE-032S_A02-24D5
```

When we run the `pyBlueZ` service enumeration example (`pybuez/exemples/sdp-browse.py D5:24:02:10:01:17`), the services get enumerated at a lower level of detail than with `sdptool`, and the joystick doesn't crash!

Let's look a little bit more into the device with BlueZ. Let's enumerate the RFCOMM services (we can normally connect with the RFCOMM services to look for trouble):

```
// on the joystick
$./rfcomm_enum_services.py D5:24:02:10:01:17
found 2 services on D5:24:02:10:01:17
found RFCOM service:
Service Name: Port
    channel/PSM: 1
      svc classes: 0x1101
// on salty, a lot more since it is a phone
```

```
$./rfcomm_enum_services.py C0:EE:FB:21:9B:2D
found 15 services on C0:EE:FB:21:9B:2D
found RFCOM service:
Service Name: Headset Gateway
     channel/PSM: 2
        svc classes: 0x1112
        svc classes: 0x1203
found RFCOM service:
[...snip...]
Service Name: OBEX File Transfer
     channel/PSM: 20
        svc classes: 0x1106
```

Let's connect to the joystick RFCOMM:

```
$./rfcomm_enum_port.py D5:24:02:10:01:17 0x1101
found 1 port(s)
service 'Port' available on port(s): [1]
connected.  type stuff
```

At this point, the device-specific search starts, which means you can try to type in certain commands, such as modem-style AT commands. The accepted commands depend on the device (you will have to search the device manual or look into the device's BT profile definition, and maybe even sniff the connection or the activity of an application to find out more about how the device is used), but you can now connect to an arbitrary RFCOMM service from your device.

## BlueZ – getting down and dirty with libbluetooth

So, what is `sdptool` doing differently? Let's clone the BlueZ source tree:

```
git clone https://git.kernel.org/pub/scm/bluetooth/bluez.git
```

Let's `git checkout` to the adequate version (the one installed on your system so that you don't have any issues with tools and libraries) and build it but don't install it:

```
./bootstrap && ./configure --enable-testing --enable-
experimental --enable-deprecated && make
```

Now, let's have a look at `sdptool`.

By slightly patching `sdptool`, we can see that the device is crashing when it looks into a service sublevel with a sublevel ID of `0`.

Now, let's patch it a bit more, like so:

```
// if (sdp_get_group_id(rec, &sub_context.group) != -1) {
if (sdp_get_group_id(rec, &sub_context.group) > 0) {
```

Now, the device doesn't crash anymore! This indicates that not only the records in SDP are returned by the device incorrectly, but that it crashes on this particular value! Now, let's see if it crashes on any unused values. Let's patch `sdptool` again:

```
if (sdp_get_group_id(rec, &sub_context.group) != -1) {
// patch start
            if(sub_context.group.value.uuid16 == 0) {
                sub_context.group.value.uuid16 = 0x1003; //
patched value
            }
// patch end
```

As we can see, the device crashes (on multiple values, such as `0x1003`, `0xabab`, and so on).

With that, we've found that the device crashes (DoS) if you try to enumerate SDP services that don't exist on the device! The main goal here was to show that we can instrument legitimate tools (in this example, by adding a few `printf` calls and changing some tests) so that we can look at our devices and find problems.

## Sniffing the BT activity on your host

We can use `btmon` to trace what is happening on our machine when we are connecting to the device.

Let's run `btmon` and associate it with the joystick (`btmon` is very verbose and you can write a trace to a file with `-w`). The trace file can be opened with Wireshark:

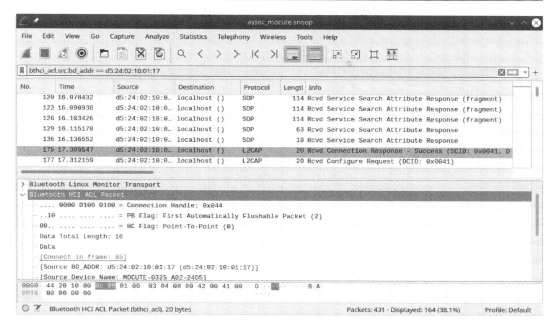

Figure 8.2 – Trace file opened in Wireshark

Use `bthci_acl.dst.bd_addr` and `bthci_acl.src.bd_addr` as display filters (in Wireshark, this is the line on top of the packet list) to remove what you don't need.

But *how is this useful to me?* you will say...:

- If your device is conforming to normal profiles, it will allow you to look into how it works.

- If it doesn't, this means that you will need an app or a driver to snoop on. Since most devices that need an app to interact with will be available on Android, we can leverage the fact that all Android phones are Linux devices that rely on BlueZ (until KitKat) and can produce `btmon` style files with the Bluetooth HCI Snoop Log (I'll let you search the internet about how to enable and retrieve it with `adb`).

# Sniffing raw BT

Let's plug in our Ubertooth ONE, install the host tools and then update it to the correct firmware to it (that is, `bluetooth_rxtx`; the `dfu` process is described in the Ubertooth documentation here: `https://github.com/greatscottgadgets/ubertooth/wiki/Firmware`).

Ubertooth comes with a variety of command-line tools (the manuals for them can be found at `https://github.com/greatscottgadgets/ubertooth/tree/master/host/doc`; we will be using `ubertooth-rx`) to receive Ubertooth frames. Let's try it out:

```
$sudo ubertooth-rx
systime=1563641019 ch=62 LAP=d695ef err=0 clkn=60351 clk_
offset=5001 s=-42 n=-55 snr=13
systime=1563641019 ch=62 LAP=d695ef err=0 clkn=60383 clk_
offset=4995 s=-42 n=-55 snr=13
systime=1563641019 ch=34 LAP=d695ef err=0 clkn=61554 clk_
offset=1826 s=-42 n=-55 snr=13
systime=1563641019 ch=66 LAP=d695ef err=0 clkn=61602 clk_
offset=1829 s=-40 n=-55 snr=15
<turning on Fruity>
systime=1563641085 ch=69 LAP=9e8b33 err=0 clkn=6929 clk_
offset=4937 s=-31 n=-55 snr=24
systime=1563641085 ch=69 LAP=9e8b33 err=0 clkn=6961 clk_
offset=4946 s=-35 n=-55 snr=20
systime=1563641085 ch=69 LAP=9e8b33 err=2 clkn=7025 clk_
offset=4938 s=-35 n=-55 snr=20
systime=1563641085 ch=39 LAP=9e8b33 err=2 clkn=7548 clk_
offset=1822 s=-30 n=-55 snr=25
systime=1563641085 ch=71 LAP=9e8b33 err=1 clkn=7577 clk_
offset=4949 s=-31 n=-55 snr=24
<turning Fruity off and Salty on>
systime=1563641212 ch=31 LAP=9e8b33 err=2 clkn=35228 clk_
offset=1810 s=-44 n=-55 snr=11
systime=1563641212 ch=31 LAP=9e8b33 err=1 clkn=35260 clk_
offset=1812 s=-44 n=-55 snr=11
systime=1563641212 ch=31 LAP=9e8b33 err=1 clkn=35292 clk_
offset=1802 s=-43 n=-55 snr=12
systime=1563641212 ch=31 LAP=9e8b33 err=1 clkn=35324 clk_
offset=1807 s=-43 n=-55 snr=12
systime=1563641212 ch=37 LAP=9e8b33 err=0 clkn=37140 clk_
offset=1811 s=-42 n=-55 snr=13
systime=1563641212 ch=37 LAP=9e8b33 err=0 clkn=37236 clk_
offset=1811 s=-42 n=-55 snr=13
```

```
systime=1563641213 ch=28 LAP=f5a32f err=1 clkn=39324 clk_
offset=1820 s=-41 n=-55 snr=14
```

```
systime=1563641213 ch=28 LAP=f5a32f err=0 clkn=39356 clk_
offset=1823 s=-41 n=-55 snr=14
```

```
systime=1563641213 ch=28 LAP=f5a32f err=1 clkn=39420 clk_
offset=1829 s=-40 n=-55 snr=15
```

```
systime=1563641213 ch=60 LAP=f5a32f err=0 clkn=39448 clk_
offset=1821 s=-43 n=-55 snr=12
```

First, the joystick (which is paired to Fruity) is looking for its master (the LAP 0xd695ef is pretty recognizable – look at the lower bytes of Fruity's address). Then, Fruity sends packets with a LAP of 0x9e8b33, but there is nothing like that we are aware of. This is normal and this is the General Inquiry Access Code, which is used by all devices to search for other devices. After a few attempts, Fruity will try to connect to another device it has in memory, which means we can look into a connection in a more specific way. Let's try to spy on the watch connection.

Let's turn on the Bluetooth on Fruity and try to connect to the watch while dumping the traffic. However, we will see nothing! bluetooth-rx only sees BT3, and the connection with the watch happens to be on BLE. We will come back to this later when we look at BLE.

Let's have a look at the connection between the joystick and Salty:

```
$sudo ubertooth-rx -l 219b2d
```

```
systime=1563643388 ch=34 LAP=219b2d err=0 clkn=790 clk_
offset=1908 s=-48 n=-55 snr=7
```

```
offset < CLK_TUNE_TIME
```

```
CLK100ns Trim: 5908
```

```
systime=1563643391 ch=43 LAP=219b2d err=1 clkn=8818 clk_
offset=2321 s=-40 n=-55 snr=15
```

```
[...]
```

```
systime=1563643394 ch=51 LAP=219b2d err=1 clkn=21418 clk_
offset=2616 s=-63 n=-55 snr=-8
```

```
offset > CLK_TUNE_TIME
```

```
CLK100ns Trim: 366
```

```
Clock drifted 366 in 6.446250 s. 5 PPM too fast.
```

```
systime=1563643396 ch=78 LAP=219b2d err=0 clkn=24984 clk_
offset=2250 s=-42 n=-55 snr=13
```

```
[...]
```

```
systime=1563643400 ch=15 LAP=219b2d err=0 clkn=40282 clk_
offset=2175 s=-44 n=-55 snr=11
UAP = 0xfb found after 12 total packets.
```

Here, we can see that, even though Ubertooth only knew the LAP, it has been able to find the UAP (UAP = 0xfb, which was found after 12 total packets):

```
$sudo ubertooth-rx -l 219b2d -u fb
Calculating complete hopping sequence.
Hopping sequence calculated.
26446 initial CLK1-27 candidates
[...]
systime=1563644251 ch=50 LAP=219b2d err=0 clkn=56554 clk_
offset=2276 s=-39 n=-55 snr=16
[Snip...hugely random time it is luck dependent, sometimes
it's seconds, sometimes 10min, the more traffic the better,
sometimes unplugging the Ubertooth and relaunching helps]
Acquired CLK1-27 = 0x05d95a7
```

Now, we are capturing a lot more! However, most of the information has been cyphered (and the link key is stored on the device you're associated with; for example, with an Android device, it is available in the developer tools).

Ubertooth One is very practical if you wish to view BT traffic that is not directly visible with higher-level tools. When it comes to attacking lower-level Bluetooth signals, the documentation is sometimes a little bit terse – but again, read and learn!

# BLE

Now, let's have a look at BT 4.x (low energy /smart). The main introduction, from a security point of view, is the **Generic ATTributes (GATT)** profile. These GATTs are key/value stores that allow us to interact with the device very easily.

## Scanning for BLE

To find BLE devices, we can use `hcitool lescan`:

```
$sudo hcitool lescan
LE Scan ...
FC:45:96:C1:4C:99 Grayson 9915  /*my watch*/
```

```
D9:F2:25:36:4C:76 (unknown)
72:35:46:95:30:89 (unknown)
72:35:46:95:30:89 (unknown)
D9:F2:25:36:4C:76 Braceli5-9574 * interesting, that's my
girlfriend's activity tracker and she D9:F2:25:36:4C:76
(unknown)        * turned her phone off, let's look into it
D9:F2:25:36:4C:76 Braceli5-9574
D9:F2:25:36:4C:76 Braceli5-9574
```

As you can see, we found a few different devices from the scan.

## Enumerating BLE GATTs

Now that we have found some devices (my watch and an activity tracker), let's look at their attributes and services:

```
$sudo gatttool -i hci0 -t random -b D9:F2:25:36:4C:76 --primary
attr handle = 0x0001, end grp handle = 0x0007 uuid: 00001800-
0000-1000-8000-00805f9b34fb
attr handle = 0x0008, end grp handle = 0x0008 uuid: 00001801-
0000-1000-8000-00805f9b34fb
attr handle = 0x0009, end grp handle = 0x000f uuid: 0000ff20-
0000-1000-8000-00805f9b34fb
attr handle = 0x0010, end grp handle = 0xffff uuid: 0000fee7-
0000-1000-8000-00805f9b34fb
```

Since there are thousands of different UUIDs available, we must look at the Bluetooth website or at the GATT identification tools to find their meanings. (I made a small script that builds a CSV from a folder with XML GATT characteristics and services descriptions – bgparser2csv.py can be found in this book's GitHub repository. There is also the excellent nRF mobile connect application for Android that has a pretty good database of UUIDs.)

attr handle and end grp handle define handle groups per service.

Let's identify our services:

```
$sudo gatttool -i hci0 -t random -b D9:F2:25:36:4C:76 --primary
|cut -d' ' -f 11 | while read -r line; do echo -n "$line ";grep
$line gatt_uuid
.csv;echo; done
00001800-0000-1000-8000-00805f9b34fb "00001800-0000-1000-
800[...],"Generic Access'
00001801-0000-1000-8000-00805f9b34fb "00001801-0000-1000-
800[...],"Generic Attribute'
0000ff20-0000-1000-8000-00805f9b34fb  *unknown in our db
0000fee7-0000-1000-8000-00805f9b34fb  *unknown in our db
```

Let's identify their characteristics:

```
$sudo gatttool -i hci0 -t random -b D9:F2:25:36:4C:76
--characteristics
handle = 0x0002, char properties = 0x0a, char value handle =
0x0003, uuid = 00002a00-0000-1000-8000-00805f9b34fb
handle = 0x0004, char properties = 0x02, char value handle =
0x0005, uuid = 00002a01-0000-1000-8000-00805f9b34fb
handle = 0x0006, char properties = 0x02, char value handle =
0x0007, uuid = 00002a04-0000-1000-8000-00805f9b34fb
handle = 0x000a, char properties = 0x84, char value handle =
0x000b, uuid = 0000ff21-0000-1000-8000-00805f9b34fb
handle = 0x000d, char properties = 0x10, char value handle =
0x000e, uuid = 0000ff22-0000-1000-8000-00805f9b34fb
handle = 0x0011, char properties = 0x12, char value handle =
0x0012, uuid = 0000fea1-0000-1000-8000-00805f9b34fb
handle = 0x0014, char properties = 0x02, char value handle =
0x0015, uuid = 0000fec9-0000-1000-8000-00805f9b34fb
```

Here, we can see the following:

- There are two handles by characteristics (the first contains the value attributes listed here, while the second contains its value)

- The characteristics have properties in that they have bit fields (that is, values can be ORed) that describe the operations supported (described in the BLE core 4.2 specification).

Here are the values of the characteristic bitfield:

| Value of bit in the field | Name | Signification |
|---|---|---|
| 0x01 | Broadcast | Broadcasts the characteristic value to the client (that is, us, the device is the server) |
| 0x02 | Read | Read allowed |
| 0x04 | Write without response | Write allowed without response |
| 0x08 | Write | Write allowed with response |
| 0x10 | Notify | Can be notified to the client without acknowledgement |
| 0x20 | Indicate | Can be notified to the client and must be acknowledged |
| 0x40 | Authenticated signed writes | Only signed writes are allowed |
| 0x80 | Extended properties | More information is available in another descriptor |

Let's identify the characteristics:

```
$sudo gatttool -i hci0 -t random -b D9:F2:25:36:4C:76
--characteristics|cut -d ' ' -f 15|while read -r uuid;do echo
-n "$uuid ->";grep $uuid gatt_uuid.csv|cut -d ',' -f 4 |tr -d
'\n' ;echo;done
00002a00-0000-1000-8000-00805f9b34fb ->"Device Name'
00002a01-0000-1000-8000-00805f9b34fb ->"Appearance'
00002a04-0000-1000-8000-00805f9b34fb ->"Peripheral Preferred
Connection Parameters'
0000ff21-0000-1000-8000-00805f9b34fb ->
0000ff22-0000-1000-8000-00805f9b34fb ->
0000fea1-0000-1000-8000-00805f9b34fb ->
0000fec9-0000-1000-8000-00805f9b34fb ->
```

With that, we have identified the services and the characteristics we can use to communicate with the joystick.

## Interacting with BLE GATTs

At this point, we don't know what the characteristics do, nor how we can interact with them. Let's read and write some values so that we can make educated guesses about what they do:

```
#the handle of device name

$sudo gatttool -i hci0 -t random -b D9:F2:25:36:4C:76 --char-
read -a 3

Characteristic value/descriptor: 42 72 61 63 65 6c 69 35 2d 39
35 37 34

#the long uuid of device name

$sudo gatttool -i hci0 -t random -b D9:F2:25:36:4C:76 --char-
read -u 00002a00-0000-1000-8000-00805f9b34fb

handle: 0x0003    value: 42 72 61 63 65 6c 69 35 2d 39 35 37 34

#the short id of device name

$sudo gatttool -i hci0 -t random -b D9:F2:25:36:4C:76 --char-
read -u 2a00

handle: 0x0003    value: 42 72 61 63 65 6c 69 35 2d 39 35 37 34

#all the handles listed in characterstics, the characteristic
and the value handle

$sudo gatttool -i hci0 -t random -b D9:F2:25:36:4C:76
--characteristics|tr ' ' '\n'|tr -d ','|egrep '^0x[0-9a-f]
{4}'|while read -r handle; do echo -n "$handle -> "; sudo
gatttool -i hci0 -t random -b D9:F2:25:36:4C:76 --char-read -a
$handle;done

0x0002 -> Characteristic value/descriptor: 0a 03 00 00 2a

0x0003 -> Characteristic value/descriptor: 42 72 61 63 65 6c 69
35 2d 39 35 37 34   *Braceli5-9574*

0x0004 -> Characteristic value/descriptor: 02 05 00 01 2a

0x0005 -> Characteristic value/descriptor: 40 14

0x0006 -> Characteristic value/descriptor: 02 07 00 04 2a

0x0007 -> Characteristic value/descriptor: 28 00 20 03 00 00 f4
01

0x000a -> Characteristic value/descriptor: 84* 0b 00 21 ff *
read will fail, extended, write

0x000b -> Characteristic value/descriptor read failed:
Attribute can't be read

0x000d -> Characteristic value/descriptor: 10* 0e 00 22 ff *
read will fail, notify
```

```
0x000e -> Characteristic value/descriptor read failed:
Attribute can't be read
```
```
0x0011 -> Characteristic value/descriptor: 12 12 00 a1 fe
```
```
0x0012 -> Characteristic value/descriptor: 07 00 00 00 00 00 00
00 00 00
```
```
0x0014 -> Characteristic value/descriptor: 02 15 00 c9 fe
```
```
0x0015 -> Characteristic value/descriptor: d9 f2 25 36 4c 76
```

Now that we can read them, let's delve a bit deeper into reading the descriptors of the services and their characteristics.

Services basically only show a short UUID (2, 4, or 16 bytes); for example:

```
handle 01 value is 00 18  for
00001800-0000-1000-8000-00805f9b34fb.
```
```
handle 03 value is 2a 00  for 00002a00-0000-1000-8000-
00805f9b34fb.
```

Characteristics are a bit more interesting since they hold their attributes, the descriptor number for their value, and their UUID (see the values in bold in the preceding code block).

Let's read a value, change it, and then read it back to see if the writing went wrong:

```
$sudo gatttool -i hci0 -t random -b D9:F2:25:36:4C:76 --char-
read -a 3
```
```
Characteristic value/descriptor: 42 72 61 63 65 6c 69 35 2d 39
35 37 34
```
```
$sudo gatttool -i hci0 -t random -b D9:F2:25:36:4C:76 --char-
write-req -a 3 -n 0x4242424242
```
```
Characteristic value was written successfully
```
```
$sudo gatttool -i hci0 -t random -b D9:F2:25:36:4C:76 --char-
read -a 3
```
```
Characteristic value/descriptor: 00 42 42 42 42 42
```

Well, that was a lot to learn about Bluetooth LE! Now, it's your turn to play with some Bluetooth devices. Try out the following to test your BLE devices:

- Try to write to attributes you are not supposed to
- Write values you are not supposed to (and link your writes to the behavior of the device, along with the different attributes and anything interesting you may have found)
- Check if you can find values that are damaging to the user's privacy
- And a lot of other things – get creative!

## BLE connection security

Just like BL classic, BLE supports pairing and connection cyphering. As for many devices in a classic that lack input for the user, a large number of BLE devices don't implement anything. This gives an attacker free rein to connect to and interact with the device.

This lack of BLE security should already be a finding in itself, and I encourage you to read more about the BLE security modes, levels, and pairing/bonding possibilities so that you can propose adequate remediations.

# Summary

In this chapter, we looked into the two main wireless networking protocols that are used by embedded systems and how to attack them. Probing network activity is always very interesting and can point you toward some relevant security elements, such as keys and certificates that were identified during the S.T.R.I.D.E. exercise (*Chapter 4, Approaching and Planning the Test*). This is also a good starting point when your interactions with the system are limited because you cannot damage the system, or you only have a very limited number of test systems. In the next chapter, we will look into attacking other radio interfaces that can't easily be reached with common tools.

# Questions

1. What is the DHCP configuration directive for giving a proxy to the test system?

2. Do you think that other DHCP parameters could be leveraged for security testing? Can you think of some examples?

3. In the DNS part of the netmasq config, I added a list of DNS "spoofed" hosts. What do you think they can be used for?

4. In the DNS part of the netmasq config, I added logging for the queries. What do you think this can be used for?

5. What does GATT stand for?

6. What is the main security problem with the common implementation of BLE?

# 9
# Software-Defined Radio Attacks

Modern embedded devices communicate a lot over radio interfaces in order to be independent of cables. It is very common for them to use the well-established protocols (such as Wi-Fi or Bluetooth) that we already looked into in previous chapters. There are numerous systems that don't need such complex protocols (or are constrained due to other design considerations, such as cost, complexity, processing power, and more) but still have a need for radio communications. In this case, they tend to use other protocols that are not necessarily easy to interface with out of the box. In this case, we need to be able to interact with these custom protocols in order to be able to test the communication's security. This is the domain of **Software-Defined Radio (SDR)**.

We will go over the following topics in this chapter:

- Introduction to arbitrary radio/SDR
- Understanding and selecting the hardware
- Looking into the radio spectrum
- Finding back the data

- Identifying modulations
- Demodulating the signal
- Sending it back

# Technical requirements

You will need at least an SDR adapter. The bare minimum hardware requirement is an RTLSDR stick that I will talk about in the next section. You will also need the following software tools:

- GNU Radio
- Gqrx
- baudline
- Audacity
- Python

Check out the following link to see the Code in Action video: `https://bit.ly/3uKVsRz`

# Introduction to arbitrary radio/SDR

SDR allows you to receive (and emit if you have the adequate license and hardware) arbitrary radio signals. The adapter acts as a device that can sample (some can also emit) radio signals around a frequency you can specify and that is it. All the signal processing is done on the software. The theoretical aspects of the sampling and how the samples represent the radio data is a little complicated; it is not absolutely necessary to understand it to start but it will become very useful later when you start to develop your own scripts and signal processing chains in GNU Radio.

> **Note**
> To understand the theoretical principles of SDR and basic usage of GNU Radio, I strongly advise looking at this excellent series of videos by Michael Ossman: `https://greatscottgadgets.com/sdr/1/`.

# Understanding and selecting the hardware

As usual, the hardware capabilities and costs are linked. Here is a list of the main domains that the hardware selection impacts, with a list of the main SDR adapters and their capabilities per domain.

The hardware will mainly define the following:

- The frequencies you can access are as follows:

  - **RTL-SDR (receive only)**: 20 MHz–1.75 GHz

  - **HackRF**: 10 MHz–6 GHz

  - **BladeRF**: 300 MHz–3.8 GHz

  - **USRP**: 70 MHz–6 GHz

- The width of the spectrum you can cover in one shot is as follows (the sample rate in MS/s is the number of samples it takes per second. It is also the width of the spectrum that is captured):

  - **RTL-SDR**: 2.4 MS/s

  - **HackRF**: 20 MS/s

  - **BladeRF**: 40 MS/s

  - **USRPs**: 61 MS/s

  The higher the sample rate you have, the faster you can explore the spectrum, but it will (most of the time) not impact your capability to analyze signals since most of the signals have a bandwidth of a few dozens of KHz in the lower frequencies.

- The price range is as follows:

  - **RTL-SDR**: ~25€

  - **HackRF**: ~300€

  - **BladeRF**: ~400€

  - **USRPs**: ~1,000€+

Once you have decided on your hardware, let's use it to look into a radio device.

# Looking into a radio device

First, get yourself one of the multiple radio-emitting simple gadgets that are currently on the market (such as a garage opener or a radio-commanded relay box) and see whether information is available in the FCC documentation (`https://www.fcc.gov/oet/ea/fccid` or `https://fccid.io/`). Since the Furby does not use radio, I'll look into an IKEA radio-controlled LED lighting device (ANSLUTA). There is no apparent FCC number on the emitter or receiver, but a simple internet search lends the FCC ID as FHO-E1205. Opening the emitter (using the same approach we used in previous chapters) shows a TI CC 2500 chip. Looking into the CC2500 documentation, we can see that the frequency should be ~2.45 GHz (2.4–2.48 from the CC2500 datasheet: `https://www.ti.com/lit/gpn/cc2500`) and this is confirmed by the FCC documentation.

If you are using an RTL-SDR, this frequency will be out of your reach. Pick a wireless garage door opener in the lower ISM bands (433 MHz–800 MHz, depending on where you live). The principles will be the same.

# Receiving the signal – a look at antennas

When looking into an antenna to receive your signal, there will be two cases:

- The device emits on a frequency for which commercial antennas are available. Just buy an antenna; you can reuse it later and it will be nicely designed, and you won't have to worry.

- The device emits on a frequency for which commercial antennas are not available. Most of the time, we will be working quite close to the device we will be testing. That means we won't need a very performant antenna to be able to receive the signal, but we will need something that works at least half-decently in our target band.

  Antenna design could cover two or three books on its own (it is a very complex domain on its own), their pros and cons too (look into antenna books on your favorite bookseller's website if you want confirmation). For our usage, we can just use simple, throwaway dipole antennas that I stick to a length of PVC tube, or buy a ready-made antenna that matches our frequency range of interest.

Now, let's look at what to do when you don't have a commercial antenna.

## Making a quick and dirty dipole antenna

The dipole antenna is very simple. It is two lengths of wire forming an antenna of a fractional length of the signal wavelength.

Usually, half-wavelength works great (but 1/4, 1/8, and more can be used if 1/2 is too big). The wavelength is *C x (1/(Frequency))*.

Let's imagine something emitting at 520 MHz (in my country, that can be medical devices, radio microphones on onboard vehicular communication, and so on).

Now, let's calculate the antenna parameters for 520 MHz:

| Wavelength: 520 MHz | = 0.576 m (299792458 m/s * (1/(520e6/s)) ) |
|---|---|
| Length of a half wavelength: 520 MHz | = 0.2882 m (good) |
| Length of a quarter wavelength: 520 MHz | = 0.1441 m |

Next, we build the antenna by measuring two adequate lengths of wire for the target frequency (for a half-wave, measure two quarter wavelengths, for a quarter-length, measure two eighths, and so on).

For a half-wave 520 MHz antenna, that is 2 x 14.4 mm.

In the following figure, we can see how the wires are connected to the SDR device:

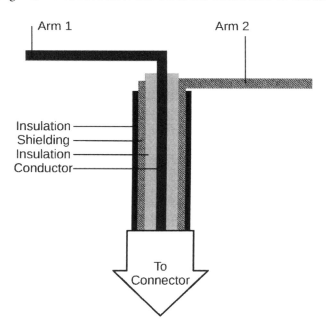

Figure 9.1 – Dipole antenna connection

This should be enough for correct reception. Just keep in mind that the dipole antenna is unbalanced; you should (it helps but is not mandatory) use a **balun** (**bal**anced/ **un**balanced) right before the dipole in order to balance it (to overly simplify, it avoids unwanted currents coming into your receiver and correctly references the signal). Either buy one that fits your transmission line impedance (depends on your coax type and length) or make an air-choke by making a coil of a few turns of your coax (this is a bit more complicated to do but is basically free; it requires you to measure the capacitance to determine the correct length of coax to coil up). To do so, look into this: `https://www.instructables.com/id/Air-Choke-Ugly-Balun-for-Ham-Radio/`.

Here is the (not) very fancy 75 cm/branch half-wavelength antenna I use for 100 MHz:

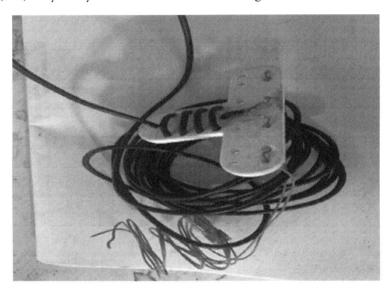

Figure 9.2 – Antennas don't have to be fancy to work

This uses an ugly 3D-printed balun from `http://www.dk0tu.de/users/DB4UM/c3d1pole/`.

# Looking into the radio spectrum

Gqrx is a GNU Radio application that allows you to have a nice GUI to set the frequency of your hardware and have a visual representation of the radio spectrum around the set frequency. It also allows you to hear some common modulations, such as narrow- or **wide-band FM (WFM)**, **lower and upper side band (LSB and USB)**, and others.

Let's fire up Gqrx and set up the source (`hackrf` for `hackrf`, RTLSDR for RTLSDR, and so on):

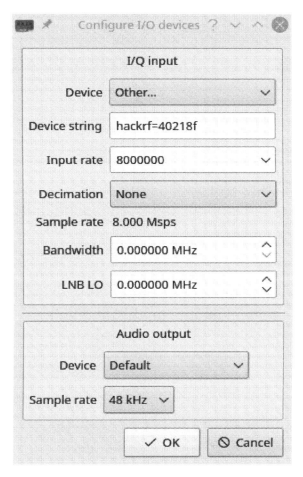

Figure 9.3 – Selecting the source: a HackRF example

The following screenshot shows the Gqrx main window:

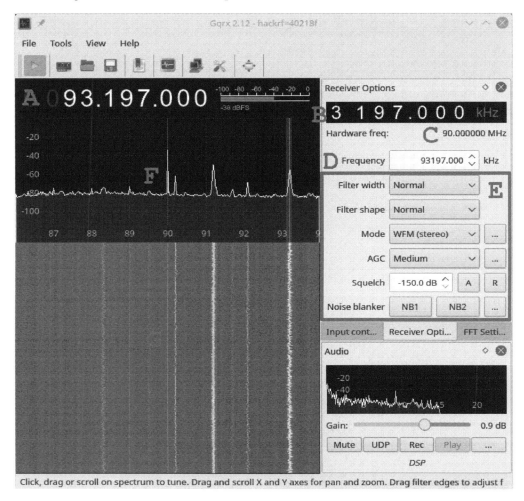

Figure 9.4 – Gqrx main window

The frequency you are listening to is as follows:

- **A**: The frequency you are listening to
- **B**: The frequency delta between the hardware-centering frequency and the part of the captured data the software processing is focusing on
- **C**: The frequency the hardware is centered on (that is, the frequency it will be capturing data around)
- **D**: Same as **A**

- **E**: The signal processing chain that will be applied to the data (here, set up to listen to (W)FM radio)

- **F**: The FFT scope

- **G**: The cascade scope (that is, the history of the FFT scope that flows down like a cascade)

Now, let's have a look at ~90 MHz. Normally, you can see two subwindows: a top one (the FFT) and a bottom one (the cascade) where you see peaks at frequencies that are emitting signals in the FFT and the history of these peaks in the cascade. Set the mode to **WFM** (right side of the GUI) and move the cursor to one of these peaks. You should now hear music (such as songs or someone speaking)! Wonderful, this is your first SDR use!

Now, look at the FFT plot in the following figure and you can see you have a big, thin peak right in the middle. This is your hardware center frequency (the big peak at 2.429 GHz in the following example). This peak comes from the hardware and cannot be removed. It would pollute your signals and that is the reason why you always have a shift next to the center frequency (the vertical line at 2.4355 GHz in the following figure) to listen to a specific frequency.

If we move to 2.45 GHz (go on the frequency and use your mouse wheel), we can have a look at our radio controller (not shown in the figure for clarity purposes). Here, our main problem is that the portion of the spectrum we are looking at (2.45 GHz) is pretty crowded (it's an ISM band after all; plenty of devices (including Wi-Fi) are emitting there):

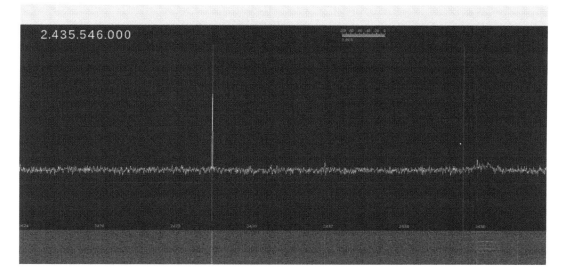

Figure 9.5 – FFT and cascade plots in Gqrx

So, let's go from 2.4 to 2.48 GHz by a step of our 1/2 sample rate and click on the device to see it emitting.

I find that mine is emitting around 2.436 GHz. Can you see the horizontal lines in the cascade? These are radio pulses you see when you click the remote control buttons.

# Finding back the data

GNU Radio is a set of software tools that allows you to create a signal processing chain for the data that comes from your SDR hardware (or a file) to either your hardware again (to emit) or a file. The blocks in its GUI (`gnuradio-companion`) are individual processing steps in the signal processing chain. Data comes from a source toward a sink (both are files or your SDR hardware driver, your sound card, or... well, it can be a lot of things: another program, a network endpoint, and so on).

> **Note**
>
> **gnuradio-companion (grc)** has two main GUI frameworks it can talk to: QT and WX. Depending on your installation, you may have to change the framework in the generate options block. The GUI-related processing blocks will also have to be changed in the processing flow itself.

So, let's fire up `gnuradio-companion` and make a receiver.

First, let's replicate Gqrx and let's have an FFT visualization. FFT is a visualization of the signal in the frequency domain (that is, the strength of the different components as a function of their frequency).

Add a source (depending on your hardware, the `osmocom` source for `hackrf`, for example; right column, *Ctrl + F* to search) and an FFT sink (it can be named `FFT` or `Frequency sink`, depending on the version; for now, default values should be fine, just change your sample rate variable to the best your hardware can do) and link them (by drawing from the output of your source to the input of the FFT).

All `.grc` files describe a signal processing chain in GNU Radio and are available in the Git repository of the book. I will also provide a file with the samples that are coming from my receiver so that you can replicate these steps (you will need to replace the `osmocom` source with a file source pointing to the sample file).

Open `fft.grc` and run it:

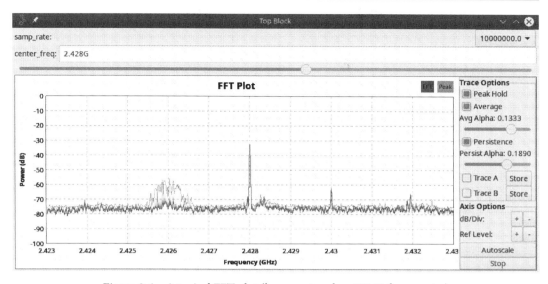

Figure 9.6 – A typical FFT plot (here, centered on Wi-Fi frequencies)

Now, let's center on our emitting channel:

- Focus on it by reducing the sample rate (it removes signals from higher and lower frequencies) in the Osmocom source block.

- Add a low-pass filter, a width around what the signal you receive seems to be (it focuses even more sharply). This is the low-pass filter block.

- Add two scopes: one on our raw signal and one on our mag^2 (the square of the magnitude will make emissions "pop out"). These are the time sink blocks.

It should look like this:

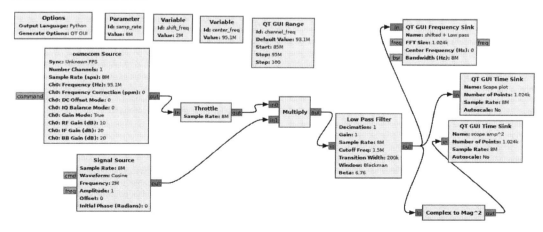

Figure 9.7 – Our flow graph with additional visualizations

Run it to see the size of the received samples on the time domain (use `fft-scope.grc` if you can't make it work on your own):

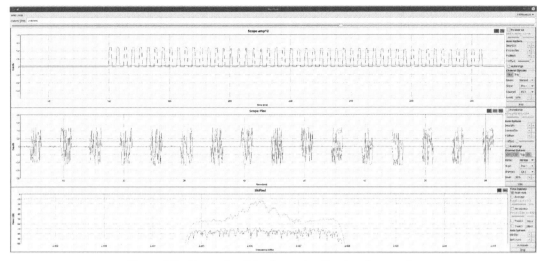

Figure 9.8 – Example of the three visualization flowgraphs

Here, we can see that the trains of magnitude (top scope) have the same width and spacing. If we zoom closer into one, it is not clear at this point whether it is a repeated signal, but they don't seem to contain clear on/off sequences inside. This is not **on-off keying** (**OOK**), and in the bottom FFT, we cannot see "spikes" that could indicate **frequency shift keying** (**FSK**). So now, what is the modulation?

# Identifying modulations – a didactic example

What we now have is a very common question when looking into unknown signals: what is the modulation? Finding the correct modulation and parameters can require a bit of detective work, even if you know the parameters. This section is more of an illustration of the process of reversing a signal modulation than directly a recipe (since there is no recipe). Some people are currently working in an academic context on projects to train neural networks to do signal classification, meaning there is no straightforward way to recognize modulations.

In the case of the light controller, we can already reduce the candidate's number because we know (from the FCC documentation and opening the device) that it embeds a CC2500. The datasheet tells us that it supports a few modulation schemes: 2-FSK, GFSK, MSK, and OOK. We already eliminated two (OOK and FSK) but how do we tell the difference between them?

First, let's talk about what modulation is. Modulation is a way to transmit information in a radio signal. It can be digital (OOK, FSK, G-FSK) or analog (AM, FM, and more). Modulation is the way the information is "inserted" in the physical characteristics of the signal (changes in frequency, phase, amplitude, and others).

Second, let's talk about what modulation is not.

Modulation is not encoding. Encoding is the way to describe data, not the way data is inserted in the signal. Let's take an example with a very simple modulation: OOK. OOK is basically knowing whether a signal is on or off. Now, how can you encode data over OOK? You can do it in multiple ways, actually! Take the following examples:

- You can have long pulses for 0 and short for 1 (or vice versa).

- You can have data encoded in the transition of the modulation. For example, if a modulated signal changed in the symbol time slot from low to high, it's a 1, and if from high to low, it's a 0 (this is called Manchester encoding).

- You can use the length of the pause in between high pulses to encode the information.

- And others...

When looking into a signal, you will also have to understand how that data is encoded.

Here are a few common modulations (there are plenty of modulations), as well as a brief explanation of how they work and how to recognize them.

# AM/ASK

The main points related to AM/ASK are as follows:

- **Modulation**: Amplitude modulation/amplitude OOK.

- **Type**: Analog/digital.

- **How it works**: The signal amplitude (for AM/ASK) or the fact that it is there or not (OOK) carries the information.

- **How to recognize it in GNU Radio**: In a scope view coming from a mag or a mag^2 block, we can see trains of data.

Visual examples of modulation (sending 1,0,0,0,1,1,0,1) are shown in the following figure:

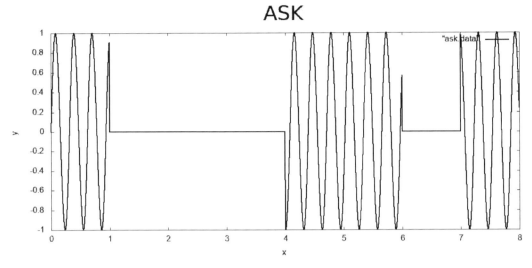

Figure 9.9 – ASK modulation

Next, let's look at FM/FSK.

# FM/FSK

The main points related to FM/FSK are as follows:

- **Modulation**: Frequency modulation/FSK.

- **Type**: Analog/digital.

- **How it works**: The carrier frequency is modulated to carry the information, going a little up or down to carry the information (for example, in FM radio, this is done in a continuous way (as opposed to a discrete way in FSK) to carry the sound frequency.

- **How to recognize it in GNU Radio**: In the FFT, for FSK, you will see two (or more; two spikes is 2-FSK, three is 3-FSK, and so on) peaks very close to each other when looking at the signal up close. For analog FM, the peak of the carrier frequency will be consistently wide.

Visual examples of modulation (sending 1,0,0,0,1,1,0,1) are shown in the following figure:

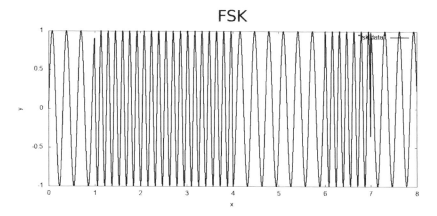

Figure 9.10 – FSK modulation

Next, let's look at PM/**phase shift keying (PSK)**.

## PM/PSK

The main points related to PM/PSK are as follows:

- **Modulation**: Phase modulation/phase shift keying.

- **Type**: Analog/digital.

- **How it works**: The phase of the carrier is shifted to carry the information.

- **How to recognize it in GNU Radio**: When you use a Complex to Mag phase block and output the results to a scope, you can see brutal changes in the signal phase.

Visual examples of modulation (sending 1,0,0,0,1,1,0,1) phase changes are hard to see in the signal itself, but see how the sine jumps:

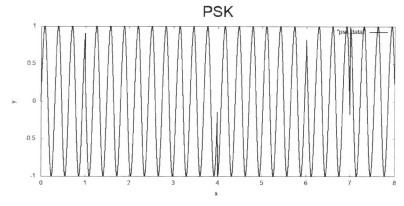

Figure 9.11 – PSK modulation

Next, let's look at **minimum shift keying (MSK)**.

## MSK

The main points related to MSK are as follows:

- **Modulation**: Minimum shift keying.

- **Type**: Digital.

- **How it works**: The amplitude and phase of the carrier are shifted to carry the information.

- **How to recognize it in GNU Radio**: You will see both magnitudes and phase change in the output of a Complex to Mag phase block and quite often, the changes will be in sync. MSK acts on two variables (magnitude and phase) and transmits symbols instead of just bits.

Since MSK is very hard to see in the signal itself (phase jumping especially), here is an AM modulation also sending symbols so that you can understand the difference between a bit and a symbol better (sending 1,0,2,3,1,2,0,1):

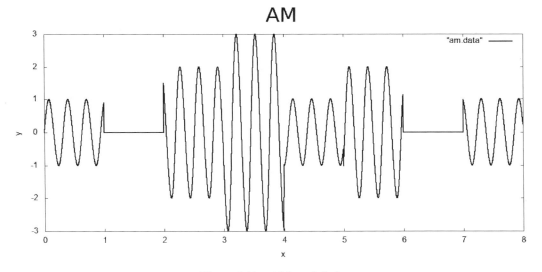

Figure 9.12 – AM modulation

Let's now learn how to get back our signal.

# Getting back to our signal

So, what about our transmitter? We see trains of transmission on the magnitude scope but no obvious variation in length or rhythms in the train; it's not really looking like OOK. Within the pulses (the wagons in the train), we see some variations in amplitude but no real on/off. We don't see clear spikes in frequency, so it's not an x-FSK. The CC2500 datasheet (`https://www.ti.com/lit/ds/swrs040c/swrs040c.pdf`) leaves us with GFSK and MSK as possible modulations.

Let's look into the signal to see whether we can identify one of these two:

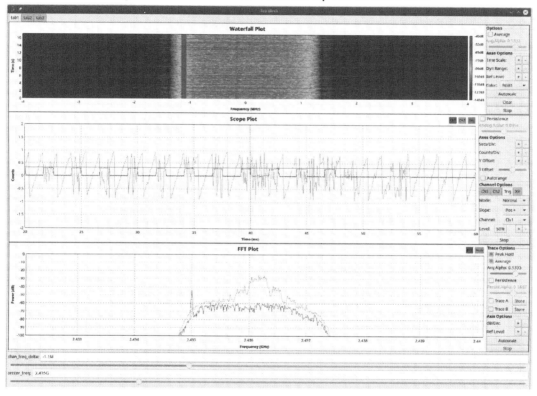

Figure 9.13 – Looking into the CC2500 signal

Let's look into GFSK. GFSK stands for Gaussian FSK; it is basically the same as FSK with a filter that ensures a smooth transition between the frequencies, hiding the very clear spikes we can see in simple FSK (in the preceding figure: FFT plot/waterfall plot).

MSK is using both amplitude and phase to carry the information and we don't see multiple "heights" in the trains that were output by the Mag^2 block (in the scope plot).

It doesn't show something that would contradict it being GFSK.

# Demodulating the signal

At this point, GFSK and MSK are still possible candidates (since we had amplitude variations in the pulses). Let's adjust our filtering to just see the signal. Add a file sink to your GNU Radio flowgraph (grab a file sync block in the GUI and route the output of the final block to the input of the file sink; the filename is in the file sink block options) and capture an emission.

Open your output file in Audacity (**File | Import | Raw data | 32-bit float**) and adjust your sample rate to the one you used in your flowgraph. The file in Audacity looks as follows:

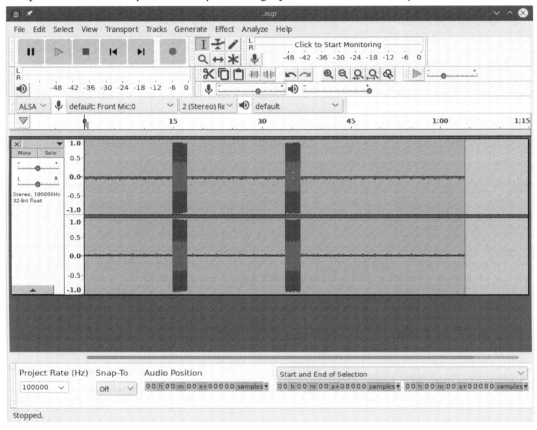

Figure 9.14 – Signal in Audacity

You can now trim the file to keep just the emission. Export it as **Other uncompressed file | RAW headerless | 32bits float**.

Now, let's work on this isolated sample to try to demodulate it.

GFSK is frequency-based, so if we try to demodulate the cut sample with a quadrature demod block, we should see something significant. Let's output it to a file sink after the quadrature demod (`sampled-simpleqdemod.grc`) and open it in baudline:

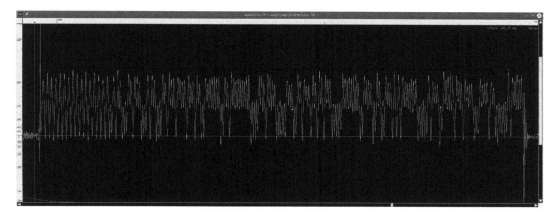

Figure 9.15 – Output of the attempted quadrature demod in baudline

Now we can see trains in the waveform window. We are going in the right direction. At this point, we have a little problem; we need to measure the time width that the smallest peaks take but the signal is so fast that baudline's ruler (on top of the waveform window) cannot go that low (it is graduated in milliseconds).

Well, we will then lie to baudline and load the file with a sample rate divided by 1,000. Let's say that I sampled the signal at 2 MS/s; that means that there are 2 million samples per second. If we load our file at 2 MS/s, it will appear 1,000 times slower in baudline, meaning that we can now use the ruler and replace the units with microseconds.

When we measure the fastest peaks (at the head of a train, they are called the preamble and are there to allow clock synchronization), we find that they are 8 µsec wide. As is, it would be 125 Kbauds, a data rate that is supported by the CC2500, which means we are still consistent! So now we have a good candidate for the baudrate. Let's refilter the demodulated signal (125e3 width and half of this in the cutoff; see `sampled-simpleqdemod-refilterbds.grc`).

It looks quite okay for the quadrature demodulation of a GFSK signal! Maybe it's still FSK but we didn't see the signal well in the FFT. When looking into an unknown signal, keep in mind that your assumptions are still assumptions; backtracking on them is not a bad thing. At this point, we don't really know whether it is GFSK or FSK. Let's keep in mind that the modulations are quite close (frequency with transition smoothing for GFSK; maybe we can get away with just treating it as FSK).

Here is how it looks in baudline:

Figure 9.16 – Checking the baudrate in baudline

Now, let's center our signal (the train is not alternating around 0 and we need that to decode it). So, let's add an `add const` block in front of a scope sink in GNU Radio and let's center it around 0:

1. Enable the scope sink.

2. Disable the file sink.

3. Enable repeats in the file source in `sampled-simpleqdemod-refilterbds.grc`.

Here is the zero-centered signal (before, the bottom of the signal was at 0, while now the signal is alternating around 0):

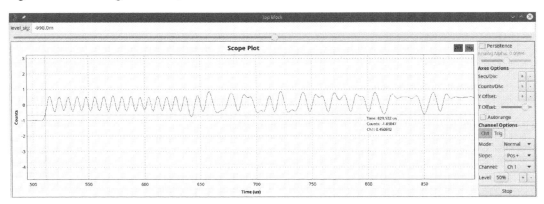

Figure 9.17 – Zero-centered signal

Now we need to use a Muller & Muller clock recovery block (Clock Recovery MM; the details are covered later in the chapter):

First, we need to know how many samples we have per symbol. I was sampling at 2 MS/s and the peak is 8 μsec: 2e6 * 9e-6 = 16 samples per symbol.

Let's bit-slice the output and sink it to a file. When we look into this file, we see that we indeed have output bits (1 byte per byte), but we don't see the preamble (usually 010101 or 101010)! We either did something wrong when processing the signal or one of our assumptions was bad. When we look back at the signal, we see that the preamble is looking just like sine, not regular pulses. This means that it is probably Manchester encoded! Do you remember Manchester encoding? The encoding is in the direction of the change.

One peak like that is 2.4 bits (to say almost 2.5 bits) in Manchester, so let's correct our baudrate to 125*2.4 = 300 Kbauds. Let's try this with our manual processing; let's add a GFSK block in parallel and plot it to see whether GNU Radio is doing a better job at this than us:

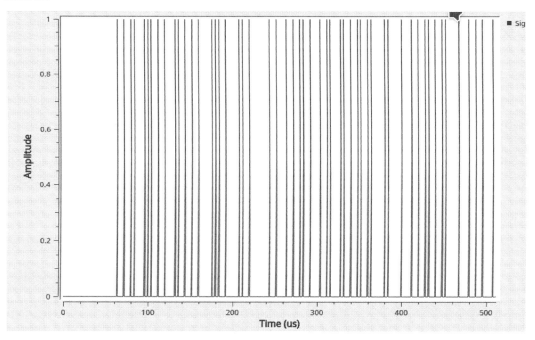

Figure 9.18 – Attempted demodulated signal

No dice, we don't get the preamble either, but when we look at the waveform, it is kind of unstable. There is something to it but there is definitely something wrong with the signal processing. Now, the waveform in the preceding screenshot is kind of looking like what I had when I was looking at the amplitude. I'll recapture the signal at a better sampling rate (10 MS/s) and look into OOK again.

When looking into it, actually the amplitude is looking more stable; was it OOK in the end and did I go on a wild goose chase? (Totally something that happens when I try to devise what modulation is in use.) If I do a complex to mag squared, with a line level correction a Clock Recovery MM, and reevaluate the baudrate ((10e6 * 9e-6)/2.5 = 36 samples per symbol, which is 277,777 bauds, which is possible but we'll try 40 samples per symbol too since humans like round numbers), then I really have something that looks like a preamble! It works at 40 samples per symbol!

This wild goose chase had the merit of allowing us to go through the different common modulations and to give us a leg up on how to identify a modulation!

# Clock Recovery MM

Muller & Muller Clock Recovery is notoriously tricky to set up (and finicky; it is sensitive to signal level, for example). Let's have a look at the parameters and documentation of Clock Recovery MM:

- The documentation says the following:

  *"The peak to peak input signal amplitude must be symmetrical about zero", " M&M timing error detector (TED) is a decision directed TED, and this block uses a symbol decision slicer referenced at zero."*

  The signal must be centered on zero.

  *"The input signal peak amplitude should be controlled to a consistent level (e.g. +/- 1.0) before this block to achieve consistent results for given gain settings; as the TED's output error signal is directly affected by the input amplitude."*

  Signal conditioning for MM is *very* important. Signal normalization is crucial (we need to have a signal that is roughly symmetrical, without "big peaks").

- **Omega (ω)**: Sample per symbol (that is, symbol rate), but it is an initial estimate. Clock Recovery MM is actually an adaptative filter; omega can and will change a little during the signal processing.

- **Mu (μ)**: Initial phase. This is not important; it will change very rapidly internally, and we don't know the phase of the signal, so leave it at 0.

- **Mu gain**: The gain in the phase feedback loop.

- **Omega gain**: The gain in the frequency/sample per symbols feedback loop.

- **Omega relative limit**: The maximum variation of omega we want.

> **Note**
>
> Wow, this is a lot to digest. The original article
> (`https://pdfs.semanticscholar.org/`
> `ef0a/539a61e05df52faeeeb8ca408e2f12575a8b.pdf`) is a
> nightmare of mathematical formulas that needs a good day to read and another
> to reread and digest. It is a lot but I really encourage you to invest the time and
> effort.

So, is there something more practical for asynchronous analysis?

# WPCR

Definitely! Let's have a look a Michael Ossmann's **Whole Packet Clock Recovery**
(**WPCR**) tool (`https://github.com/mossmann/clock-recovery`).

The tool needs files that contain one burst. I reused Michael's burst detection flowgraph
that he showed at GRCon16 (available here: `https://www.youtube.com/`
`watch?v=rQkBDMeODHc`).

Let's try the tool on our trimmed sample file:

```
./clock-recovery/wpcr.py file7_0_0.02444290.dat
peak frequency index: 230 / 9197
samples per symbol: 39.986957 *
clock cycles per sample: 0.025008
clock phase in cycles between 1st and 2nd samples: 0.104727
clock phase in cycles at 1st sample: 0.092223
symbol count: 231
[0, 0, 1, 0, 1, 0, 1, 0, 1, 0, 1, 0, 1, 0, 1, 0, 1, 0, 1, 0, 1,
0, 1, 0, 1, 0, 1, 0, 1, 0, 1, 0, 1, 0, 0, 1, 0, 1, 1, 0, 0, 0,
1, 1, 0, 1, 1, 1, 0, 0, 0, 1, 0, 1, 1, 0, 0, 0, 1, 1, 0, 1, 1,
1, 0, 1, 1, 1, 1, 0, 1, 1, 1, 0, 1, 1, 0, 0, 1, 1, 1, 1, 1, 1,
1, 0, 0, 1, 1, 0, 1, 1, 1, 1, 1, 1, 1, 1, 0, 0, 0, 0, 1, 1,
1, 0, 1, 1, 1, 1, 0, 0, 0, 0, 0, 1, 1, 1, 0, 0, 1, 1, 0, 1, 1,
1, 0, 1, 1, 0, 1, 1, 0, 1, 1, 1, 0, 0, 0, 0, 0, 1, 1, 1, 1, 1,
1, 1, 1, 0, 0, 1, 1, 1, 1, 0, 0, 1, 1, 0, 0, 1, 1, 1, 0, 1, 0,
1, 0, 1, 1, 1, 1, 1, 1, 1, 0, 0, 0, 0, 0, 1, 0, 1, 1, 1, 0, 0,
1, 1, 1, 1, 1, 0, 1, 1, 1, 0, 1, 1, 1, 1, 0, 0, 0, 1, 1, 1, 1,
0, 1, 1, 0, 0, 0, 0, 0, 0, 1, 0, 1, 1, 1, 1, 1, 0, 0, 0, 0, 0]
```

And we got it! WPCR managed to find data on and in the transmission. We got the symbol rate and the number of symbols and it extracted the data! Now you have the tools you need to start decoding radio transmissions! This is not a simple matter and a lot of trial and error is involved if you don't have a formal signal processing background (don't worry, I don't have one either).

# Sending it back

If your hardware supports it, you can record a sample file with a file sink. This can easily be played back using your device as a sink instead of a source (file source -> Osmocom sink GNU Radio block for `hackrf`, for example). Just be sure that you are keeping the same sampling rate! You can also create modulated signals from Python (or any programming language) to send arbitrary signals.

Before sending anything, be sure to check the following:

- Check that it is legal in your country depending on the frequency (on 2.4 GHz, it is (`https://en.wikipedia.org/wiki/ISM_band`) if you respect the on-air time).

- That you are not disturbing other receivers around you. Be very wary of the strength of the signal you are sending!

   You can use a Faraday cage (a metallic container to isolate radio signals) for most of your tests by using a discarded microwave (for 2.4 GHz) or find/build one yourself for cheap (ammo cans, a big metallic paint pot with a few holes for the cables, and more). There are a lot of guides available on the internet.

In order to send back data that you captured (that is, a replay attack), you can use the data you captured (from a file source in GNU Radio) and link the output to an appropriate sink.

# Summary

SDR provides you with a very powerful (albeit relatively complex) way to interact with arbitrary radio signals used by your target embedded system. In this chapter, we were able to go over the hardware you may need, building simple antennas that fit the signal frequency you want to interact with and the different signal modulations. This is a complex field that will require you to study very actively its intricacies to be used to the fullest extent of its power (and pass certifications to be able to send signals) but will allow you to interact with the communications at a very intimate level.

In the next chapter, we will go back to tinkering with circuits and will look into the typical debug interfaces we can use to interact with processors.

# Questions

1.  What is the difference between encryption and encoding?

2.  What is an FFT? What does it do?

3.  What is a modulation scheme?

4.  What are the characteristics of an SDR platform that you should take into account before buying?

5.  If the half- and quarter-wavelength antennas work, why not use a wavelength antenna?

# Section 3: Attacking the Software

After reading this section, you will know how to access debug interfaces, be familiar with the basics of reversing a firmware image, be able to identify common executable formats, and be capable of altering a system's behavior on the fly with on-chip debugging.

This section comprises the following chapters:

# 10
# Accessing the Debug Interfaces

Most **microcontrollers (MCUs)** come with some sort of debugging/programming interface. The *standard* interface is called **JTAG (Joint Test Action Group)**. It is an industry standard and is usually present in chips with a pin count high enough to support it. **Serial Wire Debug (SWD)** is a derivative of JTAG for lower-count chips. Some vendors also have their own variants (DebugWIRE for Atmels, Spy-Bi-Wire (serialized JTAG) on TI's MSP430s, PICs ICSP, and others). Now how do we find them, access them, and use them? This is what we will discuss in this chapter.

In this chapter, we will first cover the JTAG protocol and then learn how to find the JTAG pins. We will then learn how to install and use OpenOCD. Toward the end of the chapter, we will also cover some practical use cases.

In this chapter, we will cover the following topics:

- What is JTAG used for?
- The JTAG protocol
- Finding JTAG pins/test points
- ARM JTAG – TAPs and the debug engine in OpenOCD
- OpenOCD: usage and scripting

# Technical requirements

- An FDTI2232 board (with the appropriate udev rules – you know how to do it)

- A bluepill

- A JTAGulator

- An unknown device on which you found a JTAG port (WRT45G boards, a development board, and so on). Basically, go to your local flea market and buy *advanced* junk (such as modems, set-top boxes, and media players). Not only will it train you with your components opening and identification skills, but you will also have real devices to hack. Remember, these are not just knowledge-based skills but something you do with your hands!

Yes, your significant other will probably get angry at the mess. However, a good side effect is that, now, you know how to get rid of your e-waste properly.

Check out the following link to see the Code in Action video:

```
https://bit.ly/3rdYE6c
```

# Debugging/programming protocols – What are they and what are they used for?

The in-circuit debugging protocols have legitimate usages that we can use and abuse for our tests. First, let's see how they are supposed to be used.

## Legitimate usage

The debug protocols are used to achieve multiple goals and some are listed here:

- Test the physical soldering of the boards (this was the initial goal of JTAG).

- Program the chips in development or production.

- Help in debugging the programs during development.

Since the board will have the main micro-controller interact with the chips that are on the circuit board, it can be hard to develop in a completely simulated environment. This is because, unlike a general-purpose computer, there is almost no commonality between two different boards (a general-purpose computer has an OS and this OS provides a good layer of hardware abstraction).

# Using JTAG to attack a system

The test subsystem is a very interesting target for us since it will provide us with the means to interact with (and alter) the inner workings of a system.

## Understanding the JTAG protocol

Since JTAG will allow us to debug the chip, it is a very handy attack point. Let's look into it.

JTAG is a *daisy-chained* serial protocol with 4 (or 5) signals:

- **TDI (Test Data In)**: The debug data enters the chip from this signal/pin.
- **TDO (Test Data Out)**: The debug data exits the chip from this signal/pin.
- **TCLK (Test CLocK)**: The serial clock.
- **TMS (Test Mode Select)**: Manages the state of the JTAG engine.
- **TRST (Test ReSeT)**: (optional).

The following diagram shows how multiple devices are daisy-chained and the general architecture of a JTAG bus:

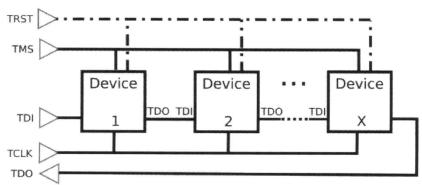

Figure 10.1 – JTAG bus architecture

Each device will have a shift register expecting data from TDI and output data on TDO (of course, clocked by TCLK). This whole structure is called a **scan chain**.

Each engine must adhere to the following state machine; the transitions (0,1) are determined by the state of the TMS signal:

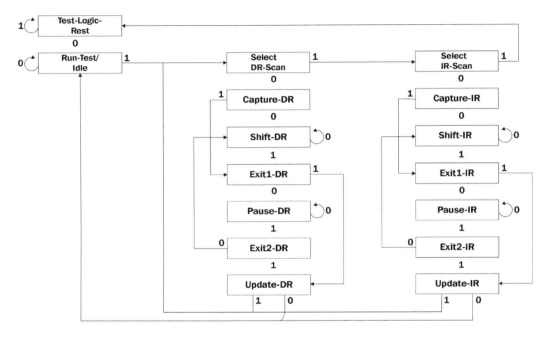

Figure 10.2 – JTAG state machine

All devices' states (and transitions) are managed by toggling the TMS state and cycling the clock, just like SPI.

The JTAG standard (IEEE 1149.1) states that the transitions are done on the falling edge of the TCLK signal, but the sampling is done on the raising edge (that is, the TMS value is read on the transition from low to high and applied on the transition from high to low).

The states mean the following:

- **Test-Logic-Reset**: Where the test logic is reset.
- **Select-IR-scan**: The state that allows entering the instruction register logic.
- **Select-DR-scan**: The state that allows entering the data register logic.
- **capture-xR**: First, state a register logic branch. It mainly allows you to enter the pause state before shifting data in the register if you want to (going through `exit1`, pause as much as you want, then `exit2`, then shift).

- **pause-xR**: Allows you to pause the shifting.

- **exit1 and exit2**: Allows you to exit or return to shifting.

- **update-xR**: Commits the data you shifted to the real register.

Let's understand the instruction register in the next section.

## Understanding the JTAG registers – instruction register

The **instruction register** (**IR**) contains (as its name implies) instructions. It is sampled in the Shift-IR state (on the raising edge).

The standard defines mandatory instructions as shown in the following table:

| Instruction name | Usual value | Description |
| --- | --- | --- |
| BYPASS | All ones (the standard advises all zeros but I've never seen it in reality) | Inserts a 1-bit register between TDI and TDO. The device becomes transparent to the scan chain. This can only be exited by resetting the device or debug engine. |
| EXTEST | Implementation defined | Outputs the value inserted with PRELOAD to the output pins. |
| PRELOAD | Implementation defined | Preloads a value to output on the pins. |
| SAMPLE | Implementation defined | Samples a representative state (can be the values on the pins or otherwise; this is defined in the device's documentation) into DR. |

Other instructions are defined but optional for standard compliance (and hence are not necessarily supported by all chips):

| Instruction name | Usual value | Description |
| --- | --- | --- |
| INTEST | Implementation defined | Internal test of the flip-flops and logic of the chip. This is targeted at the internal testing of the chip's silicon (usually used with micro probing). Sometimes it can lead to unexpected results. |
| RUNBIST | Implementation defined | Runs the chip's internal self-test logic. |
| CLAMP | Implementation defined | Clamps the outputs to the values set in the DR register and sets the chip in bypass mode (1-bit register between TDI and TDO). |
| IDCODE | Implementation defined | Returns the 32-bit IDCODE of the chip (that is, a 32-bit model number if you want). |
| USERCODE | Implementation defined | Returns the 32-bit USERCODE of the chip (that is, a 32-user programmable identification number if you want). |
| ECIDCODE | Implementation defined | Returns the 32-bit ECIDCODE of the chip (that is, a factory-programmed chip (silicon die) identification number). |
| HIGHZ | Implementation defined | Sets the in/output pins in high resistance (high impedance) mode: (almost) no current can flow through them. |
| INIT_SETUP | Implementation defined | Configures on-chip resources for I/O. |
| INIT_SETUP_CLAMP | Implementation defined | Configures on-chip resources for I/O and clamps (like the CLAMP instruction). |
| INIT_RUN | Implementation defined | Exists when INIT_SETUP needs some time before the initialization sequence (then it starts the sequence). |
| CLAMP_HOLD | Implementation defined | The **Test Mode Persistence** (**TMP**) controller clamps I/O. |
| CLAMP_RELEASE | Implementation defined | The TMP controller releases I/O. |
| TMP_STATUS | Implementation defined | Returns the status of the TMP controller. |
| IC_RESET | Implementation defined | Resets the chip. |

Let's now look at the data register.

## Understanding the JTAG registers – data register

The **data register** (**DR**) holds, well... data. It is used to enter the data needed by an instruction or to read the data returned by an instruction. The data is shifted in and out of the register in the Shift-DR state machine state.

## JTAG adapter

As I indicated in *Chapter 1, Setting Up Your Pentesting Lab and Ensuring Lab Safety*, in the different lab levels, there are a lot of JTAG adapters available. The main difference between them lies in the software packages (or lack thereof) that are provided, the list of chips supported by the vendor (for closed source software packages, if your target chip is not supported, you are out in the cold), their speed, and their price. Here is a small comparison of the adapters I know and use/have used:

- **SEGGER J-Link**:

  - **Pros**: One of the most popular in the professional world. It is fast and supports a large variety of chips. The software is available for all three major OSes (Windows/Linux/macOS).

  - **Con**: Price; closed source.

- **Black Magic Probe**:

  - **Pros**: Acts as a GDB server; open source. It's possible to use the firmware on a bluepill with some fixes.

  - **Cons**: Only supports ARM chips.

- **FTDI based adapters (FTDI2232 breakouts, JTAGkey, Olimex's JTAG, and others)**:

  - **Pros**: Very common, very cheap, very flexible; supported by OpenOCD; no firmware (chip support is done on the PC, allowing you to easily add/change things).

  - **Cons**: Needs manual setup; can be intimidating the first few times.

To be honest, you should start by buying an FTDI2232H breakout board (in the $10-15 range on your favorite bidding website). Not only is this what I will use in the examples but it is cheap (so you have no fear of killing it) and it will allow you to learn the most since everything happens because you set it up. It is the adapter that gives you a good opportunity to learn since there is almost no "behind-the-scenes" magic happening.

## A note on SWD

**Single wire debug** (**SWD**) is common on chips where the pin count is reduced (pin count is tightly linked to chip price). This version is used to reduce the number of pins used for debugging. To simplify, SWD is a serialized version of JTAG where the TDI/TDO/TMS signals are multiplexed in the serial data. SWD signals are data (SWDIO) and clock (SWDCLK); an SWDO (trace port) signal is optional. Please note that the SWD topology is not serial (the chips are not one after the other in a daisy-chain) but a star topology.

## Other debug protocols

Sometimes, you will evaluate a product that doesn't seem to use JTAG or SWD. Some other (non-ARM) vendors sometimes have specific debug/programming protocols and the companion hardware and software packages:

- **Spy-by-wire**: Texas implementation of a serialized JTAG (mainly used on MSP430)
- **DebugWIRE**: ATMEL SPI debug protocol for AVR microcontrollers
- Microchip PICs ICSP protocol (also SPI-like)

This is just here to make you aware of their existence and to the fact that there is more than JTAG on the market.

# Finding the pins

To connect to the JTAG pins, you first have to find them! It is a common practice among vendors not to label the pins on the debug ports, not to populate resistors on production boards to avoid JTAG access, or even not to route the pins at all! In this section, we will go through the best-case scenario (the debug port is a standard, recognizable port) to the worst practical case (pins are there but not labeled, or dispersed on test pads). It is possible that the pins are not routed at all (that is, no trace is connecting the chip's pins to an externally reachable connector), or even worse, a BGA chip has no trace when getting the debug signal from the underside of the chip (in this case, there isn't a lot you can do).

# The PCB "plays nicely"

Sometimes typical debug ports can be found on the PCBs, labeled on the silkscreen or not.

Typical JTAG ports' pinouts look like this:

- **ARM 10 pins (JTAG + SWD)**:

| 1 | VCC | TMS/SWDIO | 2 |
|---|-----|-----------|---|
| 3 | GND | TCLK/SWCLK | 4 |
| 5 | GND | TDO/SWO | 6 |
| 7 | RTCK/NA | TDI/NA | 8 |
| 9 | GND | RESET | 10 |

- **ST 14 pins**

| 1 | /JEN | /TRST | 2 |
|---|------|-------|---|
| 3 | GND | NA | 4 |
| 5 | TDI | TSTAT | 6 |
| 7 | VCC | /RST | 8 |
| 9 | TMS | GND | 10 |
| 11 | TCLK | GND | 12 |
| 13 | TDO | /TERR | 14 |

- **Infineon OCDS 16 pins**

| 1 | TMS | VCC | 2 |
|---|-----|-----|---|
| 3 | TDO | GND | 4 |
| 5 | CPUCLK | GND | 6 |
| 7 | TDI | RESET | 8 |
| 9 | TRST | /BRKOUT | 10 |
| 11 | TCLK | GND | 12 |
| 13 | /BRKIN | OCDSE | 14 |
| 15 | TRAP1 | TRAP2 (orGND) | 16 |

- **ARM 20 pins (JTAG + SWD)**:

| 1 | VCC | | VCC | 2 |
| --- | --- | --- | --- | --- |
| 3 | TRST/NA | | GND | 4 |
| 5 | TDI/NA | | GND | 6 |
| 7 | TMS/SWDIO | | GND | 8 |
| 9 | TCLK/SWCLK | | GND | 10 |
| 11 | RTCK/NA | | GND | 12 |
| 13 | TDO/SWO | | GND | 14 |
| 15 | RESET | | GND | 16 |
| 17 | NA | | GND | 18 |
| 19 | NA | | GND | 20 |

You can find more information on these connectors at the following links:

- `http://infocenter.arm.com/help/topic/com.arm.doc.faqs/attached/13634/cortex_debug_connectors.pdf`

- `https://www.infineon.com/dgdl/AP2400123_ocds_level1_jtag[1].pdf`

The debugging signals available on the typical connectors are as follows:

| /JEN | Not JTAG enabled (enabled on low; STMicroelectronics-specific). |
|------|------|
| /OCDSE | Not (Infineon's) On-Chip Debug Support enabled (enabled on low, Infineon-specific). |
| /RST | Not chip reset (reset on low, STMicroelectronics-specific). |
| /TERR | Not test error (error on low). |
| /TRST | Not test reset (reset on low). |
| /BRKIN | Not break input and OCDS configuration (break triggered on low). |
| /BRKOUT | Not break output (break happens on low). |
| CPUCLK | CPU Clock, on the Infineon connector. This is an output, allowing you to synchronize with the CPU clock. |
| GND | Ground. |
| NA | Not applicable / not connected. |
| RESET | Reset. |
| RTCK | Test clock return. This is not mandatory but allows you to verify that everything is fine with the clock. |
| SWCLK | SWD clock signal. |
| SWDIO | SWD serial data signal. |
| SWO | (Optional) SWD output, allows the CPU to output other serial data (such as human-readable text, and so on). |
| TCLK | Test Clock. |
| TDI | Test Data In. |
| TDO | Test Data Out. |
| TMS | JTAG TMS. |
| TRAP1/2 | Sometimes used by the application. |
| TRST | Test Reset. |
| TSTAT | Status of the in-circuit debugger (STMicroelectronics-specific). |
| VCC | Power. |

TDI, TMS, TRST, and TCLK expect to have a 10,000 pull-up resistor to VCC. Sometimes the PCB provides it; sometimes the PCB expects the JTAG adapter to provide it; sometimes the clip provides it on the pin. There is no rule!

To know who should provide the pull-ups (with the JTAG adapter unplugged from the circuit), do the following:

1.  Power off the PCB completely and measure the resistance between the three pins and VCC. If it in the 5,000-100,000 Ohms range, the PCB provides the pull-up. If it is open circuit (no connection), it is possible that the chip uses an internal, programmable pull-up or that the JTAG adapter is expected to provide the pull-up; continue to *step 2*).

2.  Power the system but keep the MCU in the reset state (push the **Reset** button or keep /RST low), and read the voltage on the TDI, TMS, TRST, and TCLK pins. It should read low (if this is not the case, the CPU could have an internal resistor on the pin, but you should have caught it at *step 1*). If it goes off when you release the /RST signal, the CPU uses an internal, programmable pull-up.

3.  If neither *steps 1* nor *2* are positive, you should provide an external pull-up in the 10,000-100,000 range.

## A bit harder

Sometimes, the JTAG pins will not be available in a nice recognizable connector. If you managed to find the chip's datasheet and you see on it that JTAG pins are available, you will have to get your multimeter, put it in continuity mode, and find pads or test points where the signals are available. If there are none, you can always solder magnet wires to the pins you need and make your own connector!

## Very hard – JTAGulating

Sometimes you don't have a datasheet, or the chip is in a BGA package (and hence the pins, being under that package, aren't reachable/traceable with your multimeter). In this case, you have to search for the following:

*   Test points or unpopulated component footprints (these are/may be used to program the chip with a dedicated jig after soldering) or untented vias (vias that are not covered with solder mask). These are pretty tricky since nothing prevents the designer of the PCBs from spreading the test points apart on the PCB.

*   Nonstandard connectors – most of the standard connectors are two rows but nothing prevents the designer from using a single-row or a triple-row connector; just bear in mind that the strict minimum is as follows:

    - 4 for SWD (SWCLK, SWDIO, RST, and a shared ground)

    - 6 for JTAG (TDI, TDO, TMS, TCLK, RST, and a shared ground)

- Gold finger or traces that reach the border of a PCB and seem to be cut (this can be used to program a whole panel of PCBs before the individual PCBs are broken away from the panel).

- Connector footprints that seem to lead to unpopulated component footprints. It is common to find PCBs where the debug/test connector for development was left unconnected by leaving 0 Ohm resistors unpopulated in the final version once the software and the production process are stable. This is especially common when the firmware is on an external storage chip or if the chip was already programmed before being soldered.

So, basically, you are in a situation where the following apply:

- You don't know if some pins/test points are part of the debug/JTAG.
- You don't know which pins/test points correspond to which signal.

Thankfully, there is a tool for that: Joe Grand's JTAGulator.

Basically, the JTAGulator will brute-force a set of pins in order to determine whether they are part of a JTAG interface (and whether they are a serial interface also, just as a side benefit). The JTAGulator has the benefit of having protected inputs so even if you connect to something that could be dangerous for it (within reasonable limits), there is almost no risk of damaging it.

## Understanding the JTAGulator hardware

To use the JTAGulator board, we need to know a little bit about how it works. Let's look at the board and its functionalities.

Here is a diagram of the main sections on the JTAGulator and what they are used for:

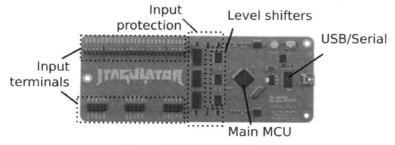

Figure 10.3 – The JTAGulator

The JTAGulator works with a very classical, text-based interface on your USB. By now, you should be pretty comfortable with them and using your favorite terminal client for it.

The first step of connecting the board to your target system is to connect the ground together, as usual (and preferably before powering them up). Then measure the power voltage of the target MCU (or find the voltage in the datasheet). The JTAGulator supports setting the I/O voltage from 1.2 to 3.3 V (the setting is done in the serial interface).

If your voltage falls outside of this range, you can do the following:

- Use one of the voltage translation circuits shown in earlier chapters.
- Use a dedicated chip such as the TI's TXS010x (used by the JTAGulator itself) or LSF10x's, NXP's NTB and LFS family, DI's PI4U family, and others. But check that the voltage range fits your need.

Again, re-read the safety instructions – especially if you are talking with a device that uses a capacitive dropper power circuit on the mains! In my *young hacker* days, I lost a USB hub to that – I could have lost my life!

So, now connect all your suspect pins to the JTAGulator. Power up both systems and connect to the JTAGulator's serial interface (the pins or screw terminals don't make a difference). The interface has a help menu (H) to select the different modes:

- i: IDCODE scan, searches for an IDCODE response (or something that looks similar). This is supposed to be the default content of the DR when the debug engine starts (but it doesn't find all the pins – since it doesn't interact with TDI, it doesn't find it).
- b: BYPASS scan, tries to set the device in BYPASS mode, and hence finds TDI.
- d: Finds all the IDCODEs of the devices in the chain.
- t: Tests BYPASS.
- v: Sets the target voltage (1.2 to 3.3 V).
- u: Searches for the serial interface.
- p: Sets the serial interface in pass-through mode so you can talk to the device through the JTAGulator.

> **Note**
> Do not connect anything to the VADJ pin of the JTAGulator!

An alternative to JTAGulator is JTAGEnum flashed on an Arduino. But this is so, so, so... slow. It is not worth it in a professional environment; invest in a JTAGulator as soon as you can.

## How does it work?

We will first identify the pins (except for TDI) with the JTAGulator. It will do so by going through the following (simplified – some back and forth may be necessary to validate candidates) sequence for all the possible pin arrangements (until a valid arrangement is found):

- Toggles a candidate test reset to have IDCODE in the DR and the state machine in a known state.

- Tries to set the device in DR shift state by wiggling the candidates' TMS and clock.

- Tries to clock the debug engine a bunch of times to see if at least one 32-bit word comes on the pins that are left. Since on reset, the IDCODE is in the DR by default, if it is the case, /TRST, TDO, TCLK, and TMS are identified.

Then we will do a BYPASS scan in order to find TDI. The sequence is quite similar, but it will try to send all ones (BYPASS) to a candidate TDI pin and see if it finds a pattern on the candidate TDO.

This works pretty similarly for UART and allows you to find candidate baud rates.

> **Note**
>
> If you use a lot of pins to scan, JTAGulating can be pretty long. Try to use other methods to eliminate as many pins as possible.

If you are interested in how the JTAGulator works internally, it is open source. Have a look at `http://www.grandideastudio.com/jtagulator/`.

# Using OpenOCD

**Open On-Chip Debugger** (**OpenOCD**), is a piece of software that acts as a bridge between your debugger interface and the JTAG interface. On one side, it will drive your JTAG interface and on the other side, present a standard GDB server that the debugger will use to drive it.

It will translate the debugger command *I want to read a 32-bit value at address X* to a series of zeros and ones your JTAG interface will clock to TDI. The interface gets the answer on TDO and sends it to OpenOCD, which translates it to an answer to GDB, *the value at X is Y*.

As much as the GDB server side is well established and standardized, OpenOCD needs to be able to talk correctly to your adapter and generate the correct series of zeros and ones for your target CPU/MCU. For this, OpenOCD will need the correct configuration. This is done in a series of configuration statements in TCL (`http://openocd.org/doc/html/Tcl-Crash-Course.html`).

OpenOCD configuration files are not simply variable affectation but a complete programming language (we will go through a few examples on our own).

## Installing OpenOCD

There is always an option to rely on your package manager to install OpenOCD. `sudo apt install openocd` (or any variation on the OS you've chosen) will probably work. Since the support for the different debug adapters is flagged at compile time, I will show you how to compile OpenOCD with support for the maximum number of adapters.

OpenOCD relies on a `sourceforge` Git tree: `https://sourceforge.net/p/openocd/code/ci/master/tree/`.

Install the prerequisites and clone it (or download a tarball of a release version if you don't care about the latest developments):

```
$sudo apt-get install libtool make pkg-config autoconf automake
texinfo libusb-dev libftdi-dev
[...]
$git clone --recurse-submodules https://git.code.sf.net/p/
openocd/code openocd-code
[..]
$ cd openocd-code
$./bootstrap
$./configure -help
[...]
```

In the help of `configure`, we see in the optional features that there are a lot of supported adapters, with a lot of options. So, I came up with this little terminal `magic` command that enables all the adapters (that are not deprecated on incompatibles):

```
./configure `./configure --help | egrep -e '^\s+--enable' |
egrep -v '(FEATURE|doxy|dummy|oocd)' | grep building | cut -d '
' -f3 | tr '\n' ' '`
```

It basically builds the options list from the help and disables `doxygen` documentation generation and the dummy adapter. Again, since terminal data processing will be very useful to you, I encourage you to dissect this command to understand how it works (you want to be a hacker, don't you?).

Now you can run `make && sudo make install` as usual.

## The adapter file

Let's set up our adapter and our first scan chain by hand so we can understand how the configuration files work. First, let's find the required documentation:

- The chip's documentation can be found at this link: `https://www.ftdichip.com/Support/Documents/DataSheets/ICs/DS_FT2232H.pdf`.

- Application note for FTDI pins: `https://www.ftdichip.com/Support/Documents/AppNotes/AN_184%20FTDI%20Device%20Input%20Output%20Pin%20States.pdf`.

- Application note for JTAG: `https://www.ftdichip.com/Support/Documents/AppNotes/AN_129_FTDI_Hi_Speed_USB_To_JTAG_Example.pdf`.

- The adapter setup file documentation can be found at this link: `http://openocd.org/doc/html/Debug-Adapter-Configuration.html`.

That's a lot! So, let's have a look at a real setup to understand how it works. The mode used for JTAG is called MPSSE, it is used for SPI-style interfaces. In the pin description file, we can see, in MPSSE, the following:

- ADBUS0 or BDBUS0: TCK

- ADBUS1 or BDBUS1: TDI

- ADBUS2 or BDBUS2: TDO

- ADBUS3 or BDBUS3: TMS

OpenOCD takes this into account so we don't have to make the link explicitly between the pin and the JTAG signal.

> **Note**
> Please note that nothing is preset for nTRST; we will have a general-purpose I/O for this.

Let's look at the adapter file I use for my FTDI2232H breakout board:

```
interface ftdi                         # the interface driver is ftdi
ftdi_vid_pid 0x0403 0x6010             # indicates the usb identifiers
ftdi_layout_init 0x0c08 0x0f1b                              # 1)
ftdi_layout_signal nTRST -data 0x0100 -noe 0x0400   # 2)
ftdi_layout_signal nSRST -data 0x0200 -noe 0x0800   # 3)
adapter_khz 2000                       # speed of the
adapter
```

The preceding code is explained in the following list:

1.  `ftdi_layout_init`: This allows OCD to set up the pins of the chip. Let's look at what the values mean:

| Description | Hex value | Bit7 | Bit6 | Bit5 | Bit4 | Bit3 | Bit2 | Bit1 | Bit0 | Effect |
|---|---|---|---|---|---|---|---|---|---|---|
| Output initial state high byte | 0x0C | 0 | 0 | 0 | 0 | 1 | 1 | 0 | 0 | AC2 and AC3 are high. |
| Output initial state low byte | 0x08 | 0 | 0 | 0 | 0 | 1 | 0 | 0 | 0 | AD3 is high. |
| Output direction high byte | 0x0F | 0 | 0 | 0 | 0 | 1 | 1 | 1 | 1 | AC0, AC1, AC2, and AC3 are outputs. |
| Output direction low byte | 0x1B | 0 | 0 | 0 | 1 | 1 | 0 | 1 | 1 | AD0, AD1, AD3, and AD4 are outputs. |

2.  `ftdi_layout_signal nTRST`: (Inverse) test reset signal – nTRST – is mapped on AC0 and (inverse) enabled on AC3.

3.  `ftdi_layout_signal nSRST`: (Inverse) system reset signal – nSRST – is mapped on AC1 and (inverse) enabled on AC4.

Here, we can see that this tells OpenOCD where to map which JTAG signal on the chip and how fast to use it.

# The target file

Let's have a look at a familiar target: The STM32F103 that is on the bluepill. The comments in italics are mine; the normal ones come from the OpenOCD file.

Let's see what the different steps are in the file:

1.  Defining the scan chain:

```
source [find target/swj-dp.tcl]          # defines functions
to
                                          # use either JTAG
or SWD
source [find mem_helper.tcl]              # defines shortcuts
mmw,
                                          # mrb, mrw
if { [info exists CHIPNAME] } {           # defines a _
CHIPNAME
                                          # variable
    set _CHIPNAME $CHIPNAME
} else {
    set _CHIPNAME stm32f1x
}
set _ENDIAN little        # tells openOCD the target
endianness
if { [info exists WORKAREASIZE] } {    # defines RAM used
for
                                      # flash programming
    set _WORKAREASIZE $WORKAREASIZE
} else {
    set _WORKAREASIZE 0x1000
}
#jtag scan chain
if { [info exists CPUTAPID] } {
    set _CPUTAPID $CPUTAPID
} else {
    if { [using_jtag] } {
        set _CPUTAPID 0x3ba00477          # See STM Document
                                          # RM0008 Section
26.6.3
    } {
        set _CPUTAPID 0x1ba01477      # this is the SW-DP
tap
                                      # id not the jtag tap
```

```
id
  }
}
```

2.  Defining the chips:

```
swj_newdap $_CHIPNAME cpu -irlen 4 -ircapture 0x1 -irmask
0xf -expected-id $_CPUTAPID
 #uses the function defined in swj-dp to
 #define a new test access port for jtag or
 #define a new debug access port for swd
if {[using_jtag]} {
  jtag newtap $_CHIPNAME bs -irlen 5 # for jtag defines
the boundary scan tap
}
set _TARGETNAME $_CHIPNAME.cpu
target create $_TARGETNAME cortex_m -endian $_ENDIAN
-chain-position $_TARGETNAME
$_TARGETNAME configure -work-area-phys 0x20000000 -work-
area-size $_WORKAREASIZE -work-area-backup 0
 #0x20000000 is the start of the ram
# flash size will be probed
set _FLASHNAME $_CHIPNAME.flash
flash bank $_FLASHNAME stm32f1x 0x08000000 0 0 0 $_
TARGETNAME
 #0x80000000 is the start of the flash
```

3.  Configuring our adapter's speed and target event handlers:

```
# JTAG speed should be <= F_CPU/6. F_CPU after reset is
8MHz,
# so use F_JTAG = 1MHz
adapter_khz 1000
adapter_nsrst_delay 100
if {[using_jtag]} {
 jtag_ntrst_delay 100
}
reset_config srst_nogate
if {![using_hla]} {arm6 arm7 arm8
```

```
  # if srst is not fitted use SYSRESETREQ to
  # perform a soft reset
  cortex_m reset_config sysresetreq
}
$_TARGETNAME configure -event examine-end {
  # DBGMCU_CR |= DBG_WWDG_STOP | DBG_IWDG_STOP |
  # DBG_STANDBY | DBG_STOP | DBG_SLEEP
  mmw 0xE0042004 0x00000307 0
}
$_TARGETNAME configure -event trace-config {
  # Set TRACE_IOEN; TRACE_MODE is set to async; when using
sync
  # change this value accordingly to configure trace pins
  # assignment
  mmw 0xE0042004 0x00000020 0
}
```

That is a lot!

But if we read through it, we can see two main stages:

1. Preparation of the data for the TAP

2. Setup of the TAP

Let's connect our adapter to the bluepill based on the connections shown in the following table:

| Signal | PIN bluepill (marking) | PIN FDTI (marking) |
|--------|------------------------|--------------------|
| TMS    | PA13 / SWDIO           | ADBUS3 (ad3)       |
| TDI    | PA15                   | ADBUS1 (ad1)       |
| TDO    | PB3                    | ADBUS2 (ad2)       |
| TCK    | PA14/SWCLK             | ADBUS0 (ad0)       |
| nTRST  | PB4                    | ACBUS0 (ac0)       |
| nSRST  | Reset pin (R usually)  | ACBUS1 (ac1)       |
| GND    | GND                    | GND                |

Let's launch OpendOCD with our configuration:

```
$openocd -f ./ch10/ftdi2232h.tcl -f /usr/local/share/openocd/
scripts/target/stm32f1x.Cfg
Open On-Chip Debugger 0.10.0
[...]
adapter speed: 1000 kHz
adapter_nsrst_delay: 100
jtag_ntrst_delay: 100
none separate
cortex_m reset_config sysresetreq
Info : clock speed 1000 kHz
Info : JTAG tap: stm32f1x.cpu tap/device found:
0x4ba00477 (mfg: 0x23b (ARM Ltd.), part: 0xba00, ver: 0x4)
Warn : JTAG tap: stm32f1x.cpu UNEXPECTED: 0x4ba00477 (mfg:
0x23b (ARM Ltd.), part: 0xba00, ver: 0x4)
Error: JTAG tap: stm32f1x.cpu expected 1 of 1: 0x3ba00477 (mfg:
0x23b (ARM Ltd.), part: 0xba00, ver: 0x3)
Info : JTAG tap: stm32f1x.bs tap/device found: 0x16410041 (mfg:
0x020 (STMicroelectronics), part: 0x6410, ver: 0x1)
Error: Trying to use configured scan chain anyway...
Warn : Bypassing JTAG setup events due to errors
Info : stm32f1x.cpu: hardware has 6 breakpoints, 4 watchpoints
```

But something is wrong here! The IDCODE is wrong (UNEXPECTED: 0x4ba00477)! What is happening? Actually, I took one of my boards with a CSK STM32F103 clone instead of a genuine ST. It's convenient to show you what happens with an incorrect IDCODE, isn't it?

With the genuine ST board, it works normally without signaling the wrong IDCODE:

```
$openocd -f ./ch10/ftdi2232h.tcl -f /usr/local/share/openocd/
scripts/target/stm32f1x.Cfg
Open On-Chip Debugger 0.10.0
[...]
adapter speed: 1000 kHz
adapter_nsrst_delay: 100
jtag_ntrst_delay: 100
none separate
```

```
cortex_m reset_config sysresetreq
Info : clock speed 1000 kHz
Info : JTAG tap: stm32f1x.cpu tap/device found: 0x3ba00477
(mfg: 0x23b (ARM Ltd.), part: 0xba00, ver: 0x4)
Info : JTAG tap: stm32f1x.bs tap/device found: 0x16410041 (mfg:
0x020 (STMicroelectronics), part: 0x6410, ver: 0x1)
Info : stm32f1x.cpu: hardware has 6 breakpoints, 4 watchpoints
```

If your board has a clone, adapt the config file to use the correct IDCODE.

Now that we have seen how to connect to a device we know and already have the setup files for use with OpenOCD, let's look into how it works and what we can do with it.

## OpenOCD interfaces

OpenOCD will open three ports on your computer's local interfaces:

- A GDB server (usually port 3333): It expects connections from GDB.

- A telnet interface (usually port 4444): You can connect to it with telnet. It expects manual OpenOCD commands, which are documented here: http://openocd. org/doc/html/General-Commands.html.

- A TCL remote server (usually port 5555): You can automate things through it by connecting with a script. Templates (Python and Haskell) can be found in the contrib/rpc_example directory of the OpenOCD source.

## Defining convenience functions for OpenOCD

When invoking OpenOCD, you can add as many -f directives as you like. I find it very useful to make my own convenience functions in TCL for some basic utility functions. If you are not familiar with the TCL (pronounced tickle, hence the feather logo...) language, please refer to https://www.tcl.tk/man/tcl8.5/tutorial/ tcltutorial.html.

Please note that the tk gui functions are not available in OpenOCD's embedded TCL interpreter.

# Practical case

Let's have a look at a DSL modem (an ABB 560NM that I bought from my local flea market) that is sporting a JTAG connector. If you can't find the same modem, you will have to find a random piece of hardware with a JTAG connector. This will be a very good exercise in locating them.

Opening the case and going through the chip, I could easily identify the main CPU as a Samsung S3C4530A (the markings have not been removed; it is a big chip with Samsung and ARM markings and SC4530A is pretty visible). A bit of internet research scores the datasheet for this chip. It is sold as an *"Integrated system for embedded Ethernet applications"* and that fits the bill pretty nicely for a DSL modem. The datasheet is inside the ch10 folder of the repository.

Next to it, there is an already populated 10-pin connector that is not connected to anything on the system. It smells like JTAG!

Here, I can approach it in two ways:

- I can use my JTAGulator – it is fast and easy.

- Or I can use the fact that I have the datasheet to trace the JTAG pins of the CPU (indicated in the datasheet) to the header pins with the continuity mode of my DMM.

The Samsung ARM chip can be seen in the following figure:

Figure 10.4 – The Samsung chip

Since the chip is not BGA and I have a documented chip pinout in its datasheet, it is very easy to find out the pinout with a DMM in continuity mode only (the JTAGulator is expensive for a beginner – this is proof you don't always need it!).

Here is the pinout:

| Pin | Function | Function | Pin |
|-----|----------|----------|-----|
| 1 | 3.3V | GND | 2 |
| 3 | TDI | GND | 4 |
| 5 | TMS | GND | 6 |
| 7 | TCLK | TMODE (cf. datasheet) | 8 |
| 9 | TDO | RST | 10 |

Let's launch OpenOCD with the `scan_chain.tcl` config (this one just shows the scan chain):

```
$openocd -f ftdi2232h.cfg.tcl -f scan_chain.tcl
Open On-Chip Debugger 0.10.0
[...]
adapter speed: 2000 kHz
srst_only separate srst_gates_jtag srst_open_drain connect_
deassert_srst
adapter_nsrst_delay: 100
adapter speed: 200 kHz
  TapName Enabled IdCode Expected IrLen IrCap IrMask
-- ------------------ -------- ---------- ---------- ----- ---
-- ------
Info : clock speed 200 kHz
Warn : There are no enabled taps. AUTO PROBING MIGHT NOT WORK!!
Info : JTAG tap: auto0.tap tap/device found: 0x1f0f0f0f (mfg:
0x787 (<unknown>), part: 0xf0f0, ver: 0x1)
Warn : AUTO auto0.tap - use "jtag newtap auto0 tap -irlen 4
-expected-id 0x1f0f0f0f"
Warn : gdb services need one or more targets defined
```

`0x1f0f0f0f` is the generic ID for ARM7/TMDI. It works!

So, this time, OpenOCD doesn't come with a practical target description file; we will have to make one.

Let's define our variables:

```
transport select jtag                 # we want jtag
reset_config srst_only     # we didn't find a trst pin so, srst
only
```

```
adapter_nsrst_delay 100     # some delay after the reset
ftdi_tdo_sample_edge falling    # we want falling edge
                                # sampling in the fdti
adapter_khz 30000           # after some tests this is the fastest
set _CHIPNAME S3C45         # to have a practical name
set _ENDIAN little              # arm little
set _CPUTAPID 0x1f0f0f0f        # our jtag id
```

And define our target and actions:

```
jtag newtap $_CHIPNAME cpu -irlen 4 -ircapture 0x1 -irmask 0xf
-expected-id $_CPUTAPID
                                            # classical
arm tap
set _TARGETNAME [format "%s.cpu" $_CHIPNAME] # a nice .cpu
target for the dap
target create $_TARGETNAME arm7tdmi -endian $_ENDIAN -chain-
position $_TARGETNAME
 # target creation
$_TARGETNAME configure -work-area-phys 0x30800000 -work-area-
size 0x20000 -work-area-backup 0
 # this is the trickiest, try values for the
 # work area, keep them aligned, this is
 # trial and error mostly
telnet_port 4444 # define ports
gdb_port 3333
tcl_port 6666
init
verify_ircapture disable
halt #stop the CPU
wait_halt #wait for the stop
poll #poll it once
```

Now, we can get access to the modem memory and execution flow but... where? At what addresses? We know ARM7 is a 32-bit architecture. We could dump the whole 4 GB memory space if we were completely clueless. But let's dig a bit into the datasheet to refine our dumping (and introduce you to TCL and OpenOCD).

First, when looking at *Figure 4-1 – S3C4530A System Memory Map schema* on the datasheet, we realize that the actual memory space isn't 32-bits but 26 (so 64Mbytes $(2^{26})/(2^{10})/(2^{10})=2^{(26-10-10)}=2^6=64$)!

That should be much, much faster than dumping 4 GB!

Let's create a TCL file to do it:

```
echo "----DUMPING 0 16M"
dump_image dump_samsung_0x00000000_16M 0 0x1000000
echo "----DUMPED 0 16M"
```

echo, well... echoes text to the console, and the dump_image command... dumps memory to a file:

- The documentation of the base OpenOCD function is here (dump_image, load_image, mem2array, and so on): http://openocd.org/doc/html/Tcl-Scripting-API.html.

- TCL integrated functions (commands) and operators are documented here (if, foreach, echo, format, and so on): https://www.tcl.tk/man/tcl8.6/TclCmd/contents.htm.

Let's dump the memory space:

```
$openocd -f ftdi2232h.cfg.tcl -f samsung-S3C45.tcl -f dump16M.
tcl
[...]
Info : JTAG tap: S3C45.cpu tap/device found: 0x1f0f0f0f (mfg:
0x787 (<unknown>), part: 0xf0f0, ver: 0x1)
Info : Embedded ICE version 1
Info : S3C45.cpu: hardware has 2 breakpoint/watchpoint units
verify Capture-IR is disabled
background polling: on
TAP: S3C45.cpu (enabled)
target halted in ARM state due to watchpoint, current mode:
System
cpsr: 0x6000005f pc: 0x00b3bd60
```

```
--- DUMPING 0 16M
dumped 16777216 bytes in 39.864220s (410.995 KiB/s)
--- DUMPED 0 16M
```

Here, we have our image file of the whole memory space! We will look into code analysis in the next two chapters (of a homemade application though; since this piece of hardware is hard to find, I want you to be able to follow in the next chapters).

But we would like to know how the memory is set up and where it is "mounted" in the memory space. In order to do so, we have to parse the content of memory-mapped registers.

While reading the database, we see that the external memory is set up in multiple registers. SYSCFG configures the high-level aspect (cache mode, write buffer, and so on), the internal bus behavior (EXTDBWTH), another (ROMCON) sets up the physical layer (RAC/CAS, and so on) and specifies the external RAM base address, and one actually indicates the base address of the I/O (REFEXTCON).

I wrote code to make their content readable (samsung-S3C45-parse_and_dump.tcl). Let's have a look at it to understand tcl a little bit. Let's have a look at the main parsing function:

```
proc samsung_spe_regs {} {              # function definition
    mem2array syscfg 32 0x3ff0000 1     # mem2array: read
                                        # address in a var
    mem2array clkcon 32 0x3ff3000 1     # mem2array varname
                                        # width addr sz
    mem2array extacon 32 0x3ff3008 2
    mem2array extdbwth 32 0x3ff3010 1
    mem2array romcon 32 0x3ff3014 6
    mem2array dramcon 32 0x3ff302c 4
    mem2array refextcon 32 0x3ff302c 1

    echo [format "SYSCFG 0x%08x" $syscfg(0)]
    parse_syscfg $syscfg(0)        #this is a function call if 1
arg

    echo [format "CLKCON 0x%08x" $clkcon(0)]        #format is a
bit
                                                    # like printf
    foreach {n val} [array get extacon] {           #[] evaluates a
```

```
                                    # command,set
                                    #retun value as arg like `` in
                                                        #shell
        echo [format "EXTACON%d 0x%08x" $n $val]
        parse_extacon $n $val          #function call with
arguments
      }
      echo [format "EXTDBWTH 0x%08x" $extdbwth(0)]
      parse_extdbwth $extdbwth(0)
      foreach {n val} [array get romcon] {
    echo [format "ROMCON%d 0x%08x" $n $val]
    parse_romcon $n $val
      }
      foreach {n val} [array get dramcon] {
    echo [format "DRAMCON%d 0x%08x" $n $val]
    parse_dramcon $n $val
      }
      echo [format "REFEXTCON 0x%08x" $refextcon(0)]
      parse_refextcon $refextcon(0)
}

  samsung_spe_regs                  #function call w/o arguments
```

Just this code tidbit shows the main `tcl` and OpenOCD features/commands. A very important thing you have to know about `tcl` is that it is a functional language (like `caml`, `lisp`, `haskell`, `erlang`, `scala`, and more). To make it simple, a function cannot change its arguments; you can only process data and return it.

Go read the other functions in `samsung-S3C45-parse_and_dump.tcl` to learn more about parsing, printing, and bitwise manipulation!

If you don't find an ABB 560MN, I encourage you to write your own script for the JTAG target you find, but for you to test it, here are the static values that were in my modem. At the very bottom of the script, I parse the initial value for `syscfg`. Get inspired by it. Also, `tclsh` is a command-line interpreter that can execute `tcl` scripts (but doesn't know OpenOCD-specific commands):

| Register | Value |
|---|---|
| SYSCFG | 0xcfffff83 |
| CLKCON | 0x00000000 |
| EXTACON0 | 0x0eb70eb7 |
| EXTACON1 | 0x0eb70eb7 |
| EXTDBWTH | 0x055fff56 |
| ROMCON0 | 0x12040040 |
| ROMCON1 | 0x00000060 |
| ROMCON2 | 0x00000060 |
| ROMCON3 | 0x00000060 |
| ROMCON4 | 0x00000060 |
| ROMCON5 | 0x00000060 |
| DRAMCON0 | 0x08000182 |
| DRAMCON1 | 0x00000000 |
| DRAMCON2 | 0x00000000 |
| DRAMCON3 | 0x00000000 |
| REFEXTCON | 0x08000182 |

Now you know how to find JTAG interfaces, how OpenOCD works, how to dump memory, and so on! Find a victim and go get cracking!

# Summary

In this chapter, we saw how to interact with JTAG, how to find JTAG pins, how it works, how to use it to put a target under debugging control, how to dump its memory space, and how to interact with OpenOCD with scripts.

At this point, you should be able to make OpenOCD debug your own programs on your own boards!

In the next chapter, we will see how to reverse engineer a binary that we extracted (from JTAG or an EEPROM, or by any other means). In the chapter after that, we will put JTAG to work to directly alter the code that is executing on our target! Hang on – the best bits are still to come!

# Questions

1.  What is JTAG?

2.  What are the JTAG signals/pins and what do they do?

3.  Was JTAG initially made to debug chips?

4.  When using a JTAGulator, how come the IDCODE scan doesn't find TDI? How come BYPASS does?

5.  What is/are the OpenOCD command(s) to write a value at a specific address? Why can it be interesting?

6.  ```
    join [lmap b [lmap a [split "Bjo(u!UDM!gvo!@" {}] {expr
    [scan $a %c]-1}] {format %c $b}] ""
    ```
    ```

# 11
# Static Reverse Engineering and Analysis

In this chapter, we will look into the analysis of a piece of code, without having it execute. The approach we will use is, first, to have a look at the code while it is executing. After this, we'll manage to get the code from an external source such as a firmware update, EEPROM dump, or another source. However, we can't get debug access on the CPU because of the absence of JTAG or any other debug interface, because the emulator is unavailable, and other reasons.

In order to be able to understand the code, we will go through the following steps. First, we will understand how an operating system loads code for execution. In doing so, we will look at what an executable format is and why it is needed, the most popular formats for general-purpose and embedded systems, and an overview of common tools for finding information on executable formats. We will then understand how to deal with a raw dump (a bare-metal dump of a memory space or an EEPROM dump) and find relevant information to analyze them. Toward the end of the chapter, we will look at a dedicated reverse engineering program (Ghidra).

In this chapter, we will look at the following topics:

- Executable formats
- Dump formats and memory images
- Analyzing firmware – introduction to Ghidra

# Technical requirements

For this chapter, we will need the following:

- A computer running Linux
- Ghidra (`https://ghidra-sre.org/`)
- `readelf` (in the `elfutils` package usually)
- `pev` (also usually packaged)
- `qemu-system-arm` if you don't have a Raspberry Pi

The code files for this chapter can be found in the repository you cloned initially.

Check out the following link to see the Code in Action video:

`https://bit.ly/2OfFSwu`

# Executable formats

On a modern (after 1975) computer, the operating system is roughly split into two main parts:

- **The kernelland**: This is the memory space of the code that manages both the hardware and what happens in the userland. It generally doesn't have internal memory protection and any crash here can crash the computer (or even damage the hardware). It is also called **ring 0** as an abuse of the memory protection rings on x86 CPUs.

- **The userland**: This is the (virtual) memory space where the user executable lives. The executables cannot access the hardware directly, they don't have a direct view of the physical memory addresses, their execution can get interrupted by the kernel scheduler, and they can crash happily without too much risk to the system. Also known as **ring 3**, the least privileged of the x86 CPUs.

Since the kernelland can manage a myriad of userland programs (that it has no clue about beforehand), there must be a standard way to describe these programs so they can be given what they need to run smoothly by the kernelland. This is basically what an executable format is. An executable format will tell the OS the following:

- I contain a program made for this OS or another. (Does the OS recognize the executable format?)

- I contain a program made for this CPU architecture. (Is the program compatible with the current CPU architecture?)

- My program needs this list of external libraries to work. (Are they available locally? Does the OS need to load them in the memory space that it will create for the executable?)

- For each library, the program will need these exported functions (since the functions can be at different addresses between two compilations or two versions of the library, it will need a way to resolve these addresses – this is dynamic linking).

- You will be able to find the code of the program at this offset (this is called the entry point).

It is very clear that, from a security point of view, the executable formats are a rich environment to hide and hijack things, and from a defensive point of view (the programmers trying to hide things from you) and an offensive point of view (you are relying on information they provide to exploit a vulnerability). Just so you know, executable format manipulation is the historical way viruses replicate on an operating system.

Now we've seen why we need standardized executable formats, let's have a quick look at the most popular ones.

## Understanding operating system formats

Since executable formats are OS-dependent, there are of course some competing standards (`https://xkcd.com/927/`). Let's start with the most popular one in embedded systems, the king of flexibility, the one that in the darkness binds them.

## The Executable and Linkable Format

The **Executable and Linkable Format** (ELF) has been the standard on (most) *NIX systems since the late 90s (besides OSX grandstanding alone in its corner, as usual). It is relatively simple but powerful and allows embedding much more than executables. It can contain libraries, object code, core dumps, debugging symbols, operating system and CPU-specific "things"... anything short of the kitchen sink. It can target more than 16 **Application Binary Interfaces** (**ABIs**), more than 100 architectures, and more...

The first thing that comes in an ELF file is the file magic:
`\x7fELF`(0x7f,0x45,0x4c,0x46).

Let's have a look at a typical ELF header with `readelf`:

| `readelf -h` | On a Linux x64 ELF | On an intermediate ELF for the bluepill (from ch5 for example) |
|---|---|---|
| Magic | 7f 45 4c 46 02 01 01 00 00 00 00 00 00 00 00 00 | 7f 45 4c 46 01 01 01 00 00 00 00 00 00 00 00 00 |
| Class | ELF64 | ELF32 |
| Data | Two's complement, little-endian | Two's complement, little-endian |
| Version | 1 (current) | 1 (current) |
| OS/ABI | UNIX – System V | UNIX – System V |
| ABI Version | 0 | 0 |
| Type | DYN (Shared object file) | EXEC (Executable file) |
| Machine | Advanced Micro Devices X86-64 | ARM |
| Version | 0x1 | 0x1 |
| Entry point address | 0x6130 | 0x8000c5d |
| Start of program headers | 64 | 52 (bytes into file) |
| Start of section headers | 137000 | 229664 (bytes into file) |
| Flags | 0x0 | 0x5000200, Version5 EABI, soft-float ABI |
| Size of this header | 64 (bytes) | 52 (bytes) |
| Size of program headers | 56 (bytes) | 32 (bytes) |
| Number of program headers | 11 | 2 |
| Size of section headers | 64 (bytes) | 40 (bytes) |
| Number of section headers | 29 | 21 |
| Section header string table index | 28 | 20 |

This is the general information about these ELF files, what CPU and OS they can run on, where the sections start, and more. Just by reading the header, we already have a lot of very interesting information!

If we dig a bit deeper into comparing them, we can look into the segments they need and see the following:

- The bluepill needs very little. Actually, it is not relying on anything provided by the kernel (which is normal since it is not a real executable but more of a container for our compiled code). But look at our familiar addresses (flash @0x08000000, RAM @0x20000000) with the correct access flags... A thing of beauty and joy forever:

```
Elf file type is EXEC (Executable file)
Entry point 0x8000c5d
There are 2 program headers, starting at offset 52
Program Headers:
  Type           Offset   VirtAddr   PhysAddr   FileSiz
MemSiz  Flg Align
  LOAD           0x010000 0x08000000 0x08000000 0x00d44
0x00d44 R E 0x10000
  LOAD           0x020000 0x20000000 0x08000d44 0x0000c
0x0000c RW  0x10000

 Section to Segment mapping:
  Segment Sections...
   00      .text #text is usually the segment with
                 # the code we want to analyze inside
   01      .data
```

- The Linux executable, on the other hand, needs a lot of kernel-provided things:

```
Elf file type is DYN (Shared object file)
Entry point 0x6130
There are 11 program headers, starting at offset 64
Program Headers:
  Type           Offset            VirtAddr
PhysAddr
                 FileSiz           MemSiz
Flags  Align
  PHDR           0x0000000000000040 0x0000000000000040
0x0000000000000040 [...]
```

```
   INTERP              0x00000000000002a8 0x00000000000002a8
0x00000000000002a8 [...]

[this is too long and of little value outside of
comparison right now, run readelf on your /bin/ls...
snip...]
 Section to Segment mapping:
  Segment Sections...
   00
   01      .interp
 [...snip...]
   10      .init_array .fini_array .data.rel.ro .dynamic
.got
```

All the ELF information is stored as a series of *records* that are described here: https://refspecs.linuxfoundation.org/elf/gabi4+/ch4.eheader.html. You can interact with them directly in C or with the excellent pyelftools in Python.

Please run readelf with the other options (-S, -g, -t, or -a to see everything) on the "blink" ELF file for bluepill (in the Ch5 directory) and look into their signification. Normally, the tools we are going to use later will take care of loading everything properly, but sometimes the people that make your targets can be sneaky and use the executable format to try to hide things from you.

Let's now look into PE, the format for Windows.

## The Portable Executable format

The **Portable Executable (PE)** format is the one used by Windows and is more common in embedded systems than you would think. Sure, in modern systems, Linux is all the rage, but older systems are often based on Windows CE or a full-fledged version. The basic functions that can be found in ELF are all here but it is a bit more restricted in terms of supported CPUs.

An example of using readpe (in the pev package) on a calc.exe file copied from a Windows 10 machine is shown here:

```
$readpe calc.exe
DOS Header
   Magic number:              0x5a4d (MZ)
   Bytes in last page:        144
   Pages in file:             3
   Relocations:               0
```

| Size of header in paragraphs: | 4 |
| Minimum extra paragraphs: | 0 |
| Maximum extra paragraphs: | 65535 |
| Initial (relative) SS value: | 0 |
| Initial SP value: | 0xb8 |
| Initial IP value: | 0 |
| Initial (relative) CS value: | 0 |
| Address of relocation table: | 0x40 |
| Overlay number: | 0 |
| OEM identifier: | 0 |
| OEM information: | 0 |
| PE header offset: | 0xf8 |

COFF/File header

| Machine: | 0x8664 IMAGE_FILE_MACHINE_ AMD64 |
| Number of sections: | 6 |
| Date/time stamp: | 1615788109 (Mon, 15 Mar 2021 06:01:49 UTC) |
| Symbol Table offset: | 0 |
| Number of symbols: | 0 |
| Size of optional header: | 0xf0 |
| Characteristics: | 0x22 |

Characteristics names

| | IMAGE_FILE_EXECUTABLE_ IMAGE |
| | |
| | IMAGE_FILE_LARGE_ADDRESS_ AWARE |

[...]

Imported functions

Library

Name: SHELL32.dll

Functions

Function

Name: ShellExecuteW

Library

Name: KERNEL32.dll

| Functions |
| --- |
| Function |
| Name: GetCurrentThreadId |
| Function |
| [...] |

As you can see, the PE format provides roughly the same kind of information that can be found in ELF since it covers the same need (loading an image, linking libraries, and more).

# Dump formats and memory images

The first thing to know about *raw* formats is that they are not as raw as you think. When you dump an EEPROM (SPI or I2C) or dump a chip's memory space, there is always an underlying structure. A chip cannot magically turn a soup of bytes into something it can use and run internally. To understand the structure of such an image, you will have to dig into the chip's documentation.

When analyzing a dump, the following applies:

- There is always an underlying organization.
- Read the chip's documentation and its underlying architecture documentation.
- If it is a dump that is external to a device (that is, from a firmware update), then the following applies:

  - It can pack multiple updates for multiple chips.

  - It can be applied in multiple passes (update chip1, then chip2, and so on) that are necessarily reflected in the structure, but are not necessarily targeting your chip of interest.

- If it is a dump that is internal to a device and internal to a chip (that is, MCU flash), then the following applies:

  - It can reference code that is externally stored (in an EEPROM, for example).

  - It may be launched or used by internal boot microcode; do not assume it executes first.

- It is very common to have code that is not linked to other pieces of code (there's no jump to it, while a normal function will be jumped to via the architecture's relevant instruction such as B, BL, JMP, or ARM) and that seems dead, but is actually run by internal structures of the chip because it is sitting at a predetermined address (interrupt service routines, for example).

If it is a dump that is internal to a device but external to a chip (that is, from an EEPROM or an SD card):

- It is most probably launched or used by internal boot microcode or code running inside an onboard flash; assume it does not execute first.

- If you have a full-fledged operating system to analyze, look into the possible candidates for executables that are implementing the different services that the device exposes or uses. When in this situation, there is an immense amount of code available but most of it is only here to support the execution of a handful of core services. The way you should focus your effort is this:

- Only reverse code that is specific to the device, not the supporting code:

   - Reverse the interpreted scripts first (Python, Perl, Bash, and others) since the effort needed to find problems is less.

   - Reverse compiled code last and focus on the portions that handle external input.

- Harvest all the versions of the libraries and programs that act as support and run them against the NIST's CVE database to identify vulnerable versions.

Let's look into typical formats for code dumps.

# Dump structure – the bluepill as an example

If we look into our trusted bluepill, we already know that the memory space is divided into different areas (we saw two sections in the ELF headers: flash @0x08000000, and RAM @0x20000000) but how did we know that it was flash and RAM? This is because the STM32 chip on the bluepill is actually an ARM Cortex chip and that all Cortex M of the same range (M0, M0+, M1, M3, and others) share a (general) memory map where the address range indicates a type of memory (both flash and RAM are two types of memory).

The STM32F103 is based on the Cortex M3 architecture. For the different architectures (ARM or otherwise), the memory map will be described in the chip's (or the architecture's) documentation.

Cortex M chips can be compliant with different architectures :

| Architecture | Cortex family |
|---|---|
| ARMv6-M | M0, M0+, M1 |
| ARMv7-M | M3 |
| ARMv7E-M | M4,M7 |
| ARMv8-M | M23, M33, M35P |
| ARMv8.1-M | M55 |

For our STM32, if we look into the Cortex M3 technical reference manual (search it on the internet – ARM keeps moving it around; providing you with a link isn't worth it, as it would be obsolete very fast), we can see that `0x08000000` is just described as *Memory with write-through cache attribute*, while `0x00000000` is described as *Typically ROM or flash memory*. So STMicro decided to place the flash at `0x08000000`. But this is stated in the STMicro documentation (the STM32F103C8 datasheet, page 34)! This is a perfect example of the decisions an ARM implementer can have to make, which create fundamental variations while staying within the architecture's specification (that is, NXP's Cortexes have their flash at `0x0`, as it is verbatim in the architecture documentation).

# Analyzing firmware – introduction to Ghidra

Ghidra is an open source tool that will allow you to reverse engineer executables on a lot of different CPU architectures for free. It also gives you a very nice feature when you compare it to the most popular proprietary tool: C decompilation for free.

Its main proprietary competitor (IDA Pro) is very popular in the security community but is extremely expensive and, all in all, only has one feature that Ghidra lacks: native debugger integration (Ghidra support some level of integration with the usual debuggers with external bridges). Given the extremely high license costs involved in IDA (this can be explained, but I will not enter into this debate here), I have chosen to use Ghidra in this book for you to be able to use a modern reverse engineering software suite.

I use IDA at work and Ghidra in my free time. Both are very good but Ghidra is open source.

## Getting to know Ghidra with a very simple ARM Linux executable

The first thing we will look into is an ELF executable for a Raspberry Pi.

The image it is running on is in this chapter's folder (`Ch11`).

Let's launch the file:

- On a Raspberry Pi (if we have one, copy it over with `scp`)
- Or within `qemu`, if we don't have a Raspberry Pi (follow this tutorial to do so: https://azeria-labs.com/emulate-raspberry-pi-with-qemu/)

Launching the ELF, we can see that it expects a password as the first argument:

```
pi@raspberrypi:~ $ ./1.elf
arguments needed : ./1.elf password
bye !
pi@raspberrypi:~ $ ./1.elf test
no !
```

Obviously, we want to find the password!

Let's launch the `strings` command on the ELF, to see if there is anything that looks like a password:

```
pi@raspberrypi:~ $ strings 1.elf
[...]
arguments needed : %s password
bye !
yes !
no !
[...]
.ARM.attributes
```

We can see a lot of strings, but some look like what we saw when we launched the executable (`arguments needed : %s password`), which looks like a `printf` format string.

Let's launch Ghidra. The first window will allow us to manage the different files that can come into a project. For this, let's import the `1.elf` file (using **File | Import**).

When we look at the loading messages, we can see that it fails to load some external symbols:

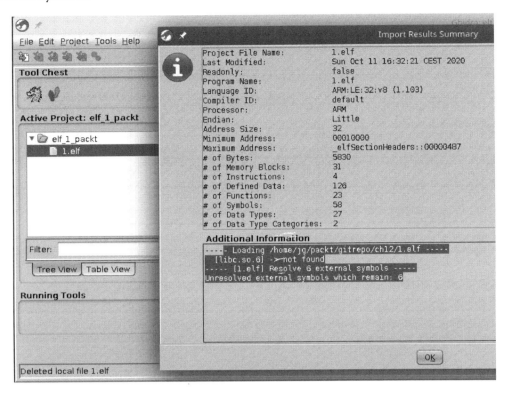

Figure 11.1 – Ghidra loading an ELF

This means that the program uses functions in shared libraries and that Ghidra has not been able to load them.

Let's mount the image to be able to load these libraries. Since there is more than one partition in the image, our first step will be to find out where the root partition starts in the image:

```
$fdisk -lu <path>
Disk <path>: 1.7 GiB, 1845493760 bytes, 3604480 sectors
Units: sectors of 1 * 512 = 512 bytes
[..]
Device   Boot   Start       End Sectors Size Id Type
<path>1          8192    532479   524288 256M  c  W95 FAT32 (LBA)
<path>2        532480   3604479  3072000 1.5G 83  Linux
```

Our root `fs` partition starts at *512 \* 532480 = 272629760* bytes in the image.

Let's set up our loop accordingly and mount it:

```
sudo losetup -o 272629760 /dev/loop0 <path>
sudo mount /dev/loop0 /mnt/tmp/
```

Now let's delete `1.elf` from the project and reimport it into Ghidra and indicate the location of the libraries:

- You may need to relaunch Ghidra as a superuser to be able to read the content of the mount point.

- It is easier to just make a copy of the usual library path (`lib/` and `usr/lib/`) and change the ownership of this:

```
~/raspilibs$ sudo cp -r /mnt/tmp/lib/ ./
~/raspilibs$ mkdir usr
~/raspilibs$ sudo cp -r /mnt/tmp/usr/lib/ ./usr/
~/raspilibs$ sudo chown -R jg:jg ./*
```

Now let's reimport the file with the proper library path:

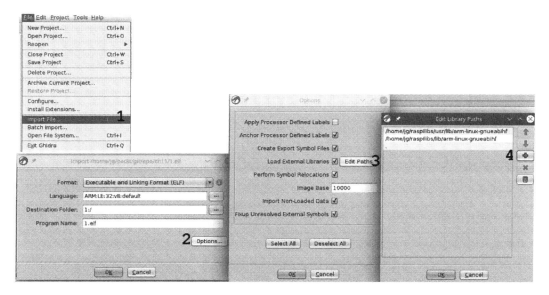

Figure 11.2 – Ghidra – loading with external libraries

Please follow these steps:

1.  Import the target file.

2.  Go to **Options**.

3.  Check **Load external libraries**.

4.  Set up the import path to the copied files (or directly to the place you mounted the image if you launched Ghidra as root).

Both `elf` and the libraries it uses are loaded as shown in the following screenshot:

Figure 11.3 – Loaded elf and libraries

Let's double-click on the name of `elf`. Ghidra will launch its reversing interface and propose to analyze the binary file. Select **Yes** and launch it with the default options.

Here are the main sections of the Ghidra interface:

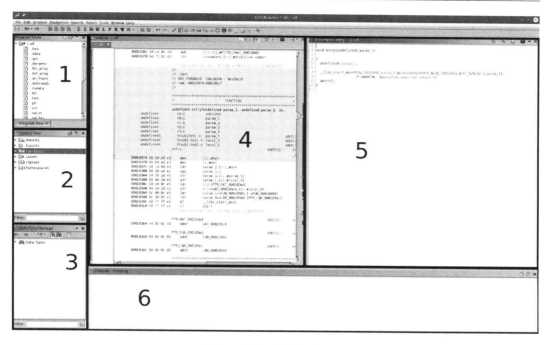

Figure 11.4 – Ghidra layout

The different sections are as follows:

- **Section 1**: Sections of the loaded executable.

- **Section 2**: Symbols used by the executable (imported or exported, functions, classes, and others).

- **Section 3**: The data types that Ghidra identified in the executable (if Ghidra identifies datatypes in libraries, you have to import them here).

- **Section 4**: The disassembly window. Here, the assembly opcode (the human-understandable mnemonic corresponding to the binary in the file) is displayed.

- **Section 5**: The C equivalent code generated from the disassembly (known as the decompiled code).

- **Section 6**: The output of the scripts.

Here, the executable has been stripped. This means the function names are not available to us. We will have to find a way to identify the functions that are interesting to us.

We have multiple solutions to do that. We can follow the execution flow. We know that the elf format defines an entry point. On a Linux executable, this will call a special function in libc. This is the main library on Linux where all the base system functions are managed. This special function will initialize the executable space and load libraries in the memory space, and everything that puts the executable in an environment where it can execute. The main function is usually provided as an argument to the libc initialization so it can call it once the initialization is done. This is the case here:

```
00010374 00 b0 a0 e3    mov    r11,#0x0
00010378 00 e0 a0 e3    mov    lr,#0x0
0001037c 04 10 9d e4    ldr    param_2,[sp],#0x4
00010380 0d 20 a0 e1    cpy    param_3,sp
00010384 04 20 2d e5    str    param_3,[sp,#param_5]!
00010388 04 00 2d e5    str    param_1,[sp,#local_4]!
0001038c 10 c0 9f e5    ldr    r12,[PTR_DAT_000103a4]                = 000105c4
00010390 04 c0 2d e5    str    r12=>DAT_000105c4,[sp,#local_8]!     = 1Eh
00010394 0c 00 9f e5    ldr    param_1=>FUN_00010464,[->FUN_00010464]  = 00010464
00010398 0c 30 9f e5    ldr    param_4=>LAB_00010564,[PTR_LAB_000103ac]  = 00010564
0001039c e8 ff ff eb    bl     __libc_start_main                    undefined __libc_start_
000103a0 f0 ff ff eb    bl     abort                                void abort(void)
                   -- Flow Override: CALL_RETURN (CALL_TERMINATOR)
```

Figure 11.5 – Initialization of an ELF file – jumping the libc initialization

When we look at the function labeled FUN_00010646, we can see in the decompiled C code that it references a string that looks like what we saw in the execution.

Wait... what? How do I know that? These are the points to find out:

- You have to know how to read the disassembly view. The columns are as follows:

  - Address

  - Hex values in the file

  - Disassembled opcode (you can find what it means here: https://developer.arm.com/architectures/instruction-sets)

  - Disassembled parameters for the opcode

  - Ghidra comments

- You have to know that this is how the loader works in Linux.

- You have to know that parameters 1, 2, 3, and 4 are synonyms for r0, r1, r2, and r3 when Ghidra disassembles ARM ELF files (because in the ARM call convention, these are the argument registers and r0 is the return value register). For other CPUs, they can be synonyms for other registers.

If we have no clue where the entry point is, or if it goes through a lot of strange initialization code, we can always search for strings that we have seen with the string search tool. Here is an example of searching for `password`:

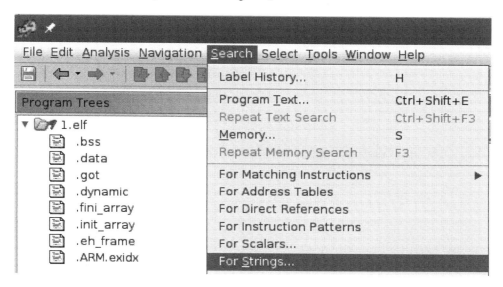

Figure 11.6 – Searching for strings

After this, the next step is searching for `passw`:

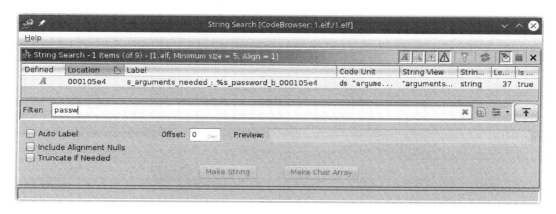

Figure 11.7 – Searching for a specific string

Double-clicking on the found string leads us to `FUN_00010646`.

When we look at the decompiled C code for this function, we don't see real variable names (they have been stripped from the executable), but we have a very good approximation of the code that generated the function:

```
void FUN_00010464(int param_1,undefined4 *param_2)
{
  bool bVar1;
  int local_c;
  local_c = 0;
  bVar1 = true;
  if (param_1 < 2) {
    printf("arguments needed : %s password\nbye !",*param_2);
    exit(-1);
  }
  while (PTR_DAT_00021030[local_c] != '\0') {
    if (*(byte *)(param_2[1] + local_c) != (byte)~PTR_
DAT_00021030[local_c]) {
      bVar1 = false;
    }
    local_c = local_c + 1;
  }
  if (bVar1) {
    puts("yes !");
    exit(0);
  }
  puts("no !");
  exit(-1);
}
```

If this is a main function in C, param_1 should be argc (the number of command-line arguments) and param_2 should be argv (an array of string pointers on the arguments). This is very likely, since if param_1 <param_2, the message we saw when we launched 1.elf without arguments will be displayed.

Here, we can see that it references an external variable: PTR_DAT_00021030. This is addressed as an array of bytes that is compared, byte by byte, to the entered password. But, as usual, the devil lies in the details. It is comparing the value of ~byte! If you remember the introduction to C (*Chapter 5, Our Main Attack Platform*), this is a binary NOT (it flips all the zeroes and ones of the value). If we double-click on the PTR_DAT_00021030 string in the disassembled code (it is in light turquoise and is a label reference), we can see it in the disassembly window:

Figure 11.8 – Disassembled assembly

This actually points to another place where the data is. How do I know this? Because Ghidra named the first variable PTR_DAT. This means this is a pointer (PTR) to data (DAT). Additionally, to help us, Ghidra put the pseudo instruction addr here. This pseudo instruction is normally used to fetch the address of a piece of data. Here, it is not really the case. We can see in the second column that this actually is the direct address of the data.

So... what is at DAT_000105d4? If we double-click on it, Ghidra will show us what is there, as shown in the following screenshot:

```
                    DAT_000105d4              XREF[4]:   FUN_00010464:000104e4(R),
                                                         FUN_00010464:00010510(*),
                                                         FUN_00010464:0001051c(R),
                                                         00021030(*)

    000105d4 8c              ??        8Ch
    000105d5 8a              ??        8Ah
    000105d6 8f              ??        8Fh
    000105d7 9a              ??        9Ah
    000105d8 8d              ??        8Dh
    000105d9 8f              ??        8Fh
    000105da 9e              ??        9Eh
    000105db 8c              ??        8Ch
    000105dc 8c              ??        8Ch
    000105dd 88              ??        88h
    000105de 90              ??        90h
    000105df 8d              ??        8Dh
    000105e0 9b              ??        9Bh
    000105e1 de              ??        DEh
    000105e2 00              ??        00h
    000105e3 00              ??        00h
```

Figure 11.9 – Looking at data at the pointer's location

So, now let's try to binary NOT it byte by byte:

```
$echo -n -e
'\x8c\x8a\x8f\x9a\x8d\x8f\x9e\x8c\x8c\x88\x90\x8d\x9b\xde
'| perl -ne 'for $c (split(//,$_)){print(~$c);}'
superpassword!
```

Let's try it:

```
pi@raspberrypi:~ $ ./1.elf 'superpassword!'
yes !
```

Clearly, this very easy example is here to make you a little more familiar with Ghidra. Now, let's go with something more complicated: a little crackme I wrote for the bluepill.

## Going into second gear – Ghidra on raw binaries for the STM32

The source code is available in a password-protected archive. The password will be given by beating the crackme!

Let's connect the bluepill in the same configuration we used for the first serial/UART exercise in *Chapter 6*, *Sniffing and Attacking the Most Common Protocols*, and load the bluepill with the binary and see what the UART interface says:

```
$screen /dev/ttyUSB0 115200
---
UUID:ff5706708448535150398708
PASSWORD:test
NO!
```

If we run strings on the bin, we can find the PASSWORD: and YOU WIN! strings, but that's pretty much it.

Let's load the `.bin` into Ghidra:

1. The first thing that is different is that Ghidra has no clue what kind of processor the binary is for (there is no ELF header to help it). We know it is a little-endian Cortex, so let's select this in the **Language** menu:

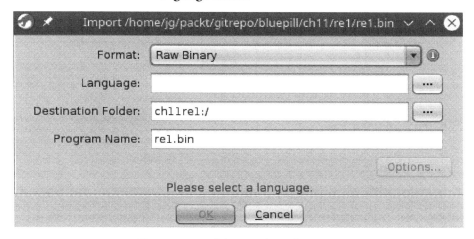

Figure 11.10 – Selecting the architecture

2. This is the updated screenshot:

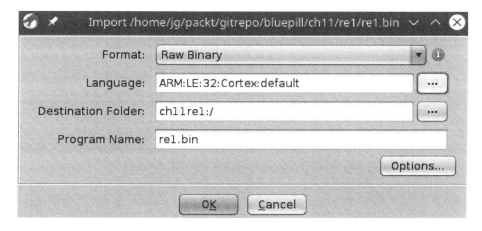

Figure 11.11 – Architecture selected

3. Now, in the options, we can tell it that the image has a base address of `0x08000000` (remember this from the ELF header and the compilation flash process?):

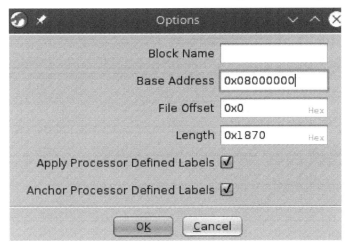

Figure 11.12 – Setting the base address

4. Now, let's open the binary and let Ghidra analyze it (add both aggressive instruction options, so Ghidra will try to find instructions even if they are not directly in the detected execution flow).

5. And now... ouch... there is a lot of assembly. And we don't know where to start looking... Let's search for the PASSWORD string (**Search | For Strings**):

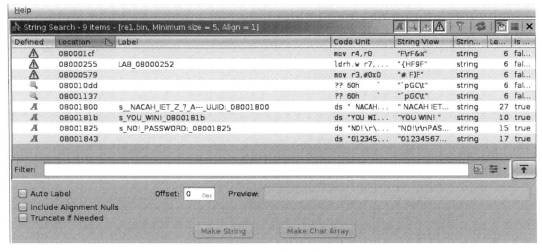

Figure 11.13 – Searching for strings

6. Strangely, there is no real PASSWORD: string... Strange, but it is a starting point. Let's look there:

Figure 11.14 – The strange password string

So, this is the place where the string is stored in memory. We have the reverse situation of the one we had for the first ELF (a pointer to the place where the string is stored). Ghidra will allow us to take the reverse path by using the cross-references (XREFs) in the fourth column. Let's click on FUN_080001f0 to see what is happening there.

If we look into the decompiled C code, we can see a lot of variable affectation from values that are on the program – a few function calls but most importantly, the following:

- A cross-reference to a PASSWORD: string and to a NO!\r\nPASSWORD: string (but we didn't find it in the existing strings – maybe a clever compiler optimization stored PASSWORD: as a pointer on NO!\r\nPASSWORD: offset to spare space!).

- A cross-reference to a YOU WIN! string.

- Three imbricated do{}while() loops with the outermost being a do{} while(true): an infinite loop, very usual in microcontroller programming as the main processing loop!

This is very probably our main function with some setup and the main control loop! Let's rename the function main (with the *L* key while the function name is selected):

Figure 11.15 – Renaming a function

We can rename functions and variables like that, which will help us quite a bit in understanding the program!

Now let's look into the three functions that are called one after the other before the outermost `main` loop.

From what we have seen in the previous STM32 programs, they are probably doing some kind of peripheral setup!

## First identification pass

First, we will make a fast pass to try to identify the functions rapidly to make sense of the general structure of the program. At this point, we will not delve too much into the details. We will try our first approach and we will mainly rename the functions. If we find out that we were wrong, we will rename them afterward.

Let's go through the functions.

### FUN_08000e54();

Let's try to understand what this function does. We can see that it calls a lot of functions with fixed arguments:

```
void FUN_08000e54(void)

{
  undefined4 uVar1;
  undefined4 uVar2;

  FUN_080009b8(4);
  FUN_080009a8(4);
  FUN_08000a84(0);
  FUN_080009b8(3);
  FUN_080009a8(3);
  FUN_08000a84(1);
  FUN_08000be8(0);
  FUN_08000bac(3);
  FUN_08000bd4(4);
  FUN_08000bc0(0);
  FUN_080014d0(2);
  FUN_08000a98(7);
  FUN_08000ad4(1);
  FUN_08000ae8(0);
  FUN_080007b4();
  FUN_080009a8(0);
  FUN_08000a84(2);
  uVar2 = DAT_08000ed4;
  uVar1 = DAT_08000ecc;
  *DAT_08000ed0 = DAT_08000ecc;
  *DAT_08000ed8 = uVar2;
  *DAT_08000edc = uVar1;
  return;
}
```

Figure 11.16 – First function's decompiled listing

When we look into the first one, we can see that it selects something to do based on the fixed argument in a switch:

```
void FUN_080009b8(undefined4 param_1)

{
  uint *puVar1;
  uint uVar2;

  puVar1 = DAT_08000a00;
  switch(param_1) {
  case 0:
    FUN_080007b4();
    return;
  case 1:
    uVar2 = *DAT_08000a00 | 0x4000000;
    goto LAB_080009d4;
  case 2:
    uVar2 = *DAT_08000a00 | 0x10000000;
    goto LAB_080009d4;
  case 3:
    uVar2 = *DAT_08000a00 | 0x10000;
    goto LAB_080009d4;
  case 4:
    break;
  case 5:
    puVar1 = DAT_08000a04;
    break;
  case 6:
    puVar1 = DAT_08000a08;
    break;
  default:
    return;
  }
  uVar2 = *puVar1 | 1;
LAB_080009d4:
  *puVar1 = uVar2;
  return;
}
```

Figure 11.17 – Selection switch

This is strange in itself, as you wouldn't select something to do in a switch based on a fixed test case, right? This means that this probably comes from a library that the programmer used with a fixed argument. This is a clue – let's keep that in mind.

Then we see that this is setting binary flags to a memory location that is stored in the DAT_08000a00 variable. When looking at what it is pointing at, by double-clicking on it, we can see that it points to 0x40021000:

```
        DAT_08000a00                    XREF[4]:    FUN_080009b8:080009cc(R),
                                                    FUN_080009b8:080009d8(R),
                                                    FUN_080009b8:080009e2(R),
                                                    FUN_080009b8:080009ec(R)

08000a00 00 10 02 40    undefined4 40021000h
```

Figure 11.18 – A strange address pointer

Since we looked at the memory map in the Cortex M3 technical reference manual (You did, right? I asked you to look into it in the *Dump structure – the bluepill as an example* section. Yes, I know that it was a short paragraph, and I would have skipped that too, but now it is important!), we know that 0x40021000 is actually in a memory region that is hosting the peripherals! So I was right – this function is doing some sort of setup! But what exactly? What is at 0x40021000?

Let's continue exploring this function. After a little digging, we see that it doesn't really write outside of the region (But maybe I am lying or I am wrong? You should really explore by yourself; I will not be here to hold your hand on your engagements!).

If we look at the SMT32F103 technical reference (https://bit.ly/3oo0gq0), we can see (page 50) that we are in 0x4002 1000 - 0x4002 13FF: **Reset and clock control (RCC)** region.

FUN_08000e54(); is setting up some clock functionality! Let's rename it clock_setup for now.

## FUN_08000154();

I strongly encourage you to reverse engineer this function by yourself. You will discover some funny compiler tricks that are used to calculate addresses, which you will find useful to know in the future! We'll follow the same logic as the logic of the previous function.

Going through the different addresses (double-clicking) and the code of the function, we see that the function writes to 0x4002 1000 - 0x4002 13FF: RCC region, and 0x4001 1000 - 0x4001 13FF: GPIO Port C region.

If you remember what we usually to do enable a GPIO port, we start by enabling its clock, and then we set up its exact function. This function most probably sets up the GPIO! Let's rename it gpio_setup for now.

## FUN_080003a8();

We follow the same logic as for the previous function. Here, the function writes to the following:

- 0x4002 1000 - 0x4002 13FF Reset and clock control RCC region

- 0x4001 3800 - 0x4001 3BFF USART1

Again, it starts by enabling the USART1 clock, and then we set up its exact function. This function is setting up USART1! Let's rename it USART1_setup for now.

## FUN_0800041c();

This function starts with this function call:

```
FUN_0800041c(DAT_08000324,PTR_s_---_UUID:_08000320);
```

Let's understand this further:

- **First argument**: Here, we have a pointer to UART1
  (*DAT_08000324=0x40013800).

- **Second argument**: The string that is printed on UART1. This is a function that
  prints a string on UART, let's rename it UART_print.

## First loop

This is the first loop:

```
do {
  puVar10 = puVar10 + 1;
  uVar1 = *puVar10;
  FUN_0800060e(uVar2,(uint)uVar1);
  uVar11 = uVar11 ^ (uint)uVar1;
  puVar10 = puVar10;
} while (puVar10 != puVar4);
```

Figure 11.19 – Listing of the first loop

We can see the following:

- puVar10 is initialized at 0x1FFFF7E8.

- puVar4 is initialized at 0x1FFFF7F4.

So, the loop is going through pointers at 0x1FFFF7E8, but this is not in the peripheral
memory space (0x4000 0000), nor in RAM (0x20000000), nor in flash (0x08000000).
When we check the STM32F103 technical reference manual (pages 50-52), it doesn't show.

If we search 0x1fff... Ah! We find that 0x1FFFF7E8 is actually the position of the
device's 96-bit unique device ID register. 96 bits = 96/8 = 12 bytes, so from 0x1FFFF7E8
to 0x1FFFF7F4.

Given the fact that on the serial interface the UUID is displayed, FUN_0800060e is
actually printing a hex value on the UART, we can see uVar11 is XORed with the value of
the unique identifier (it is initialized at 0). Strange. Why is it doing this? We may will find
out later...

## The big while (true) loop

This is the main loop of the application. From here, everything is set up, so this will be the main piece of code that will check the validity of our password and display the winning string.

Here, we will continue renaming the functions and understanding how they work. At this point, we will see that it is easier to attack the password validation or the displaying of the flag (the winning string).

## The deepest subloop

This is doing nothing for `0x000927C0` iterations. This is just a waiting loop.

## The shallowest subloop

This is testing the value stored at `0x20000014` (in RAM) and loops again on the waiting loop if this equals 0. This is probably a flag that is set when we enter something as a password. This very probably means that what follows will be what is interesting to us.

## The main loop

There are a few aesthetic/management functions (printing a carriage return, getting a pointer to the `receive` buffer, and others).

Then a function (`FUN_080001cc`) return value is tested in order to print a `YOU WIN!` string and calls the same function (`FUN_08000174`) five times (probably to decipher the flag string).

Let's rename the following:

- `FUN_080001cc` as `validate_password`
- `FUN_080001ccFUN_08000174` as `decipher_flag`

So now that we have quickly covered the general behavior of the program, let's look at our potential victim functions.

# Reversing our target function

First, let's quickly look at the difficulty of reversing `validate_password` versus the difficulty of reversing `decipher_flag`. It is always better to go for the easier path first and attack the harder functions if you don't succeed with the easy ones:

| validate_password | decipher_flag |
| --- | --- |
| ```uint validate_password(byte *param_1,uint param_2)

{
  byte bVar1;

  bVar1 = *param_1;
  while (bVar1 != 0) {
    param_2 = param_2 - (uint)bVar1 ^ (uint)bVar1 << 8;
    param_1 = param_1 + 1;
    bVar1 = *param_1;
  }
  return param_2;
}``` | ```void decipher_flag(uint *param_1,int *param_2)

{
  int iVar1;
  uint uVar2;
  uint uVar3;
  uint uVar4;

  uVar2 = *param_1;
  uVar3 = param_1[1];
  iVar1 = DAT_080001c4;
  do {
    uVar3 = uVar3 - (param_2[2] + uVar2 * 0x10 ^ param_2[3] + (uVar2 >> 5) ^ uVar2 + iVar1);
    uVar4 = uVar3 + iVar1;
    iVar1 = iVar1 + DAT_080001c8;
    uVar2 = uVar2 - (*param_2 + uVar3 * 0x10 ^ param_2[1] + (uVar3 >> 5) ^ uVar4);
  } while (iVar1 != 0);
  *param_1 = uVar2;
  param_1[1] = uVar3;
  return;
}``` |

Just at a first glance, we see that `validate_password` is much less complex than the flag deciphering. When we look at the deciphering function, we see a lot more XORing and shifting. We will start with `Validate_password` and only look into `decipher_flag` if we don't manage to generate a valid password.

## validate_password

First things first, let's find out what the function's arguments are.

In the main loop, we can see that the second argument is `uVar11`, the initial result that was calculated by XORing the chip's unique identifier values.

Still looking in the main loop, we can see that `uVar7` (the first argument), is a RAM address (`0x20000040`). Well, since the other argument isn't the password, that must be a pointer to a buffer that holds it. The fact that the loop test variable (`bVar1`) is tested for 0 after receiving the value stored in `*param_1` (and `param_1` being incremented in the loop) also points to `param_1` holding a pointer to a null terminated character string.

Now, for every character, the XORed UUID is decremented by the character's value and then XORed with (character value << 8) ). It is not obvious here but ^ has less precedence in C than -: see https://en.cppreference.com/w/c/language/operator_precedence.

The value that is left after doing that with all of the password's characters is returned. If it is 0, the main loop prints the flag.

It is actually not that hard to find a password that will succeed the tests for your chip's own unique identifier. You will have to first calculate the XOR value of all the 16-bit halfwords in your UUID (it's a good thing the program gives you the hex value of it) and find a password that when subtracted, and its characters values are sequentially subtracted, shifted, and XORed from the initial value, ends up being 0.

I cannot provide you with a password since the UUID of your bluepill's STM32F103 chip will certainly be different from mine. It's almost as if I designed this reversing challenge to make you think and program!

Don't worry if you don't manage to do it by yourself – I give a good way to achieve it in the questions. In the solution archive file, you'll be able to find a keygen for this crackme, but going straight for it would be missing a good opportunity for learning.

Additionally, I tested that every possible XORed UUID value actually has a solution. Some XORed UUIDs (very, very rare) may require more time for generation than others, but they *all* have a solution.

In our next chapter, I have prepared another little crackme, with some additional difficulties and tricks that will force us to do some dynamic analysis! I strongly suggest that you go through all of the sections in this chapter on Ghidra and ensure you understand the details of how I came to identify the functions well.

# Summary

In this chapter, we saw the basic structure of the most common executable formats you will encounter in your tests. There are others but you should now have at least an idea of how executable formats work and how to approach an unknown format. We saw how to look into the structure of a program without having the source code and how to use this knowledge to bypass basic security mechanisms.

In the next chapter, we will add everything we learned in this chapter to what we learned in the previous chapter to allow us to dig into the program's behavior while it is executing, allowing us to bypass some more complicated security schemes.

# Questions

1.  We looked into ELF and PE as executable formats. Can you give me two more formats? What are they used for?

2.  In an ELF file, what are these sections: `.text`, `.debug`, `.plt`, `.dynamic`, and `.got`?

3.  What peripheral is at `0x40013000` on the bluepill?

4.  We didn't really look into the `Decipher_flag` function. Its first argument is a very random-looking array and its second argument is this very strange string: `NACAH IET Z ? A`. With all of the shifting and XORing, this is most probably a cyphering function. What algorithm is that?

5.  Other clues regarding the `Decipher_flag` should be in there but aren't. What clues and why?

6.  In the first reverse engineering exercise (`re1.bin`), instead of reversing the password validation string, we could just have patched the binary to accept an incorrect password and flashed the patched version on the bluepill. How? What is the offset of the instruction to patch? Patch it with what tool? With what instruction?

# 12
# Dynamic Reverse Engineering

In this chapter, we are going to look at dynamic reverse engineering. The first question is what is dynamic reverse engineering and how does it compare with static reverse engineering? What are the advantages and requirements of dynamic engineering? And how can you interact with a program that is executing on the chip while it is executing, look at (and change) memory content, alter the execution flow, step through the program instructions, and more?

We will cover the following topics in this chapter:

- What is dynamic reverse engineering and why do it?
- Leveraging OpenOCD and GDB
- ARM assembly – a primer
- The usefulness of dynamic reverse engineering – an example

# Technical requirements

We will pretty much need the same things as in the previous chapter for this dynamic reverse engineering chapter:

- A Bluepill board and programmer
- Ghidra
- `gdb-multiarch`

As usual, the code files for this chapter can be found in the book's repository, which you have already cloned in an earlier chapter.

Check out the following link to see the Code in Action video:

`https://bit.ly/3bQz6FP`

# What is dynamic reverse engineering and why do it?

Mainly, dynamic reverse engineering looks into code behaviors during execution.

There are multiple reasons this is more efficient than static reverse engineering:

- You can look at the variables while the program is executing.
- You can step through the code to better understand the different sections and steps.
- You can inspect the memory to extract things that are deciphered if you need to.
- In the case of self-modifying or dynamic code, you can directly inspect the modified code.

But the requirements for dynamic reverse engineering are also more stringent than for static reverse engineering:

- You need to have a platform that can execute the software (either real or emulated).
- The execution platform must allow you to debug the program (either with a hardware or software debugger).
- You need to have a basic understanding of how the software works to look into the execution flow.

- Most platforms will provide a good disassembly of the software but not necessarily a decompiled version (that is, a translation from binary instructions to assembly opcode but rarely a higher-level language like C). This means that you will need to understand (or research) what the different processor instructions do.

Now, how can we achieve dynamic reverse engineering? Where do we start?

# Leveraging OpenOCD and GDB

First, what do we want to do and how?

We want to achieve control over the target chip, and we want to be able to do the following:

- Control the execution flow in a typical debugger fashion (have a breakpoint, inspect and change variables, and so on).

- Change the execution flow (change the result of a branching test, change CPU flags, and so on).

- Have access to the RAM and possibly the ROM.

How can we achieve that? We saw that we can have very low-level access to the chip with OpenOCD, but using it to achieve all of our goals is a pretty harrowing, complex, and repetitive task. And what do we do about harrowing, complex, and repetitive tasks? We automate them. Since debugging is such a common task, we will use tools that other people built and leverage them to achieve our goals as depicted here:

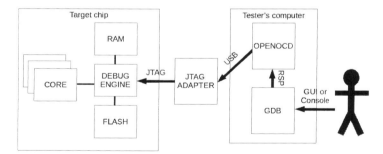

Figure 12.1 – Debug chain

We saw that OpenOCD is opening a port that can be used as a GDB server. GDB servers are the way for the **GNU Debugger (GDB)** to do remote debugging. They can run on remote computers to allow for the debugging of machines that are of a different architecture or, for example, on machines where the thing that is debugged could interfere with the debugging process (the kernel, for example). In our situation, we use it to abstract both the architecture and the fact that the target environment will not allow us to debug directly on it.

Let's flash our bluepill with the `ch12` program in your cloned folder and, once flashed, connect our bluepill to our JTAG adapter (as indicated in *Chapter 10, Accessing the Debug Interfaces*) and create a clean debug environment with the appropriate OpenOCD configuration files (you can find the clean environment in the GitHub cloned folder).

Load the target binary for this chapter (`make flash` in the chapter directory) and connect the FTDI2232 board to the bluepill as indicated in *Chapter 11, Static Reverse Engineering and Analysis.*

To start the debug session, launch the following command (adapt the second file to fit your platform – genuine STM32 or clone):

```
openocd -f ./ftdi2232h.cfg.tcl -f ./clone_CSK.cfg &
gdb-multiarch -x ./gdbinit
```

The `gdbinit` file contains the necessary `gdb` commands to make it connect to the OpenOCD `gdb` server:

```
set architecture arm          #tells gdb-mutiarch which
                              # architecture to use
target extended localhost:3333    #tells gdb to connect
                              # to openOCD's gdb server
monitor reset halt            #tells gdb to tell
                              # openocd (monitor talks
                              # directly to openocd) to
                              #reset and stop
monitor reset_nag enable      #... to enable the reset_nag
                              # (if setup could
                              # have been better on reset)
```

Let's launch it with the indicated command:

```
#openocd launching
Open On-Chip Debugger 0.10.0
Licensed under GNU GPL v2
For bug reports, read
        http://openocd.org/doc/doxygen/bugs.html
adapter speed: 2000 kHz
Info : auto-selecting first available session transport "jtag".
To override use 'transport select <transport>'.[...]
#gdb launching
```

```
GNU gdb (Debian 8.2.1-2+b3) 8.2.1
Copyright (C) 2018 Free Software Foundation, Inc.
License GPLv3+: [...]
The target architecture is assumed to be arm
Info : accepting 'gdb' connection on tcp/3333
[..]
Info : JTAG tap: stm32f1x.cpu tap/device found: 0x4ba00477
(mfg: 0x23b (ARM Ltd.), part: 0xba00, ver: 0x4)
Info : JTAG tap: stm32f1x.bs tap/device found: 0x16410041 (mfg:
0x020 (STMicroelectronics), part: 0x6410, ver: 0x1)
JTAG tap: stm32f1x.cpu tap/device found: 0x4ba00477 (mfg: 0x23b
(ARM Ltd.), part: 0xba00, ver: 0x4)
JTAG tap: stm32f1x.bs tap/device found: 0x16410041 (mfg: 0x020
(STMicroelectronics), part: 0x6410, ver: 0x1)
target halted due to debug-request, current mode: Thread xPSR:
0x01000000 pc: 0x080013b8 msp: 0x20005000
[...]
(gdb)
```

If you tracked the content well, you will see that both the output of GDB and OpenOCD are mixed. If you want to avoid this, just launch the two commands in separate terminals.

And here we go – we now have a gdb invite. The target is halted (not blinking anymore) so we have a live debug session on the actual bluepill! Neat, right?

Now let's have a look at the new program in Ghidra (repeat the instructions from *Chapter 11*, *Static Reverse Engineering and Analysis*, to launch the Ghidra analysis with the new .bin).

# GDB? But... I know nothing about it!

But learning about it is why you are here!

GDB is a complex beast that could be (and is) the subject of books on its own.

There are actually a few things, such as the main commands, you have to know (they are the most useful).

Commands can most of the time be shortened to their first letter(s): typing d for display, p for print, x for examine, and more, is really useful. In the following table, the optional parts are between parentheses.

## Here are the main commands you will be using all the time:

| | |
|---|---|
| h (elp)<br><br>command | The most useful command ever! It displays, well... help about the command (that is, you can type h  d for help with the d (isplay) command. |
| p (rint)<br><br>(/format)<br><br>expression | Prints the value of an expression. Expressions are a C style, well... expressions such as:<br><br>• a+b (if your executable contains debug symbols that will tell GBD where to find the variables a and b in memory) will print the sum of the a and b variables.<br><br>• *0x1FFFF7E8 will print some bytes of your unique identifier.<br><br>• $ can be used as register names (for arm, $r0, $r9, $pc, and so on; for x86_64, $rax, $rcx, $rip, and so on).<br><br>• You can call program functions as in C.<br><br>The format is something you will use a lot while debugging/reversing programs since GBD (without the debugging symbols – our usual use case) has no idea of the type of the variable.<br><br>The format usually prints the formatted value (x for hexadecimal, t for binary, d for decimal, o for octal, f for a float).<br><br>It is interesting to note that print will decode a de-referenced pointer (for example, to a structure) if it knows the type you type-casted it to. |
| (e) x (amine)<br><br>(/format)<br><br>expression | Basically, the same deal as print but it actually takes the expression value as an address to be displayed.<br><br>The (optional) format usually comes in three parts:<br><br>1. A numeric repeat value (that is, show me x size things starting from the address expression).<br><br>2. A printing format value (like print but with the additional i format to decode assembler instructions).<br><br>3. A size value (for anything else than i), which will tell GDB how to access and display the value at the address. It is very interesting to us since (without symbols) GDB has no clue about the type of data stored at the address. Interesting sizes are the following:<br><br>- g: A 64-bit double-word<br><br>- w: A 32-bit word<br><br>- h: A 16-bit half-word<br><br>- b: An 8-bit byte<br><br>- c: An 8-bit byte decoded as an ASCII character<br><br>- s: A 0 terminated string starting at the target address |
| b (reakpoint)<br><br>expression | Will place a breakpoint at the address of the expression (can be an address like *0x08000123 or a function name if we have debug symbols). The execution will stop and GDB will prompt you for action when this address is reached. |
| c (ontinue) | Resume execution until the program ends or a breakpoint is reached. |
| next | Execute until the next line of code (only works if debug symbols are present). |
| stepi<br><br>(n) | Execute one (or n if the n argument is present) assembler instruction. It is extremely practical to follow an execution instruction by instruction (if you don't know the assembly very well, for example). |
| d (elete)<br><br>(n) | Delete all (without an n argument) breakpoints. If an n argument is present, it deletes the breakpoint number n (for example, if you understood a loop you were looping through and want to let it execute and break after it, or if you are running out of breakpoints on a platform where they are limited in numbers like ARM). |
| wa(tch)<br><br>expression | Watches for an expression to evaluate as true and then breaks. It is very practical to see where a variable of interest is changed in the code. |
| i(nfo) | Info is shorthand to get plenty of information on the running program and comes with a *ton* of possible information. Please launch gdb and type h  i. My favorites are the following:<br><br>• i(nfo) r(egisters): Displays all the registers of the platform<br><br>• i(nfo) f(rame): Displays stack frame info<br><br>• i(nfo) br(eakpoints): Shows info about the existing breakpoints |
| fr(ame)<br><br>(number) | Shows the successive stack frames, holding the successive function call information (which function with which arguments called which function with which arguments called...) that leads to the place in code where you are currently breaking.<br><br>When called with a number, it sets the scope to the function called at the frame number, which allows you to look into the execution state at that point. |

Whoof! That's a lot! And only a small subset of the commands, but these are the ones you will be using all... the... time. Don't forget, this is actually a skill that requires practice to acquire. Don't be discouraged; persist and keep this in mind: I selected open source software for everything in this book not just because it is free but also because it is incredibly well-documented – read the manuals!

At this point, we know how to debug a program live on a chip and (a bit about) how to manage the debugging process. Your fingers should be itching to hit the keyboard and your mind boiling with hacking possibilities! Let's put that into practice, shall we?

# Understanding ARM assembly – a primer

Wait... assembly? What? Wasn't C low-level enough?

Well, in short... No. In our case, Ghidra decompiles to C but Ghidra cannot (some things are in development but at the time of writing are not mature enough to be regularly used) directly act as a debugger frontend.

Additionally, it is very important for you to understand one or two assembly languages in order to understand how an MCU/CPU actually executes code. Once you have integrated one assembly language, all the others will be very, very similar in structure.

Between the assembly code for two different architectures, the mnemonics can be different (mnemonic is the name for a binary instruction that the CPU understands), but the way they interact will largely follow the same principles.

Also, the base operations are largely the same! After all, a CPU is nothing more than a very fast calculator. You can expect all of them to be able to do integer additions, subtractions, multiplication, tests, comparisons, and memory manipulations.

Wait! Didn't I forget division in there? And what about floating-point numbers? Well, sometimes, you have to know that division is the worst enemy of a CPU – especially floating-point division. The first thing you have to know is that the smaller ARMs don't even support integer hardware division (`https://community.arm.com/developer/ip-products/processors/b/processors-ip-blog/posts/divide-and-conquer`)! And that floating-point math is also an option the ARM chip maker has to pay for (look up for ARM **floating-point unit** (**FPU**) and that comes as a kind of separate co-processor! Fascinating, isn't it?

# General information and syntax

Here is some general information about the ARM architecture. You have to keep this in mind when reading ARM assembly code:

- Instructions come in two flavors: ARM (four byte instructions) and thumb (either two or four instructions). The last bit of the **PC** register (the **program counter**, holds the address of the current instruction) is used to indicate whether the instruction mode is thumb or ARM in the CPUs that support both (0 means ARM, 1 means thumb). This means that the instructions have to be memory-aligned to at least two bytes for thumb mode (due to the last address bit being used for the mode) and four bytes for ARM mode.

- (Most) ARM chips support both a big-endian and little-endian operating mode.

- ARM chips have a barrel register for operands, making it easy to bit-shift operands and operate on them in a single instruction.

- Most instructions come with conditional forms (that is, they will only be executed if certain status flags are set) and sized forms (to indicate on what part of the target/source registers/address it applies to) and can be suffixed with s to indicate that the **Current Program Status Register** (**CPSR**) must be updated. Look into how an ARM or thumb instruction is encoded if you want more details (http://www.csbio.unc.edu/mcmillan/Comp411F18/Lecture06.pdf).

- The architectures have multiple versions and not all instructions are available on all versions. See https://www.cs.umd.edu/~meesh/cmsc411/website/proj01/arm/armchip.html and the architecture manuals relevant to your architecture version of interest.

- The architectures (depending on the version) are sometimes available in 32-bit (AARCH32) and 64-bit (AARCH64) flavors. The 64-bit version is available starting with the ARMv8 ISA.

The ARM registers are as follows:

| Register base name | Alias | Function |
| --- | --- | --- |
| R0 | | General-purpose, used as the register holding the first argument and the return value of a function by most compilers. |
| R1 | | General-purpose, used as the register holding the second argument of a function by most compilers. |
| R2 | | General-purpose, used as the register holding the third argument of a function by most compilers. |
| R3 | | General-purpose, used as the register holding the fourth argument of a function by most compilers. In the official calling convention, if there are more arguments than r0-r3 can hold, the caller must allocate memory and pass a pointer to this memory in r0. The compiler may or may not respect this official calling convention. |
| R4-R11 | | General-purpose and intra-function. If it uses it, the called function is supposed to push it to the stack and restore it on returning. |
| R12 | | General-purpose, scratchpad. In the official calling convention, this only holds temporary values, and a called function can do whatever it wants with it and doesn't have to restore it before returning. |
| R13 | SP | Stack pointer. If the ARM architecture supports it, it is banked in between the processes (that is, changing the process context will change the SP, allowing you to have different SPs per process). This is the memory address where the PUSH/POP functions will save and restore registers to/from. |
| R14 | LR | This register holds the return address of a function that is called with the **Branch and Link** (**BL**) instruction. |
| R15 | PC | This is the memory address of the next instruction (before its execution). |
| CPSR | | CPSR contains the flags that are related to the execution context of the current instruction flow. Find a complete description on ARCH32: https://developer.arm.com/docs/ddi0595/h/aarch32-system-registers/cpsr. |

At this point, the flags you are most interested in are the CPSR flags:

| Flag name | Bit | Description |
| --- | --- | --- |
| N (negative) | 31 | Set if the result of an operation is negative. |
| Z (Zero) | 30 | Set if the result of an operation is zero. |
| C (Carry) | 29 | Set if the result of an unsigned operation overflows the target register size. |
| V (Overflow) | 28 | Just like the carry flag but for signed operations. |
| Q (Saturation) | 27 | Set if saturation occurs during the execution of a saturating operation (see the instruction's definition for your architecture in ARM's documentation). You have to explicitly clear this flag with an MSR instruction. |
| GE (Greater than or Equal) | 19:16 | Used for parallel addition and subtraction. |
| E (Endian) | 9 | Controls the endianness of the CPU.<br><br>0: little-endian<br><br>1: big-endian |
| A (Abort) | 8 | *ACTS AS A MASK!*<br><br>0: **SErrors (system errors)** Not masked<br><br>1: Masked |
| I (IRQ) | 7 | *ACTS AS A MASK!*<br><br>0: **IRQ (Interrupt ReQuests)** Not masked<br><br>1: Masked<br><br>More fine control of IRQs via the **Nested vector interrupt controller (NVIC)** |
| F (FIQ) | 6 | *ACTS AS A MASK!*<br><br>0: **FIQ (Fast Interrupt reQuests)** Not masked<br><br>1: Masked<br><br>FIQs have priority over IRQs. This is used for very, very, very fast interrupts (the FIQs have their own banked register to gain time). This is very specialized and very rare. Look into it when you encounter it; the topic is too advanced for now. |
| T (Thumb) | 5 | Indicates if the processor is in Thumb mode. If set, Thumb mode is active. If cleared, Thumb mode is not active. |
| M (Mode) 5 bits | 4:0 | Indicates the current processor mode. See the following table. |

The modes (on 5 bits) are as follows:

| Bits | Mode |
| --- | --- |
| 10000 | User |
| 10001 | FIQ |
| 10010 | IRQ |
| 10011 | Supervisor |
| 10111 | Abort |
| 11011 | Undefined |
| 11111 | System |

Now that we have seen the different registers and how they govern the chip's behavior, let's look into the different instructions.

## Exploring the most useful ARM instructions

All the instructions are documented on the ARM website. When you see a strange version of an instruction pop up in GDB or an assembly dump, always refer to ARM's online documentation (*of course, the version relevant to your target architecture version*) to know what you are looking at.

I will only look into the most common instructions that are valid across all versions and will not delve into the most complicated features of the ISA (please refer to the ARM instruction documentation if you see strange things in a de-compilation, such as exclamation marks).

Also note that not all flexibility (rotations, large ranges of immediate values, CPSR updates, and so on) options and not all registers as operands are available for all instructions in thumb mode since the constraints on instruction encoding are much tighter than in ARM mode. Normally, and depending on your compiler's intelligence, you will need to do some operations by hand, or your compiler may add instructions to do the job for you. In some instances (for example, code injection), it may be a bit annoying. When you reach this point, you will know how to fix that. As per usual, please refer to ARM's documentation; these constraints will be indicated.

I will present *just a few selected instructions* that are the most common and useful for your usage. When you encounter a strange instruction, please refer to the relevant ARM manual.

If you didn't get the hint from the few preceding paragraphs:

- In case of doubt: Refer to ARM's documentation.

- Fear or a lack of understanding: Refer to ARM's documentation.

- Night terror, loss of hair, back pain, unexpected pregnancy: Refer to ARM's documentation (or your local physician).

Here are the instructions:

- Memory and register transfer instructions:

| | |
|---|---|
| MOV | Moves a register or an immediate (fixed) value to another register. Due to how the immediate values are encoded in the instructions, you sometimes must do it in multiple steps to load the final value (depends on the value). |
| LDR | Loads a value in a register from memory. It can increment the address register. |
| STR | Stores a value from a register to memory. It can increment the address register. |

These instructions come with size modifiers and condition modifiers. Note that the [] syntax indicates a memory address and can indicate an additional offset.

For example:

| | |
|---|---|
| mov r1, #128 | Puts 128 in r1 without updating the CPSR. |
| movs r1, r2 | Copies the value of r2 in r1 and updates the CPSR accordingly. |
| ldrh r1, [r2] | Puts the lower 2 bytes of the value at the memory address held in r2; 0 extended to 32 bits in r1. |
| ldrs r1, [r2] | Puts the value at the memory address held in r2 in r1 and updates the CPSR accordingly. |
| strb r1, [r4, #4] | Stores the lowest byte of r1 at the memory address held in r4 + 4. |
| strb r1, [r5], r3,ror #4 | Stores the lowest byte of r1 to the address held in r5, then increments r5 by r3 rotated right four times. |
| strbs r1, [r4] | Stores the lowest byte of r1 at the memory address held in r4 and updates the CPSR accordingly. |

- Integer math instructions:

| ADD | Adds two registers together or an immediate value to a register. |
|---|---|
| MUL | MULtiply registers together (also comes in accumulative flavors such as MLA, MLSMultipLy and Accumulate, Multiply and Subtract). |
| SUB | Subtract two registers together or an immediate value to a register.<br><br>**WARNING:** SUBS can be read as subtract and update the CPSR. In most cases, it is true, but if it is SUBS pc, lr, then *in this case, it is special and means* exception return, without stack popping. It may be just me pulling weird shenanigans but I lost multiple nights over this one trying to calculate the offset of where I was compared to my calling function while injecting assembly. |

For example:

| add r1, r2 ,r3 | r1 = r2+r3 |
|---|---|
| adds r1, r1 ,r2 | r1 = r1+r2 and update the CPSR accordingly |
| adds r1, r1 ,#1 | r1++ and update the CPSR accordingly, often used in loops |
| muls r1, r1 ,r2 | r1 = r1*r2 and update the CPSR accordingly |
| subs r1,r1,#1 | r1-- and update the CPSR accordingly, often used in loops |
| subs pc, lr | *It's a trap!* |

- Bit-wise operations instructions:

Whether you like it or not, these operations *always* update the N and Z flags in the CPSR:

| AND | Bit-wise AND between two registers |
|---|---|
| ORR | Bit-wise OR between two registers |
| EOR | Bit-wise **Exclusive OR (XOR)** between two registers |
| BIC | BIt Clear (that is, AND NOT) between two registers |
| LSL | Left-shifts a register by a number of bits (the number can be either an immediate value or a value in a register). As per usual with the << operator in C, overflowing bits are **lost**. |
| LSR | Right-shifts a register by a number of bits (the amount can be either an immediate value or a value in a register). As per usual with the >> operator in C, overflowing bits are **lost**. |
| ROR | Rotates the bits in the register right. This means that the overflowing bits are put on the other end of the register. You remember when I talked about a barrel register in ARM? It works just like the loading chamber of a revolver: it "rotates" around a central pivot, just changing the starting read point and rolling around. |

For example:

| | |
|---|---|
| `and r1, r1, r2` | `r1 = r1 & r2` |
| `orr r1, r1, r2` | `r1 = r1 | r2` |
| `eor r1, r1, r2` | `r1 = r1 ^ r2` |
| `bic r1, #0xff` | NOT WORKING, for BIC, the second operand CANNOT be an immediate value. |
| `bic r1, r2` | `r1 &= ~r2` |
| `lsl r1, #1` | `r1 <<=1` (that is `r1 = r1 * 2`) |
| `lsr r1, #2` | `r1 >>=2` (that is `r1 = r1 / 4`). Remember how division is the enemy? Not when it is a power of 2!) |
| `ror r1, #2` | `r1 = r1>>2 | r1<<30` (think about it ;) ) |

- Test instructions:

These instructions test things and update the CPSR accordingly:

| | |
|---|---|
| TST | TST compares two registers and updates the CPSR's N, Z, and C flags accordingly, *but not V*. Basically, it behaves like ANDS but discards the result. |
| TEQ | TEQ compares two registers and updates the CPSR's N, Z, and C flags accordingly, *but not V*. Basically, it behaves like EORS but discards the result. |
| CMP | CMP compares two registers and updates the CPSR's N, Z, C, and V flags accordingly. Basically, it behaves like SUBS but discards the result. |

For example: (in our example, `r0 = 0xf, r1 = 0xf, r2 = 0xc, r3 = 0x3`):

| | |
|---|---|
| `tst r2, r3` | `0xc & 0x3 = 0` – the Z flag is set; the N and C flags are cleared. |
| `tst r2, r3` | `0xf & 0x3 = 0x3` – the Z flag is cleared; the N and C flags are cleared. |
| `teq r0, r1` | `0xf ^ 0xf = 0` – the Z flag is set; the N and C flags are cleared. |
| `teq r0, r2` | `0xf ^ 0xf = 0x3` – the N, Z, and C flags are cleared. |
| `cmp r3, r0` | `0x3 - 0xf = 0xfffffff4` (negatives are stored as Two's complement); the N flag is set; Z, C, and V are cleared. |
| `cmp r1, r0` | `0xf - 0xf = 0x0` – the Z flag is set; N, V, and C are cleared. |

1.  Execution flow control instructions: These instructions control the execution. They control jumping around within the code and the execution state:

| | |
|---|---|
| B | Branch to a place in code. The argument can be a `pc` relative offset or a register holding the address to branch to (**not a register**) |
| BL | Branch to a place in code and update the `lr` register with the address of the next instruction. The argument can be a `pc` relative offset or a register holding the address to branch to (**not a register**) |
| BX | Branch to a place in code. `BX` also changes the execution of the CPU depending on the lowest bit of the address.<br><br>(0 = ARM, 1 = Thumb)<br><br>The argument can be a `pc` relative offset or a register holding the address to branch to (**not a register**) |
| BLX | Branch to a place in code and update the `lr` register with the address of the next instruction. BX also changes the execution of the CPU depending on the lowest bit of the address (0 = ARM, 1 = Thumb).<br><br>The argument can be a `pc` relative offset or a register holding the address to branch to (**not a register**) |
| CBZ | Compares the first register argument and branch to a place in the code if the Z flag is set **but doesn't change the flags**.<br><br>The second argument can be a pc relative offset to branch to (**not a register**) |
| CBNZ | Compares the first register argument and branch to a place in code if the Z flag would not be set **but doesn't change the flags.**<br><br>The second argument can be a `pc` relative offset to branch to (**not a register**). |

Not all conditions are available on all versions of the architectures and the offsets can be limited. As per usual, in case of doubt: refer to ARM's documentation.

For example : (`r0` = 0 was just affected):

| | |
|---|---|
| `blx r1` | Jumps to the address held in `r1` and changes the instruction set (ARM/Thumb) depending on the last bit of the address. |
| `b #8` | Jumps to the address at `pc+8` keeping the current execution mode (that is, ignoring the next instruction in ARM mode). |
| `cbz r1, #8` | Jumps to `pc+8`. |
| `cbnz r1, #8` | Does not jump to `pc+8`. |

2.  Stack management instructions:

| | |
|---|---|
| push | Pushes a set of register values on the stack and changes sp accordingly. |
| | Very often used to save a caller context in a callee function prelude. |
| pop | Pops a set of register values on the stack and changes sp accordingly. |
| | Very often used to restore a caller context in a callee function return. |

For example:

| | |
|---|---|
| push {r4, r5, r6, r7, lr} | Pushes some used registers and the calling address that is in lr. |
| pop {r4, r5, r6, r7, pc} | Pops the saved registers and the calling address to the pc (it was in lr when the function was first called). |

Now that we have looked into the most commons instructions and how the CPU registers change the CPU's behavior, let's put that into action!

# Using dynamic reverse engineering – an example

I've prepared a variant of the previous example that will pose us some challenges. I will show you how to overcome these challenges both statically and dynamically in order for you to be able to compare the amount of effort needed in both cases.

The rule of thumb when comparing dynamic and static approaches is that 99% of the time, dynamic approaches are just easier and should be given priority if possible (don't forget that you may not be able to get access to JTAG/SWD or other on-chip debugging protocols).

In this section, we will also learn how to break where we want, inspect memory with GDB, and all this good stuff!

The target program is located here in the folder you cloned, in the ch12 folder.

First, let's start by loading it into Ghidra and inspect it superficially. Pay attention to setting the correct architecture and base address in Ghidra's loading window (refer to the previous chapter if you don't remember how to do that or the base address value).

# First Ghidra inspection

At first glance, the main function looks very similar to the main function in the previous chapter. We can find the reference to the main function by searching a `PASSWORD` string just like in the previous chapter and look into analyzing its structure.

I will let you work on the skills you acquired in the previous chapter to find the different functions. In this executable, you will find the following again:

- A big `while (true)` loop that acts as the main event loop and blinks the bluepill's LED while acting on a password being entered

- A function to initialize the clock

- A function to initialize the GPIOs

- A function to initialize the UART

- A value depending on the chip's unique identifier is calculated again in almost the same way (calculate this value for your chip and note this value down)

- A function validates the password (just before a big `if` that triggers either the printing of *YOU WIN* or *NO*)

- A function decrypts the winning string if the validation function returns an (`uint16_t`) 0 value.

The similarity of the structure is intentional as this is your first time. If I were to repeat the exact same steps as in the previous chapter, it wouldn't give you anything new to learn, right?

Now, let's go through multiple methods of bypassing this password validation through dynamic interaction with the system. We will go from the most complex to the simplest in order to keep you focused and acquiring know-how (if you are anything like me, if there is an easy way to bypass something, why go for the hard way?).

# Reversing the expected password

The first thing we're going to do is try to see how the password is validated to understand how to generate a password that passes the tests.

Let's have a look at the validation function equivalent C code that is output by Ghidra:

```
undefined4 validate_password(undefined4 param_1,undefined2 param_2)

{
  undefined4 uVar1;
  int local_c;

  local_c = 0;
  while (local_c < 0x47) {
    *(undefined *)(local_c + DAT_08000304) = ~PTR_DAT_08000300[local_c];
    local_c = local_c + 1;
  }
  uVar1 = (*(code *)(DAT_08000304 + 1))(0,param_1,param_2);
  return uVar1;
}
```

Figure 12.2 – The decompiled validation function is not actually doing what you think!

Humm... this is doing nothing directly with the parameters. This is copying the content of a 0x47 (71) long static array of bytes to RAM (and NOTs it) and then calls it as a function.

This is strange.

Or is it?

This is a very common technique to camouflage code (of course, a very simple version of it). If a clear version of the opcode is not present in the .bin file (and hence not in the flash of the MCU), a reverse engineering tool like Ghidra cannot detect that it is code! Here, we have two possible approaches:

- Either we manually extract the content of the buffer from the .bin file, decipher it (here, the cipher is just NOT'ing byte by byte, it is trivial on purpose), and have this be de-compiled by Ghidra.

- Or, since we have JTAG access to the chip, we can just put a breakpoint on the correct address in memory and let the MCU do the hard work for us.

I will leave the first solution for you to implement as an exercise. It should take more or less 10 lines of Python or C code for such a simple task! You want to be a hacker? Hack away!

Me? I'm a lazy guy. If a computer can work for me, well... So be it! I'll go for the second solution.

First, let's fire up a screen session in a terminal so we can enter passwords and see how it reacts:

```
screen /dev/ttyUSB0 115200
```

Let's fire up OpenOCD and GDB in a second terminal, as we did at the beginning of the chapter, and let's poke around:

```
openocd -f ./ftdi2232h.cfg.tcl -f ./clone_CSK.cfg &
gdb-multiarch -x ./gdbinit
#openocd launching
[...]
target halted due to debug-request, current mode: Thread xPSR:
0x01000000 pc: 0x080013b8 msp: 0x20005000
[...]
```

And... and damn! It doesn't give me control back! No problem if that happens to you – a little *Ctrl + C* will give you control back straight away:

```
^C
Program received signal SIGINT, Interrupt.
0x080003aa in ?? ()
(gdb)
```

After our *Ctrl + C* (^c), gdb tells us that the execution is stopped at address 0x080003aa in an unknown function (??).

Depending on your specific state, you may break at another address.

Do not panic – put your thinking hat on and take your towel with you (always).

This is not a problem. The chances are that you will be breaking very near this address since it is in the waiting loop that blinks the LED, waiting for a password to be received on the serial interface.

First things first, let's have a look at our registers:

```
(gdb) i r
r0 0x0 0
r1 0x8001a1d 134224413
r2 0x5b8d7f 5999999
r3 0x335d7 210391
r4 0x20004f88 536891272
```

```
r5 0x8001a74 134224500
r6 0x0 0
r7 0x20004f88 536891272
r8 0x0 0
r9 0x0 0
r10 0x0 0
r11 0x0 0
r12 0xf 15
sp 0x20004f88 0x20004f88
lr 0x80003bf 134218687
pc 0x80003aa 0x80003aa
xPSR 0x81000000 -2130706432
msp 0x20004f88 0x20004f88
[...]
```

We see that `pc` is indeed where it is supposed to be, everything looks fine and dandy. So, now let's try to enter a password.

And... nothing works on the serial interface window! Thinking hat on... GDB is actually blocking the execution of the code; the serial interface will not react to your inputs. This is normal.

So, let's allow it to continue (`continue` or `c` in the `gdb` window) and see if the serial works now. Yes, it does. Let's break it again and put a breakpoint on the address of the password validation function, shall we?

In Ghidra, we can see that the address of the first instruction of the function is `0x080002b0`:

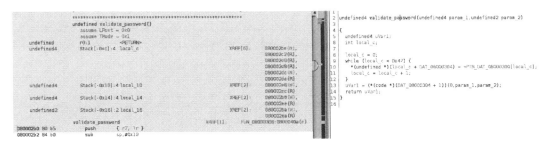

Figure 12.3 – Finding a function address in Ghidra

Let's put a breakpoint there, let gdb resume execution, and enter a dummy password:

```
(gdb) b * 0x080002b0
#1
Breakpoint 1 at 0x80002b0
#2
(gdb) c
#3
Continuing.
Note: automatically using hardware breakpoints for read-only
addresses.   #4
[entering 'aaa' in the serial console and enter]
Breakpoint 1, 0x080002b0 in ?? ()
#5
(gdb)
```

Let's dissect that:

1. b * 0x080002b0 asks GDB to put a breakpoint on the instruction stored at address 0x080002b0. Check your pointers.

2. GDB tells me, *Okay, I've put a breakpoint there.*

3. Continue the execution please, my dear GDB... and it says it is happy to do so.

4. BUT it notifies me that it can't write at address 0x080002b0 (it is in flash and flash cannot be written *just like that*; it has to be unlocked and written chunk by chunk). In order to avoid doing so much back and forth, ARM chips come with some internal debug systems that allow it to break when pc hits specific addresses that cannot be easily written to).

5. Bam! The breakpoint has been hit! The execution is stopped after I enter a dummy password.

Okay, now what can we do with that?

First things first, if you remember the code of the validation function, its arguments were passed directly to the decoded code. Let's have a look at what they can be (remember the calling convention for functions: arguments are in r0-3):

```
(gdb) p/x $r0
$2 = 0x20000028
(gdb) p/x $r1
$3 = 0x2169
```

The first argument is something in RAM, and the second is some kind of value. (This is the transformed UUID value for your chip, which you noted down, right?)

Now, what is stored at this first address? Let's examine it:

```
(gdb) x/x 0x20000028
0x20000028: 0x00616161
(gdb) x/s 0x20000028
0x20000028: "aaa"
```

Ah! Ah! Ah! (See what I did there?) This is our password. Please note the usage of the format modifier for the x command.

So, this is expected.

Now let's look into the deciphered code.

Ghidra tells us that the instruction that follows the decoding loops is at 0x080002f0. Let's break there:

```
(gdb) b * 0x080002f0
Breakpoint 2 at 0x80002f0
(gdb) c
Continuing.
Breakpoint 2, 0x080002f0 in ?? ()
(gdb) c
(gdb) x/4i $pc
=> 0x80002f0: movs r0, #0
   0x80002f2: blx r3
   0x80002f4: mov r3, r0
   0x80002f6: mov r0, r3
```

So, the address of the deciphered code is in `r3`. We saw the buffer was `0x47` (71) long. We are in thumb mode (so size 2 instructions). This should be 47/2 : about 35 instructions. The last bit of the address is for the mode; we can get rid of that:

```
(gdb) x/35i ($r3 & (~1))
    0x20000128: push {r4, r5, r6, r7, lr}
    0x2000012a: eors r4, r4
    0x2000012c: eors r3, r3
    0x2000012e: eors r5, r5
    0x20000130: ldrb r5, [r1, r4]
    0x20000132: mov r8, r5
    0x20000134: mov r6, r8
    0x20000136: lsrs r6, r6, #4
    0x20000138: lsls r5, r5, #4
    0x2000013a: orrs r5, r6
    0x2000013c: movs r6, #255 ; 0xff
    0x2000013e: ands r5, r6
    0x20000140: movs r6, #15
    0x20000142: mov r8, r4
    0x20000144: mov r7, r8
    0x20000146: ands r7, r6
    0x20000148: add r6, pc, #16 ; (adr r6, 0x2000015c) #1
    0x2000014a: ldrb r6, [r6, r7]
    0x2000014c: eors r5, r6
    0x2000014e: adds r0, r0, r5
    0x20000150: adds r4, #1
    0x20000152: ldrb r5, [r1, r4]
    0x20000154: cmp r5, r3
    0x20000156: bgt.n 0x20000132
    0x20000158: eors r0, r2
    0x2000015a: pop {r4, r5, r6, r7, pc}
    0x2000015c: str r5, [r4, #36] ; 0x24
    0x2000015e: ldrb r4, [r6, #5]
    0x20000160: ldr r7, [r6, #32]
    0x20000162: subs r2, #55 ; 0x37
    0x20000164: ldr r4, [r2, r5]
    0x20000166: ldr r5, [r1, #100] ; 0x64
```

```
0x20000168: add r3, r12
0x2000016a: adds r4, #68 ; 0x44
0x2000016c: vqadd.u8 q0, q8, <illegal reg q15.5>
```

That's more like it! We see a normal function prelude (saving intra-function registers to the stack), some processing, and a function return. But GDB warns us about illegal instruction parameters (0x2000016c).

When looking at the listing, we see that GDB indicates the usage of a PC relative piece of data:

```
#1 : commented : adr r6, 0x2000015c)
```

This is very often used to store data in an assembly program. adr is a pseudo instruction that tells the assembler, *please add the offset to a label (a named position) in the code.*

Let's look at what is stored there:

```
(gdb) x/4wx 0x2000015c
0x2000015c: 0x79746265 0x3a376a37 0x6e4d5954 0x34444463
(gdb) x/s 0x2000015c
0x2000015c: "ebty7j7:TYMncDD4"
```

This is indeed a string that is used in the process somehow.

Let's step through the first instructions, as an example of how to follow an execution flow. We will first set up gdb so it shows us the interesting registers, content on each step:

```
(gdb) disp/x $r0
1: /x $r0 = 0x20000028
(gdb) disp/x $r1
2: /x $r1 = 0x20000028
(gdb) disp/x $r2
3: /x $r2 = 0x2169
(gdb) disp/x $r3
4: /x $r3 = 0x20000129
(gdb) disp/x $r4
5: /x $r4 = 0x20004f88
(gdb) disp/x $r5
6: /x $r5 = 0x8001a74
(gdb) disp/x $r6
```

```
7: /x $r6 = 0x0
(gdb) disp/x $r7
8: /x $r7 = 0x20004f70
(gdb) disp/x $r8
9: /x $r8 = 0x2
(gdb) disp/i $pc
10: x/i $pc
=> 0x80002f0: movs r0, #0
=> 0x80002f2: blx r3
```

Now we are ready to use `stepi` (step instruction) to see what is going on:

```
0x2000012b: eors r4, r4
0x2000012d: eors r3, r3
0x2000012f: eors r5, r5
```

This zeros r4, r3, and r5 (x^x = 0):

```
0x20000130: ldrb r5, [r1, r4]
0x20000132: mov r8, r5
0x20000134: mov r6, r8
```

This loads the first character of the password string in r5 (r1 is the address and r4 is zeroed at this point) and copies it to r8 and r6:

```
0x20000136: lsrs r6, r6, #4
0x20000138: lsls r5, r5, #4
0x2000013a: orrs r5, r6
0x2000013c: movs r6, #255 ; 0xff
0x2000013e: ands r5, r6
```

This shifts r6 4 bits to the right, r5 4 bits to the left, and puts their ORed value in r4. It then masks out the ORed result with `0xff`, basically exchanging the 4 lower and 4 higher bits of the password character and cleaning out the excess bits!

```
0x20000140: movs r6, #15
0x20000142: mov r8, r4
0x20000144: mov r7, r8
0x20000146: ands r7, r6
```

This moves 15 in r6, copies r4 in r8 and r7, and masks r7 with 15. But why? At this point, r4 is 0! This may be used later – since we saw that r4 was used as an offset on the loading of the password character, r4 is probably a counter! If that is the case, this masking can be used as a kind of modulo... (it's very common to use masking for modulo a power of two -1):

```
0x20000148: add r6, pc, #16 ; (adr r6, 0x2000015c)
0x2000014a: ldrb r6, [r6, r7]
```

This loads the first character of the string that was hidden in r6 and uses r7 and an offset! r4 is definitely a counter here and r7 a modulo'ed version of it. This is a very typical programming way to approach this:

```
0x2000014c: eors r5, r6
0x2000014e: adds r0, r0, r5
0x20000150: adds r4, #1
```

This is XORing the value of the bit swapped password character with the current ranks of the strange string, adding this to r0 and incrementing the r4 counter:

```
0x20000152: ldrb r5, [r1, r4]
0x20000154: cmp r5, r3
0x20000156: bgt.n 0x20000132
```

This loads a new password character with the new offsetting r5. r3 is 0 so the cmp checks r5-r3 and ... Wait ... bgt.n? What is that? Do you remember what to do when you have doubts? Go read the documentation here: https://community.arm.com/developer/ip-products/processors/b/processors-ip-blog/posts/condition-codes-1-condition-flags-and-codes.

So, it jumps if r5 > r3. And r3 is 0, so? This is testing for a 0 terminated string!

This is the main validation logic loop!

Once this is done, it does this:

```
0x20000158: eors r0, r2
0x2000015a: pop {r4, r5, r6, r7, pc}
```

It XORs this sum with the UUID depending on the value it calculated, restores the caller register values, and returns this value. The C code then checks whether this value is null to actually display the winning string. We then just need to arrange it so that our sum is equal to the UUID dependent value for the XOR to be null!

We have the whole logic!

Now let's write a keygen for this. This is very simple – you can do it. I will explain to you how I approached this.

## Making a keygen

So, we need to achieve the highest value possible per byte of the password in order to be slightly under the target value and use a few bytes to reach it.

The first step will be to find, for each byte of the strange string, which nibble swapped printable character (a half byte can be called a nibble) achieves the highest value. This gives us a maximal value string.

Once we have this string, we know that by repeating it $x$ times ($x$ being the largest integer divisor of the UUID dependent value by the max string value), we only have the reminder to complete. We can almost finish that by adding more characters to the maximum value string until we reach a reasonable value that we can finish with a few new characters. The finishing characters follow the same principle to reach the target value.

I will give myself three characters (or four if needed, but three works for all possible values of the UUID dependent value) and brute-force through the possible values to get three printable characters.

This is doable. I've done it, and so can you. :)

As stated before, I am lazy. And I don't want to write a keygen, so let's just make the test succeed, shall we?

# Of course, I aced the test

Okay, so this is the easy solution.

Let's start from scratch and put a breakpoint on the final validation test:

```
(gdb) b * 0x08000428
Breakpoint 1 at 0x8000428
(gdb) c
Continuing.
```

```
[enter any password]
Breakpoint 1, 0x08000428 in ?? ()
(gdb)x/i $pc
=> 0x8000428: bne.n 0x8000492
(gdb)p/x $xPSR
$6 = 0x81000000
(gdb)set set $xPSR = ($xPSR | (1<<30))
(gdb) p/x $xPSR
$5 = 0xc1000000
(gdb)c
-> On serial you will see "YOU WIN! decompress w/ this : ...."
```

And this is why the security of something should never ever rely on a simple test. A way to make it secure could have been to use a key derived from the password to decipher the content of the string.

### What is the added value over binary patching as in the previous chapter?

If the program does any kind of self-check as it should, this is not detectable. But if this was correctly protected, JTAG should be disabled. Check the STM32 manual to see how to do that and how to protect the flash against readback. Be aware that these are not endgame protections; they can be bypassed in multiple ways. Given enough money and motivation, there is always a way.

## Summary

In this chapter, we saw how an attacker can take complete control of the execution flow if they have access to the JTAG interface. We used it to inspect memory while the firmware was executing, and we managed to completely change the behavior of an executable.

In the following chapter, we will see how we can protect a device against all the different problems we have found.

# Questions

1. Give me the name of one band I like a lot. There is a pretty good source in something that is written in this chapter – investigate!

2. ARM is a RISC architecture. How do you think there can be a RISC architecture with such rich instructions and tests?

3. When typing i r (info register) in GDB, it shows other registers – msp, psp, primask, basepri, and faultmask – and controls what they are.

4. Why did I choose to mask the highest bit in the UUID dependent value?

5. Let's say that you want to extract some code for a chip you don't have access to or for which the JTAG was blocked. How could you approach that?

# 13
# Scoring and Reporting Your Vulnerabilities

Now that you have managed to find a lot of problems in your target system, how do you give a score to them and present them to your client? And even more importantly, how do you actually explain the vulnerabilities so it makes sense to your client (both business- and risk-management-wise)?

The most important aspects of scoring and reporting are the following:

- Be consistent (in scoring and format)
- Be clear
- Separate the information based on the audience
- Use a scoring system that is formally agreed on by the client

- If they want to adjust the scoring of a vulnerability, **they own their risk** but this change must leave a written trace

- All the vulnerabilities must be discussed with the client. You may perceive something as being critical, but the clients may have mitigation or countermeasures in place you may not be aware of (for example, they could have a contractual clause with their network provider that actually prevents your wonderful abuse of SMS sending from getting out of hand).

Don't forget, the reporting and scoring part is very human and subjective – do not get stuck or bitter because a client wants to score something lower than your perceived score. They are the risk owner. But, keep a written record – always. Their bad decisions must not come back to bite you on the backside!

We will cover the following topics in this chapter:

- Scoring your vulnerabilities

- Being understandable to everyone

- When engineers don't want to re-engineer

Now let's have a look together at the how.

# Scoring your vulnerabilities

Remember how we used the "gut feeling" we had about the kind of attacker that could compromise a system (In *Chapter 4, Approaching and Planning the Test*) to gauge the time per scenario? We can use the same approach to build a scoring matrix that can be formally validated upfront with our client.

Our scoring matrix is usually a two-dimensional array along the following two dimensions:

- Technical complexity or probability of occurrence of the risk (depending on the specific circumstances)

- Impact

For the technical complexity, it could very well happen that we over- or under-evaluated the effort put into a specific scenario. With the actual vulnerabilities in hand, we can be much more precise about the actual technical complexity that was necessary to compromise the device's function.

The actual impact has to be discussed in advance with the client. It is very clear that an SME and a giant, multinational group will cope with a financial impact in a very different way. For example, the big fish will probably have a lot more financial resources than an SME but could be far more sensitive to reputational risk (stock valuation impact and so on).

When agreeing on an impact scale with a client, the following impact dimensions have to be considered:

- **Financial loss**: Direct or through missed opportunities.

- **Legal risk**: With special attention to the fact that multiple legal frameworks and punishments may be of concern:

  - **Privacy laws**: Especially if European citizens are concerned.

  - **Environmental laws**

  - **Consumer protection laws**: But explicitly exclude safety and electromagnetic disturbance laws – these are highly specialized.

  - **Loss of life or "organic damage"**: Bodies getting cold on the floor can cost a pretty penny and be terribly bad for the company's image.

  - **Contractual risk**: Could the company be sued by consumers or other companies due to the contract in place?

  - Other specific regulations...

- **Reputational risk**: The company image at large. Do you want to run the risk of being seen as selling bad quality products?

- **Operational risk**: Could the company infrastructure and resources be impacted by the vulnerability in a way that would compromise its normal operations?

- **Strategic risk**: *Will the vulnerability*: Allow the product to be duplicated or faked by a third party? Disrupt the financial model of the service? Provide an unfair advantage to a competitor? Leak proprietary processes?

For each of the identified risks, the client will have to agree on its relevance and their perception of the risk's scale. This perception can vary widely from client to client. For example, an SME could see losing a million dollars as critical while a multinational company could score this as medium. This can also vary widely between companies depending on their risk appetite.

For each of these dimensions, you should have a list of corresponding factual measures, for example:

- Regarding the privacy law, looking at 1 record is a 1, 10 records is a 2, 20 is a 3... 100,000 is a 9, and over 1 million is a 10.

- Reputational risk: one device being hacked is a 1, 5% of the pool is a 5, 20% is a 10...

There is a wide variation depending on the company's risk appetite, scales, granularity, and so on.

Here are a few examples of matrices: (1 being considered as irrelevant, 2-3 low, 4-6 medium, 7-8 high, and 9-10 critical).

This is an example of a matrix for a client with a balanced risk appetite:

| | | Complexity/probability (Higher = more complex, less probable) | | | | | | | | | |
|---|---|---|---|---|---|---|---|---|---|---|---|
| | | 1 | 2 | 3 | 4 | 5 | 6 | 7 | 8 | 9 | 10 |
| | 1 | 5 | 5 | 4 | 4 | 3 | 3 | 2 | 2 | 1 | 1 |
| | 2 | 6 | 5 | 5 | 4 | 4 | 3 | 3 | 2 | 2 | 1 |
| | 3 | 6 | 6 | 5 | 5 | 4 | 4 | 3 | 3 | 2 | 2 |
| | 4 | 7 | 6 | 6 | 5 | 5 | 4 | 4 | 3 | 3 | 2 |
| **Higher=** | 5 | 7 | 7 | 6 | 6 | 5 | 5 | 4 | 4 | 3 | 3 |
| **more** | 6 | 8 | 7 | 7 | 6 | 6 | 5 | 5 | 4 | 4 | 3 |
| **impact** | 7 | 8 | 8 | 7 | 7 | 6 | 6 | 5 | 5 | 4 | 4 |
| | 8 | 9 | 8 | 8 | 7 | 7 | 6 | 6 | 5 | 5 | 4 |
| | 9 | 9 | 9 | 8 | 8 | 7 | 7 | 6 | 6 | 5 | 5 |
| | 10 | 10 | 9 | 9 | 8 | 8 | 7 | 7 | 6 | 6 | 5 |

This is an example of a matrix for a client that is more risk-adverse:

|  | | Complexity/probability (higher = more complex, less probable) | | | | | | | | | |
|---|---|---|---|---|---|---|---|---|---|---|---|
|  | | 1 | 2 | 3 | 4 | 5 | 6 | 7 | 8 | 9 | 10 |
| **Higher= more impact** | 1 | 5 | 5 | 4 | 4 | 3 | 3 | 2 | 2 | 1 | 1 |
|  | 2 | 6 | 6 | 5 | 5 | 4 | 4 | 3 | 3 | 2 | 2 |
|  | 3 | 7 | 7 | 6 | 6 | 5 | 5 | 4 | 4 | 3 | 3 |
|  | 4 | 8 | 8 | 7 | 7 | 6 | 6 | 5 | 5 | 4 | 4 |
|  | 5 | 9 | 9 | 8 | 8 | 7 | 7 | 6 | 6 | 5 | 5 |
|  | 6 | 10 | 10 | 9 | 9 | 8 | 8 | 7 | 7 | 6 | 6 |
|  | 7 | 10 | 10 | 10 | 10 | 9 | 9 | 8 | 8 | 7 | 7 |
|  | 8 | 10 | 10 | 10 | 10 | 10 | 10 | 9 | 9 | 8 | 8 |
|  | 9 | 10 | 10 | 10 | 10 | 10 | 10 | 10 | 10 | 9 | 9 |
|  | 10 | 10 | 10 | 10 | 10 | 10 | 10 | 10 | 10 | 10 | 10 |

There are multiple ways to transcribe risk appetite. The scoring can be adapted or the classification of the score can be adapted.

For example, an aggressive risk appetite can be seen as a change in the classification, like so:

- 1-2 Considered irrelevant
- 2-5 Low
- 6-7 Medium
- 8-9 High
- And 10 as critical

There are as many ways to arrange this as you will have clients. The only critical point for you is that this must be set in stone from the start.

Once this is agreed upon, you will turn to the part of engagement that is universally loved by all testers – we all get the most fun from it… Well, actually, we all hate it with a passion, to be honest, but… The section that is actually the most important in order to transmit the right message to our clients is the report.

# Being understandable to everyone

The report is actually the trickiest part of engagement. You may have found the slickest, the smartest, the most impactful vulnerabilities of your whole career on a device, but if you are not able to deliver your message in a clear and understandable way, finding that and nothing is exactly the same... Let's see how we can minimize the risk of being misunderstood by the client.

# Building your report template

The first fundamental thing is: use a template. Not only is reinventing the wheel for every report a waste of time but just imagine yourself in the client's shoes. If they receive two entirely different documents, with different structures and a different approaches, they will have a lot of trouble understanding the point. And if this is a re-test (very common after you have found problems and they want to ensure that the vulnerabilities are actually covered correctly), they won't be able to compare the reports to understand what was done rightly or wrongly.

The template I use, outside of the purely a esthetic and contractual elements, flows like this:

- Management overview: After a given hierarchical level, turning pages and reading becomes hard – put it in first. Additionally, they are the ones signing the checks – better keep them happy!

- Presentation of the device and the test's objectives

- Presentation of the execution of the test: Where, when, meeting dates, and architectural overview.

- A risk management section:

  - For each vulnerability, a non-technical explanation of the vulnerability, the complexity of the attack and impacts, and nice, visible risk scoring.

  - At the end, a reporting matrix: The name and reference number of the vulnerability and final scoring. Risk management likes to see a nice recapitulation table to see a lot of green or a lot of red. Management in general is a very color-sensitive species.

- A separate technical description section, just in order for the company to be able to ventilate the technical descriptions and the various pieces of evidence (screenshots, files, and so on) to technical people. Keep the technical details away from management – this is complicated and could cause a headache. Management is very sensitive to mental strain in general; the less they have to think, the better they feel. For each vulnerability, have the following:

  - A technical description

  - A piece of evidence (a screenshot, for example)

  - If possible, a script for the technical personnel to be able to replicate the findings

  - A recommendation on how to solve the issue of remediating the impact of its realization

- A lexicon: You have to explain every technical word; people shouldn't have to search the internet for technical words. If a word is explained in the lexicon, style it in a specific way so your reader knows that they can find out what it means there.

- A legal section that is standard for your company and validated by your legal team. This can be a pretty sensitive document and may end up being used in court. Cover your bits!

We will talk at length about the types of remediation and controls and the effects they can have in the last chapter.

For your mitigation's recommendations, do not necessarily focus on technical security controls; physical and administrative controls can be just as effective (as a control objective). Also keep in mind that preventive, detective, and curative controls (as a control type) can be applied.

## Usage of language in a report

Your language to be simple – overly simple, such as *"Explaining a vulnerability to your mom"* simple. This is actually a test we use internally in my team: if your mom wouldn't understand, it is too complicated.

You can be detailed in the explanation (at least in the technical section), but you have to pay attention to the way you say things:

- A sequence of events and their consequences (business or technical) have to be explicit.

- Use short sentences and keep the information density low. Your sentences must be easy to digest information chunks.

- Use simple English words. You cannot assume that your reader is a native speaker or is reading your report with translation software at the ready.

- Text must be agreeable to read and agreeable to the teams. You are talking about somebody's work. If you antagonize them in your report, they will antagonize you in the reporting meetings. For example, do not say "this is not implemented correctly;" say "this may not have been taken into consideration in the design or implementation phase."

- Never ever point the responsibility to a specific team, and even less so a specific person. Creating something is a team effort and failures should be shared as much as successes!

You also have to pay attention to the things you say, such as:

- Do not count on the technicality of your reader: Everything with a technical consequence must be explicit (not only might your reader not be very technically gifted but, if they were as security aware as you, they wouldn't need you).

- Do not count on the intelligence of your reader: Everything with a business consequence must be explicit (if something is bound to happen, write it explicitly – something that is clear to you will not necessarily be clear to someone that has their nose in financial reports all day long!).

- Be direct: Do not imply information or "things." If it is in the report, it must be explicit.

# Report quality

You must have a quality control process in place for your report.

After all, you engage your company's reputation and relationship with your client when you deliver a report. These are the precautions we take every time:

- This seems to be self-evident but modern word processors have pretty good grammar and spelling checks: always use them.

- Always have someone else re-read the report before delivery. You may find something that you have written completely clear, but it could be pretty obscure to someone who isn't you.

- Always explain the scoring, vulnerability per vulnerability, to the proofreader and note down the explanations in order to prepare for the delivery meeting.

- The delivered documents should not allow the client to modify the content on their own. Always deliver a signed PDF.

- The more reports you write, the more common vulnerabilities you will find. Compile your findings and reuse the most efficient text for a specific kind of vulnerability. If you are in a company where security tests are a staple activity, automated tools to assist you in drafting standardized reports are available on the market.

Now that your report is written, let's go to the next step of report delivery, the validation meeting.

# When engineers do not want to re-engineer

When delivering your findings, there will always be a pre-delivery meeting. This meeting exists in order to confirm your findings with the product teams and the management. During these reviews, the engineering teams being on the defensive and/or claiming that something can't be fixed (often for budget reasons or because an early go-to-market is desirable) is a common trope.

Always keep minutes of these meetings and have them validated by the client.

For this meeting to have real value for both the testing team and the client, a few select actors have to be present.

From the client's side:

- The security owner of the device from the client's side (most probably the party that requested the assessment)

- A representative of the client's business side (the risk owner on the client's side)

- A representative of the client's compliance or legal side (that is, the party at the client that is in charge of risk management)

- A representative of the client's device technical development team

From the testing team's side:

- A testing team responsible with knowledge of the business relationship between your company and theirs (this is usually their commercial contact)

- A senior member of the testing team (in a small team, this is usually the same person as the previous responsible)

- The actual testers – you have to have the actual person that was doing the test

I will go through the main common explanations for *not going back to the drawing board* and try to give you some key pointers to help clients make better decisions. You should be able to defend your stance, but always keep in mind that, in the end, your client is the owner of their own risk and that you are there to help them find a suitable solution:

- *"The remediation solution you specify isn't the right one for us"*: This can be a fair point. Listen to your client's teams; they know their product and their infrastructure. If they come up with a better remediation plan (or one that is a better fit for them), it's also good. Don't fall into the "my solution is the best because it is mine!" fallacy.

- *"The remediation solution you propose is too expensive/complex/hard/incompatible with our go-to-market date"*: Then, it is up to them to find a cheaper/simpler/faster alternative. Although you can still help them to do so; this is called consulting and has a price. Do not let your client try to drain your life force or financial resources. If push comes to shove, always tell them that it is their risk, and they can always accept the risk, but this is their internal processes at play. You are there to provide an expert opinion, not to skew your opinion to satisfy some of their current constraints (in an assessment context of course, when you are in a consulting context, you are paid to find solutions).

- *"We want to reduce the scoring because we think you scored the impact too high"*: This can be a valid claim, but they have to demonstrate their claim. If they cannot demonstrate the claim, just refuse to lower the scoring. You are acting as a trusted advisor, and sometimes standing your ground is the best advice you can give them. If they have a valid point and it fits the matrix that was agreed upon from the start, then proceed. As per usual, keep a written record.

- *"We want to reduce the scoring because we think you scored the technicality too low"*: This is generally not a valid claim, but, in all fairness, you have to demonstrate your position. At this point, keeping extensive documentation of the test and actually having the tester in the room is invaluable. Answering this kind of challenge can be as simple as *"I have a master's degree in IT and I am not a state-sponsored team. I broke your thingy anyways; your claim is invalid"*.

- *"There are easier ways to achieve the result; we don't see why this is relevant"*: This, for example, often comes in the context of denial of service against the application layer (for example, when leveraging a compromised device to create artificial loads on the backend servers if they are in scope). The engineering team will often argue that a volumetric **Denial of Service (DoS)** against the servers (creating a lot of traffic through a botnet is a volumetric DoS) would have achieved the same easily and hence they don't need to fix the problem. In this case, offering to add a volumetric DoS as a self-reported additional finding in the report for free is relatively efficient but actually misses the point. The fact that your mission is to find potential problems **in a specific context** should be stressed. Just because another context is problematic, it doesn't mean that your findings should be overlooked.

In any case, always stay polite, reasonable, and professional in these meetings. You might be pushing buttons that are sensitive on the internal client politics side of things...

In any case, always stay consistent, and don't lower your professional standards. The clients will pay you for your expert opinion, not to fold under the slightest pressure.

# Summary

In this chapter, we looked into giving a score to our findings that is aligned with our client's risk appetite (and how to define this risk appetite with them in a way that benefits both parties) and how to build a report template that fits our activity.

Now that we have looked into scoring our findings and putting them nicely into a report, let's look into what we can tell our clients they should do about them.

# Questions

1.  Could you give me an example of a matrix for a company with an aggressive stance towards risk?

2.  Could you give me an example of vulnerability scoring for a company with a conservative attitude towards risk (based on the balanced risk appetite matrix)?

3.  How would you reflect the threat landscape of a company that has already been the target of organized crime in the matrix?

4.  Why, in your opinion, should the impact scales be agreed upon and set in stone before the actual testing?

5.  Why, in your opinion, should the internal risk management of the client be involved in the delivery meeting?

# 14

# Wrapping It Up – Mitigations and Good Practices

Now we have found a lot of vulnerabilities, stolen secrets, and disturbed and intercepted communications, but how do we wrap up the story for our clients? How do we link this to existing industry good practices and how do we advise our clients in order for them to realize that they are not the only ones making these mistakes and, more importantly, on how to fix them? And, since this is the last chapter of the book, what do you do next and what kinds of things could you look into to satisfy your curiosity for research?

In order to advise your client on how to solve the problems you found, we will look into the sources you can rely on to relate your findings to good practices (basically to tell your client that their security is bad, and they should feel bad), then quick solutions to common problems, and, in the end, how you can continue bettering yourself at hardware.

We will cover the following topics in this chapter:

- Industry good practices – what are they and where to find them: What recognized standards can you use to take a systematic approach in your reports?

- Common problems and their mitigations: The problems you will find the most and what to do about them.

- What about now? Self-teaching and your first project.

# Industry good practices – what are they and where to find them

There isn't really an OWASP top 10 for hardware but there are some for very closely related subjects that we can actually rely on for reference. Let's have a look at these different standards so that you are aware of them and can select the ones that are the most adequate for your project. Depending on the specific device, one or more standards can apply. This has to be discussed with the client, but you can always refer to them as good practices!

Different verticals (or industries) have different standards for security, safety, and sometimes both. Let's have a look at the most common one (that is, a device targeted at the consumer market): the OWASP IoT top 10, which is very often the default standard framework you can use in most cases.

## OWASP IoT top 10

The OWASP IoT top 10 is available here: `https://wiki.owasp.org/index.php/OWASP_Internet_of_Things_Project#tab=IoT_Top_10`.

Just like the well-known web top 10, this one lists the 10 most common vulnerabilities in IoT devices. Its main downside (which could make it less applicable to your specific device) is that it focuses on IoT in the way that it is mostly understood, that is, as a consumer-targeted device that is communicating with a vendor backend somewhere in the cloud. When using it, you have to be aware that your client, if their device doesn't exactly behave like this, could not really understand how the device is concerned with this framework. The main upside of this set of good practices is that it regroups the most common problems in any device!

Let's look at the 10 items:

- **Weak, guessable, or hard-coded passwords**: Just as this suggests, weak passwords are used by the device. You will most probably find these kinds of problems when reversing the firmware or looking into the embedded filesystems. If the authentication is only relying on password hashes, for example (even if they are well salted), it can be a problem, especially if the hashes are shared across multiple devices!

- **Insecure network services**: This specific item is actually referencing the network services that the device exposes to its network, locally or remotely. You may find here things that are along the lines of usual web vulnerabilities (such as if the device onboards a web server) but also buffer overflows in network-reachable interfaces. We didn't focus on these in this book since they are not really very tightly coupled with the hardware, but you will find plenty of things about these on a lot of online challenge websites (peruse wechall.net, the phonebook for online security challenges, to train yourself on that).

- **Insecure ecosystem interfaces**: The device is using APIs (on the backend side) that are not well secured. Usually, since the API endpoints are not used outside of the device, the vendor is lulled into a false sense of security regarding them. They should also be looked into in the context of the test since attacking the backend through a device (or through knowledge acquired from device analysis) should be a major concern to the client. This is out of scope of this book, but you should also have a look at the OWASP top 10 for APIs here: `https://owasp.org/ www-project-api-security/`.

- **Lack of secure update mechanism**: As usual, the title describes it very well, but you really have to see it with all of the consequences of "secure" and "update":

  - Is there an update mechanism? Can the vendor react to a vulnerability on the device (either a vulnerability in their firmware itself or a vulnerability on an external component they rely upon)?

  - Is the update mechanism secure? Can you actually update the device with a malicious firmware (that either allows you to make it behave maliciously or bricks it)?

- **Use of insecure or outdated components**: Is the device embedding software or hardware components that are known to be insecure or have known vulnerabilities? This usually requires significant effort to harvest all of the used software components, especially if the device is running an embedded operating system such as Linux. Either you can do it manually (this is very long) but some commercial software offerings can help you scan through the libraries and embedded software. Since I don't know any open source software that can help you do that (and I refuse to put marketing material here), I will not name names, but it should be really easy to find.

- **Insufficient privacy protection**: The device, in its function or communication, is divulging (or not protecting enough!) private information about the customer. This should be a prime concern of any client since the legal repercussions can be pretty stringent (have a look into the EU's GDPR, California's Consumer Privacy Act, and so on). According to the UN's conference on trade and development, 66% of countries have a consumer privacy protection law. Data sent in plaintext, localization information, habits, and plenty of private details could be considered as private information. Regroup everything you find and, since we are not lawyers and we can't really be sure, report on everything you find to your customer. Best-case scenario, their lawyers agree but your role is to allow them to actually know what is going on!

- **Insecure data transfer and storage**: Data is sent in plaintext? Lack of ciphering of the EEPROMs? Lack of signature and data integrity measures? All of these findings fall into this section. Once again, your client will decide with living with it or not, but you told them upfront, that's most important!

- **Lack of device management**: This one is actually a little bit of a cornerstone for updating and managing the security elements (keys, customer information, and so on). This is actually maintaining a good and secure inventory of the devices. This is also a very annoying path of attack for the client's backend; imagine what would happen if a malicious actor registered millions of fake devices with fake serial numbers preventing legitimate clients from using their things. This a very funny from a pentesting point of view and will probably make your client make a lot of weird faces.

- **Insecure default settings**: As per usual, the device comes out of the box in an unsecure state, cannot use security measures that are commonplace today (such as only supporting WEP for Wi-Fi security), allows the use of admin/admin for setup, doesn't force the client to change for something secure, and so on; all of these kinds of thing fall into this category.

- **Lack of physical hardening**: Accessing the hardware was as easy as popping two screws? There is no box-opening detection. The PCB has nicely labeled Serial, JTAG, and SPI ports? This all goes in this category.

Now that we looked into the carpet bombing top 10, let's have a look a whole family of best practices that you could drown inspiration upon for looking into firmware.

## The CIS benchmarks

The CIS benchmarks are a whole family of baselines and indicators that you can draw inspiration from when evaluating a device, more specifically, the diverse components of its firmware. You will find a whole bunch of best practices here that can be applied to embedded Linux systems, web servers, and so on.

Here is a (short) list of the ones I personally use the most when reporting on the security level of an embedded system:

- Distribution-independent Linux

- Google Android

- Apache HTTP Server

- Printer devices (even when not talking about a printer, these have interesting points if you are testing for a potential user of the device and not necessarily the vendor of the device)

- **Not everything is necessary relevant but these may be of interest if the device is talking to them (especially to upsell other testing services if your company has the capabilities)**: Amazon, Alibaba, Azure, and Google Cloud Platform

This is a lot of information to consider, so I sincerely invite you to peruse them so that you can reference them in your reporting, if relevant.

## NIST hardware security guidelines

At the moment of writing, hardware security guidelines are being created by NIST. They focus on how companies can get an assurance level on the hardware they are running internally. It may or may not impact the things you will be testing for, but you should definitely keep an eye on these guidelines once they are finalized. Why? Let's see:

- When your client is a device vendor, they will want to know if their device can comply with these rules since it can be a no-go for a lot of their potential clients!

- When your client is not a device vendor but a potential user of the device, you will want to double-check whether they can (or cannot) apply these guidelines to the device you are testing.

OK... that was a lot of administrative things and frameworks. This is OK but not very cool! Let's now look into what we can tell our clients about the possible mitigations when we find a problem!

# Common problems and their mitigations

Here are some key problems that are really common and some indications on how to solve them.

## Establishing a trust relationship between the backend and a device

Here, the main problem is how to establish a trust relationship between a device in the field and the management infrastructure. In order to tackle this problem, a few elements have to be understood, not only about the device itself but also about its fabrication and enrollment process.

The main challenge in the usual situation is that the vendor will want to reduce the actions toward an individual device as much as possible in order to keep the manufacturing costs as low as possible, keep the hardware cost as low as possible, but still get the highest possible level of assurance for their money.

The questions you have to ask for the device are as follows:

- Is the MCU capable of reasonable cryptographic operations (that is, SSL/TLS)?

- Does the MCU have a secure enclave or TPM-like capabilities (ARM TrustZone, a TPM chip, crypto-authentication chips)?

The questions you have to ask for the production process are as follows:

- Do devices already go through a "per-device" process in the production process (programming, testing, and so on)?

- Is the production contracted to a single manufacturer (and how trusted is this manufacturer?

Let's start with the simplest (and also the one providing the highest level of assurance) solution, which is to actually establish this trust relationship in a controlled environment. If the devices are actually powered and tested in a trusted production plant, this is where the relationship should be established. A good example process could be to deliver unique keys to the device (for example, an enclave-stored keypair/client certificate unique to the device and issued by a specific organizational unit of the backend's PKI) based on a construction firmware, and then updating the device with the production firmware. Outside of hardware, proven, secure storage devices (such as a TPM or a secure enclave), there is no absolute guarantee that the trust-establishing element is actually secure (against the most advanced attackers).

If the manufacturer isn't actually trusted or is changing frequently, the trust establishment should be done in an environment that is controlled by the vendor. This is not as unusual as you may think and happens where serious concerns about device counterfeiting or critical intellectual property have to be protected (for example, ciphered FPGA bitstreams, expensive devices, and so on).

Then, going down in the level of assurance offered to the vendor (if the previous solutions are not possible and the device actually supports SSL/TLS operations), the generation of a device-specific client certificate on device enrolling could be envisioned (for example, based on a certificate request issued by the device on first connection to the backend, the request being granted by the backend's PKI, and the key-pair being stored in the device's secure enclave), with the chip authenticated by an enrollment-specific challenge response scheme. Then, details of the enrollment process should be erased from the device through an update to a production firmware.

Getting even lower on the trust scale, if client certificate management/secure storage by device is not possible (very cheap devices and MCUs, small sensors, and so on), the trust could be envisioned as uni-directional: the device onboards public keys for the backend PKI and only verifies the certificate chain that is embedded in the SSL certificates. This is a very low assurance level on its own, but it is better than nothing.

# Storing secrets and confidential data

Again, the only way to seriously protect these things is cryptography. Ideally, each device will have unique per-device root keys that are either provided by the process we discussed earlier and protected in an enclave (better) or derived from stable, device-specific factors (for example, using a strong key derivation algorithm such as **Password-Based Key Derivation Function 2** (**PBKDF2**) with the main chip's unique ID as the password). These root keys must *never* leave the main chip's silicon. When storing data securely on an external device (for example, an external SPI flash), it is strongly advised to use a key wrapping scheme in order to avoid exposing too many operations based on the same key (to give a very simplified example, you store a cypher-key dictionary in the first block that is ciphered with the root key and each chunk of the flash is protected with a different key stored in the encrypted dictionary).

Additionally, each ciphered chunk should have an integrity violation detection mechanism (such as a hash/HMAC, for example) in order for the system to be able to detect data corruption or alteration.

Key wrapping based on chunks of external storage also has the following advantages:

- Avoiding that losing a chunk isn't making you lose the others.

- Avoiding that, you have to rewrite everything if a piece of information is changed in a chunk "in the middle" (flash having a limited number of write cycles, this is not to be neglected, also check the cryptographic scheme that has been selected, but it is relevant for the good ones such as CBC, GCM, and so on, see `https://csrc.nist.gov/projects/block-cipher-techniques/bcm/current-modes` for more information).

# Cryptographic applications in sensitive applications

These rules are, with your current ability to execute tests, things you will have to trust me on. But if they interest you, please put everything I say in doubt and prove me wrong or try to see how you can actually mount these kinds of attacks:

- **Rule 1**: Never invent your own cryptography, That's... it... no... argument, no "yes but", NO. End of discussion. See Phil Zimmerman's *An Introduction to Cryptography* here: `https://www.cs.stonybrook.edu/sites/default/files/PGP70IntroToCrypto.pdf` (page 54) on why...

- **Rule 2**: Embedded devices have to operate in very constrained, energetic environments and all cryptographic implementations have to be checked for side-channel attacks. Read about them; they are the subjects of entire books. Also, you should yourself look into trivial examples of side channels, such as taking more or less time to answer whether a password is long or not, but there are implementations around that focus on minimizing the side channels. You can search for them (an example for AES is found at `https://core.ac.uk/download/pdf/144774958.pdf`). This kind of attack ruined the security of the first generation of MIFARE DESFire RFID chips; do not underestimate them.

- **Rule 3**: Do not rely on things you think are secure but are outside of your silicon for your randomness (and even then...). No... you may have a nice Chua's circuit connected to an ADC on your chip and think it is a "rock-hard" source of randomness (in general, this is the case), but not when your attacker can just cut the trace or solder a wire to ground on your pin. Bad randomness generation has already been the source of *big* security issues in the past (look into `https://github.com/g0tmi1k/debian-ssh`). When randomness is that important, the chip that the process is running on should come with a randomness generation internal peripheral or the harvesting of randomness for the environment (from uncorrelated multiple sources like the Linux kernel does) should be investigated.

## JTAG, bootloaders, and serial/UART interfaces

You will find active JTAG pins, serial interfaces, and all kinds of things that should be here. To put it simply... they shouldn't be here. Outside of a development board or the manufacturing plant (remember that JTAG is also used to verify soldering), they should be deactivated. There is no need for a U-Boot bootloader to wait even for a second before jumping to the actual firmware. Not only should all of these interfaces be deactivated in the chip (most chips have "fuses" to disable them that can be set in firmware in the manufacturing plant) but every means of protecting the firmware against reading and reverse engineering should be enabled. When you evaluate a device, always read the chips' manuals. There is a way to prevent this, 99% of the time.

# What about now? Self-teaching and your first project

This is all nice; you read through this whole book, played with a Furby, have a few bluepills on your desk, as well as a JTAG adapter and a logic analyzer, but... now what?

Like I said before, this is as much a craft as it is a science... so, well, you have to practice! Practice and practice again!

Here is a list of things you can play with for cheap:

- Old routers, modems, and telecom equipment in general: They are super easy to find discarded in an office corner or at a flea market. They usually run some kind of embedded operating system and you may find some things you are not used to (VxWorks, Windows CE, Symbian, and so on) and "weird" architectures (8086, Z80, 68k, PPC, MIPS, and so on).

- Old toys: If you destroy an old toy that you bought for €1 at your local flea market, you won't care! This means that you will actually learn a lot. Even when destroying it you will learn (of course, you have to investigate on how you actually did it). Another upside of old toys is that, since they're built to a price, they use big components (but also epoxy blobs)!

    - **Musical ones**: Not only is circuit bending to make them play strange noises very fun in itself (look at the "Look mum no computer" YouTube channel for basic electronics and circuit bending tip and tricks) but this is actually a good way to learn more about the analog part of the circuits, the basic operation of transistors and all.

    - **Educational toys (such as spelling toys and kid's computers)**: These are especially interesting to play with for extracting EEPROMs, training yourself at reversing storage formats, extracting and replacing strings, and so on.

    - **Radio-guided cars**: These are great for studying and reversing specific radio protocols (also, the commands are usually legal to send back even without a license).

- Old mobile phones (like really old ones) to get a sense of modern construction, small SMD components, and so on.

- Cheap IoT things such as connected doorbells, thermostats, 3/4G gateways, and so on.

Once you have found some interesting targets, just apply the methodology, make functional schemas, reverse the PCB layout, and so on... the toys are your oyster!

# Closing words

I hope you had a lot of pleasure reading this book and that I've been able to get you started on the path of messing with electronics and embedded systems. I think I can never repeat this enough, but persistence and repetition are the key to learning hardware hacking; it is a craft. You will burn yourself, cut yourself, burn components and tools, and other not-so-agreeable moments will happen. You will be stuck at 3 A.M. hunting for bugs in your code or looking for a vulnerability that may not really exist. The key thing is... don't let that stop you. Like anything hacking- or making-related, persistence and courage are actually what will allow you to succeed. A big part of this job is staying up to date on current research: keep reading articles (new ones, old ones... read all the things!), follow security conferences, read Hackaday, Y Combinator, participate in **Capture the Flags (CTFs)**, follow trainings (on a side note, having a serious training budget *must* be on your *must have* list for job hunting), and be part of the community... Who knows, maybe one day you will present research at a major conference (speaking about conferences, volunteer to help; it makes speaking with people so easy)! Stay positive! Acknowledge that we are all standing on the shoulders of giants, and help other people standing on your shoulders. And the most important: be excellent to each other!

Jean-Georges Valle

Brussels, December 2020

# Assessments

## Chapter 1

1. To be able to measure more voltage and current at the same time.

2. The bandwidth of an instrument for which the measure's voltage will be 0.7 times the real voltage.

3. 5 MHz.

4. Dangerous prototypes.

5. A tool to visualize electric signals.

6. To correctly sample a signal, you need to sample it at least at twice the frequency of the signal.

7. Passive probes are limited in frequency, so use a scope that supports active probes for signal > 200 MHz.

## Chapter 2

1. A Bluetooth service that allows object exchanges.

2. ARM

3. A frequency band available for use without licensing; yes – 2.4GHz

4. Yes

5. Yes

6. Harvard architecture has separate instructions and data buses while both are on the same bus for von Neumann architecture.

7. Usually inside but some MCUs support additional external memory.

# Chapter 3

1.  Preferably three or more:

    The first one will be used for exploratory surgery and getting familiar with the system general architecture, identifying tricky or dangerous sections/subsystems, soldering/soldering, probing, and so on without being slowed down by excessive concerns about burning a system you will need for actual testing. This doesn't mean you should be reckless with this one, nor that you will necessarily actually destroy it.

    The second one will be used in case you destroy components in the first one, either for component cannibalization to fix the first one or because the first become too damaged. This will also be used to compare two systems later to see if some security elements aren't shared when they shouldn't be (ciphering keys, certificated, and so on) or to see if you can change a system's identity if it's relevant.

    The third one will, since you are fairly familiar with the system at this point, allow you to gather pre-initialization data (for example, the content of an EEPROM or storage component before the system is provisioned or associated with a backend system, et) so that you can test scenarios along the lines of: Can I force re-enrollment while the system is supposed to prevent it ? Can I find flaws in the system's enrollment logic? Can I pose as an already enrolled system and steal keys? Can I force weak initialization of cryptography?

2.  No, absolutely not – on the contrary, you should have contractual clauses authorizing you to damage the test systems:

    First, you can fail at any point by slipping, burning a component, and so on. This is fundamentally different from software pentesting since once the magic smoke is out of a component, no re-installation in the world will solve the problem.

    Second, just imagine how limited you would be! You'd have no way to remove a chip and dump it in a controlled environment, no way to scrape the solder-mask off of a trace to probe it, and no way to replace the data in an EEPROM to see what it changes on the system. This would be the equivalent, in a software pentest, of saying "Please test this system, but you are not allowed to connect to it," which makes no sense at all.

3. When you are reading a voltage with your multimeter, you are actually using an ADC. Simply put (there are thousands upon thousands of pages of literature on them, including dedicated courses on them, their types, and so on), this electronic device will try to "guess" more and more accurately where the voltage that you are reading is compared to known voltages. It does this by sampling and comparing it repeatedly. When you have a digital bus, sometimes, it will sample with the bus in a high state, while other times, it will do so in a low state, appearing somewhere between the two. The opposite technique can be used to produce floating-point voltages too! Have a look at what ADCs are and at a technique called **pulse width modulation** (**PWM**) if you are interested (you definitely should ;)). As a side note, "real" floating-point voltage can also be produced by digital DACs.

4. At the time of writing, the price difference between the cheapest **surface mount** (**SMD**) and the cheapest **through-hole** (**TH**) packages from the same chip producer was 0.12€ per chip for the exact same die. The price of the packaging has a real impact on the chip's price; more metal, more plastic, more manipulation = more expensive. Think about the price part in the epoxy blob section and always keep this in the back of your mind, especially when it comes to security considerations. It is not uncommon for vendors to scrape a few cents here and there by selecting MCUs without floating-point hardware or a security feature, thus opening interesting possibilities for the pentester.

5. The 7400 and 4000 families are very popular for glue logic. Their main differences come to the type of transistor they are historically made from (though this is not true anymore). The 7400 family used to be made from BJT transistors, while the 4000 family used to be made from CMOS transistors. Due to this difference, the 7400 family used to be less energy efficient but faster. Today, you can find typical 7400 **integrated circuits** (**ICs**) made from CMOS or other transistor technologies (the letters after the 74 usually indicate the technology used) to balance speed and energy consumption.

6. The Federal Communications Commission keeps information about systems with wireless communication.

7. The 6502 has an address and a data bus, which means it's a Von Neumann architecture.

# Chapter 4

1.  Spoofing, tampering, repudiation, information leak, Denial of Service, escalation of privilege.

2.  From a risk standpoint, it is meant to identify the threats that are the most relevant to the product and test them. From a practical point of view, it allows the client to decide where to spend the testing budget in a way that covers the most important risks and helps us prioritize test scenarios.

3.  Who, What, Where, Why, and How.

4.  Yes and no; it depends on the following:

    a. The color of the approach (black, gray, or white) since that gives you a leg up compared to a more capable adversary.

    b. The time budget available. Being honest to your client and saying that you need more time because this specific test requires more effort is usually a reasonable way to go about this.

5.  This is very important because problems WILL be found, in the system itself or in the components it relies on. From an impact perspective, if the system producer cannot patch a vulnerability or a bug, it will impact its reputation.

6.  This is a test where you simulate an attacker with no privileges/information about the system. It is the most representative approach of attackers and will be the most common attack that's performed against the system.

7.  This is a business impact point that is especially sensitive for the client and is the end goal for an attacker.

# Chapter 5

1.  It is the **Output Data Register** (**ODR**) for the bank of GPIO, the pin that drives the LED it is attached to. The same effect can be achieved by toggling the output using the BSRR and BRR registers of the GPIOC port.

2.  No, because the PLL is only fed HDI/2 (4 MHz) and the maximum multiplier in the PLL is 16 (so a 4*16 = 64 MHz output). Since the HSI (which is an RC resonator) is less stable (frequency wise) than that of a crystal oscillator, the output clock will also be less stable.

3.  Let' search though the library code for code that start with `rcc_clock`:
    `$grep 'rcc_clock_s' bluepill/libopencm3/include/`
    `libopencm3/stm32/f1/rcc.h`:

    ```
    void rcc_clock_setup_in_hsi_out_64mhz(void);
    void rcc_clock_setup_in_hsi_out_48mhz(void);
    void rcc_clock_setup_in_hsi_out_24mhz(void);
    void rcc_clock_setup_in_hse_8mhz_out_24mhz(void);
    void rcc_clock_setup_in_hse_8mhz_out_72mhz(void);
    void rcc_clock_setup_in_hse_12mhz_out_72mhz(void);
    void rcc_clock_setup_in_hse_16mhz_out_72mhz(void);
    void rcc_clock_setup_in_hse_25mhz_out_72mhz(void);
    ```

    Note that only the `in_hsi` and `in_hse_8mhz` functions are compatible with the bluepill with an 8 MHz crystal.

4.  Here is an example of how to do it in C:

    ```c
    #include "stdio.h"
    int main(){
       char * t = "Z9kvzrj8";
       int i=0;
       while(*(t+i) != 0){ //c strings are 0 terminated
         putchar(*(t+i) ^ 0x19);
         i++;
       }
       putchar('\n');
    }
    ```

    It will print `C rocks!`.

5.  Let's go down the rabbit hole of preprocessor directives (in other words, solve what all the defined variable values are and how they relate to one another):

    ```
    $ grep -r 'ine GPIOC_ODR' bluepill/libopencm3/include/
    libopencm3/stm32/f1
    [...]/stm32/f1/gpio.h:#define GPIOC_ODR GPIO_ODR(GPIOC)
    $ grep -r 'ine GPIO_ODR' bluepill/libopencm3/include/
    libopencm3/stm32/f1
    [...]/stm32/f1/gpio.h:#define GPIO_ODR(port)
    MMIO32((port) + 0x0c)
    $ grep -r 'ine GPIOC\s' bluepill/libopencm3/include/
    libopencm3/stm32/f1
    [...]/stm32/f1/gpio.h:#define GPIOC GPIO_PORT_C_BASE
    $ grep -r 'ine GPIO_PORT_C' bluepill/libopencm3/include/
    libopencm3/stm32/f1
    ```

```
[...]/stm32/f1/memorymap.h:#define GPIO_PORT_C_BASE
(PERIPH_BASE_APB2 + 0x1000)
$ grep -r 'ine PERIPH_BASE_APB2\s' bluepill/libopencm3/
include/libopencm3/stm32/f1
[...]/stm32/f1/memorymap.h:#define PERIPH_BASE_APB2
(PERIPH_BASE + 0x10000)
$ grep -r 'ine PERIPH_BASE\s' bluepill/libopencm3/
include/libopencm3/stm32/f1
[...]/stm32/f1/memorymap.h:#define PERIPH_BASE
(0x40000000U)
```

Hence, 0x40000000 + 0x10000 + 0x1000 + 0x0c = 0x4001100c.

The simple way to do it is by using a preprocessor directive to print it when compiling a program:

```
#pragma message "The value of GPIOC_ODR: " GPIOC_ODR
```

# Chapter 6

1. The symbol time seems to be 8.8 microseconds, which is very probably 115,200 bauds.

2. Quad SPI. This is a variant of SPI where there are four data lines in order to speed up transfer. This is very common for flash storage.

3. It is used to detect errors.

4. Phillips.

5. The 24LC has address pins that can be used to set the address on the hardware level.

6. You can bit-bang the I2C protocol (it is a bit complicated but examples can be found) to accept any address on the slave side.

7. "I love binary operators !": ^ is the notation for the XOR operation (bit per bit, a^b = 1 if a!=b, 0 if a=b). This mean that if you take a string byte by byte and XOR it with a key (also byte by byte), the message is (badly) hidden. Here, it is "I love binary operators!" ^ "A very very serious key!". This is a very common method to make reverse engineering a little bit more complicated since it hides printable characters.

# Chapter 7

1. `dd`.

2. Uses a file as a block device.

3. Because modules are only loaded if they are needed. You can manually load them with `modprobe` if they are not loaded automatically.

4. **eUSB is embedded USB**. It is like a normal USB but the connector is different; it is a 2.54 mm pitch female connector. You can just strip a normal USB cable, add pins to the wires, connect D+, D- , +5 V, and ground, and connect it to a normal computer.

5. It is a multimedia card. It is possible to desolder the chip from the PCB, clean it, and use a clamshell adapter to read it from a normal computer.

6. FUSE is the "filesystem in userspace." It is a bridge between the kernel space (highly privileged, direct access to the hardware) and the user space (less privileged, access to the hardware mediated through the kernel). It is dedicated to implementing filesystems in a less-privileged area (for example, to comply with licensing constraints, refer to the history of `ntfs-3g` and `zfs` on Linux). It is very practical to make your own user space filesystem drivers for special cases where, for example, a specific system only implements a subset of a filesystem's functionalities.

# Chapter 8

1. DHCP option 252 can point out the **proxy configuration (PAC)** file in option 252: `ex : dhcp-option=252, http://192.168.0.2/proxy.pac and serve it over http`.

2. Actually, a lot! We can set up the timeserver (to make certificate checks fail, for example), try to make it boot to an external file (if it supports remote booting), make it forward IP traffic, change its static routes, and more. Look at the supported options list on the IANA website for more information.

3. Change the IP it associates with a legitimate server so that it talks to us instead.

4. It helps us identify the servers the device normally talks to.

5. A generic ATTribute profile.

6. A lack of security features being implemented in BLE allows an attacker to interact freely with a device.

# Chapter 9

1.  Encryption: The goal of encryption is to make it impossible to read for someone who does not have the keys necessary to read the signal. The goal of encoding is to make it easy or possible to transmit and receive but it does secure the information.

2.  The fast Fourier transform is used to transform a signal in a time domain (what did I receive and when?) to the frequency domain (what kind of frequencies is my signal made out of?).

3.  The modulation scheme indicates what change(s) in physical dimension(s) (change in frequency, amplitude, phase, or a combination) of the signal is used to encode the information.

4.  Sampling frequency and available frequency range.

5.  Imagine a signal as a sinusoidal of wavelength $x$. If our dipole antenna is measuring $x$, the difference between one end and the other is 0! Our receiver would have nothing to measure!

# Chapter 10

1.  It is a test interface and protocol that allows us to talk with an internal test engine. The behavior of the test engine is not defined in JTAG itself but is engine-specific.

2.  TCLK, TDI, TDO, and TMS. They respectively are Test Clock, Test Data In, Test Data Out, and Test Mode Select. TCLK clocks the debug engine; the data comes in from TDI, out from TDO, and TMS manages the state transition of the debug engine.

3.  No, it was made to test the soldering of chips and PCBs; chip debugging was added later as an afterthought.

4.  Since IDCODE is present on the DR by default, the JTAGulator doesn't have to send data to the chip to receive an IDCODE! A BYPASS scan finds it since it puts the chip in BYPASS mode and sends a test pattern through it.

5.  `http://openocd.org/doc/html/General-Commands.html`: `mwd`, `mww`, `mwh`, and `mwb`. For example, it can be used to stop a watchdog. Look at the `stm32f1x.cfg` file in OpenOCD!

6.  Yes it is! Now you can execute your own TCL and test it!

# Chapter 11

1. For example:

   Mach-O: MacOS and iOS

   a.out: Simplifier gcc output

   COFF: Older Unix executable format

   PEF: PowerPC BE/OS and MacOS classic

   There are plenty!

2. `.text`: Usually the section that holds the executable instructions. `.debug`: Usually holds the debugging symbols. `.plt`, `.dynamic`, `.got`: Sections that hold the necessary information for the linker to solve the external symbols (functions and data that come from external libraries). Reading about the linking mechanism in elf is a very good idea!

3. SPI1

4. Let's start with the strange string. When you look into how strings are stored in memory, you think of them as a list of characters, one after the other, in the order of growing memory addresses. This seems logical since you access them by incrementing a pointer. The thing is that the endianness (the direction a CPU stores numbers in its registers) can actually matter. What if I told you to break the string into blocks of four characters and read them in reverse?

```
" NAC"+"AH I"+"ET Z"+ " ? A" -> "CAN " + "I HA" + "Z TE"
+ "A ? " -> "Can i haz tea ?"
```

   Outside of a cute cat asking for a warm beverage, this should make your spidey-sense tingle. **Tiny Encryption Algorithm** (**TEA**) is a very common cypher in embedded systems. It is fast and easy to implement (and based on how it works, this string/data reversing effect can happen with the same key when you cypher and decipher on computers with different endianness). You should look into the different cypher/crypto algorithms (symetric like TEA, blowphish, CAST, IDEA, serpent, DES, and AES and asymmetric like RSA, Diffie-Hellman, and others) and, if you don't recognize them at first sight, you should at least get the feeling "this looks like a cypher" when reversing code.

5. The TEA typical initialization vector (delta=0x9E3779B9) should be here. In our code, it is replaced by 0x56455254 (VERT) because it is very common to identify cypher algorithms with their initialization vectors or constant substitution boxes (S-boxes). It is a common practice to try to hide the fact that you are using a common algorithm like that.

6. Patching the instruction at offset 0x2a8 (that is the instruction Ghidra highlights when clicking on the if in the decompiled view), **Compare and Branch Non Zero (CBNZ)** with a **Compare Branch Zero (CBZ)** would do that. In Ghidra, just right-click on the **Instruction | Patch instruction**, save it, and reflash the patched version to the bluepill. Now it should accept all incorrect passwords (and refuse the correct one).

# Chapter 12

1. Grendel, actually. Once again, the weird key string, when read in the normal endian direction reads like ytbe:7j7nMYT4DDc. You know, the online video service.

2. First, complicated instructions such as floating-point are off-loaded to a side processor. And for all the tests and conditions, this is simply implemented in the Silicon that decodes the instructions as simple switches that enable features around the additional features. Also, a lot of the instructions share a lot in common, such as how the tests actually reuse the logic operations by just ditching the results. This simplifies the decoding unit implementation a lot.

3. msp and psp are the banked sp registers for the processes. This is not supported on the STM32F103. The others are actually other core registers that are mainly used in interrupt/exception management. See https://developer.arm.com/documentation/dui0552/a/the-cortex-m3-processor/programmers-model/core-registers.

4. Because, if it is set, it will require a very long password to sum up to such a big value! And using a giant RAM buffer on a smallish MCU is never a good idea.

5. Buy a development board for the chip and flash a patched version of the binary that doesn't disable JTAG. If this is not possible, you could always use an ARM emulator (such as oaksim) to simulate the behavior.

# Chapter 13

1. This is an example of a matrix (the company is accepting a much higher overall risk level):

| | | Complexity/Probability | | | | | | | | | |
|---|---|---|---|---|---|---|---|---|---|---|---|
| | | 1 | 2 | 3 | 4 | 5 | 6 | 7 | 8 | 9 | 10 |
| Impact | 1 | 5 | 4 | 4 | 4 | 3 | 3 | 2 | 2 | 2 | 1 |
| | 2 | 5 | 4 | 4 | 4 | 3 | 3 | 2 | 2 | 2 | 1 |
| | 3 | 5 | 5 | 4 | 4 | 4 | 3 | 3 | 2 | 2 | 2 |
| | 4 | 6 | 5 | 5 | 4 | 4 | 4 | 3 | 3 | 2 | 2 |
| | 5 | 6 | 6 | 5 | 5 | 4 | 4 | 4 | 3 | 3 | 2 |
| | 6 | 6 | 6 | 6 | 5 | 5 | 4 | 4 | 4 | 3 | 3 |
| | 7 | 7 | 6 | 6 | 6 | 5 | 5 | 4 | 4 | 4 | 3 |
| | 8 | 7 | 7 | 6 | 6 | 6 | 5 | 5 | 4 | 4 | 4 |
| | 9 | 8 | 7 | 7 | 6 | 6 | 6 | 5 | 5 | 4 | 4 |
| | 10 | 8 | 8 | 7 | 7 | 6 | 6 | 6 | 5 | 5 | 4 |

   1 is considered as irrelevant, 2-3 low, 4-5 medium, 6-7 high, and 8, 9, and 10 as critical.

2. This is an example of a matrix where we reflect the possibility of a more refined attacker by reducing the impact of complexity on the reduction of the final risk (that is, the attacker is more skilled and can pull off more complex attacks easily):

| | | Complexity/Probability | | | | | | | | | |
|---|---|---|---|---|---|---|---|---|---|---|---|
| | | 1 | 2 | 3 | 4 | 5 | 6 | 7 | 8 | 9 | 10 |
| Impact | 1 | 6 | 6 | 6 | 6 | 6 | 6 | 6 | 6 | 4 | 1 |
| | 2 | 6 | 6 | 6 | 6 | 6 | 6 | 6 | 6 | 4 | 1 |
| | 3 | 7 | 7 | 7 | 7 | 7 | 7 | 7 | 7 | 5 | 2 |
| | 4 | 7 | 7 | 7 | 7 | 7 | 7 | 7 | 7 | 5 | 2 |
| | 5 | 8 | 8 | 8 | 8 | 8 | 8 | 8 | 8 | 6 | 3 |
| | 6 | 8 | 8 | 8 | 8 | 8 | 8 | 8 | 8 | 6 | 3 |
| | 7 | 9 | 9 | 9 | 9 | 9 | 9 | 9 | 9 | 7 | 4 |
| | 8 | 9 | 9 | 9 | 9 | 9 | 9 | 9 | 9 | 7 | 4 |
| | 9 | 10 | 10 | 10 | 10 | 10 | 10 | 10 | 10 | 8 | 5 |
| | 10 | 10 | 10 | 10 | 10 | 10 | 10 | 10 | 10 | 8 | 5 |

   This is to avoid the client artificially changing the scales in order to lower the scoring of vulnerabilities that they consider annoying to fix or remediate.

3. In order for you to have an internal party at the client that is acting as a neutral party (that is, compliance has no conflict of interest with the technical implementation team when it comes to do things properly) and usually have a much stricter approach to regulation compliance than the business.

`Packt.com`

Subscribe to our online digital library for full access to over 7,000 books and videos, as well as industry leading tools to help you plan your personal development and advance your career. For more information, please visit our website.

## Why subscribe?

- Spend less time learning and more time coding with practical eBooks and Videos from over 4,000 industry professionals

- Improve your learning with Skill Plans built especially for you

- Get a free eBook or video every month

- Fully searchable for easy access to vital information

- Copy and paste, print, and bookmark content

Did you know that Packt offers eBook versions of every book published, with PDF and ePub files available? You can upgrade to the eBook version at `packt.com` and as a print book customer, you are entitled to a discount on the eBook copy. Get in touch with us at `customercare@packtpub.com` for more details.

At `www.packt.com`, you can also read a collection of free technical articles, sign up for a range of free newsletters, and receive exclusive discounts and offers on Packt books and eBooks.

# Other Books You May Enjoy

If you enjoyed this book, you may be interested in these other books by Packt:

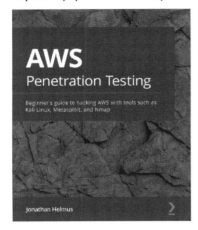

**AWS Penetration Testing**

Jonathan Helmus

ISBN: 978-1-83921-692-3

- Set up your AWS account and get well-versed in various pentesting services
- Delve into a variety of cloud pentesting tools and methodologies
- Discover how to exploit vulnerabilities in both AWS and applications
- Understand the legality of pentesting and learn how to stay in scope
- Explore cloud pentesting best practices, tips, and tricks
- Become competent at using tools such as Kali Linux, Metasploit, and Nmap

**Learn Kali Linux 2019**

Glen D. Singh

ISBN: 978-1-78961-180-9

- Explore the fundamentals of ethical hacking
- Learn how to install and configure Kali Linux
- Get up to speed with performing wireless network pentesting
- Gain insights into passive and active information gathering
- Understand web application pentesting
- Decode WEP, WPA, and WPA2 encryptions using a variety of methods, such as the fake authentication attack, the ARP request replay attack, and the dictionary attack

# Packt is searching for authors like you

If you're interested in becoming an author for Packt, please visit `authors.packtpub.com` and apply today. We have worked with thousands of developers and tech professionals, just like you, to help them share their insight with the global tech community. You can make a general application, apply for a specific hot topic that we are recruiting an author for, or submit your own idea.

# Leave a review - let other readers know what you think

Please share your thoughts on this book with others by leaving a review on the site that you bought it from. If you purchased the book from Amazon, please leave us an honest review on this book's Amazon page. This is vital so that other potential readers can see and use your unbiased opinion to make purchasing decisions, we can understand what our customers think about our products, and our authors can see your feedback on the title that they have worked with Packt to create. It will only take a few minutes of your time, but is valuable to other potential customers, our authors, and Packt. Thank you!

# Index

Made in the USA
Las Vegas, NV
04 December 2022

61155711R00210